FRICTIONAL ASCENSION

JAWN CHAEMYL

authorHOUSE®

AuthorHouse™
1663 Liberty Drive
Bloomington, IN 47403
www.authorhouse.com
Phone: 1 (800) 839-8640

Published by AuthorHouse 06/13/2019

ISBN: 978-1-5462-7345-5 (sc)
ISBN: 978-1-5462-7344-8 (e)

Library of Congress Control Number: 2018915027

Print information available on the last page.

This book is printed on acid-free paper.

Contents

Preface

Due to the unspecified threat that I pose for reasons soon to be made clear, I was forced to place ideas in the open where the public could see them. Before I knew it, a book appeared. I had made several previous attempts to place ideas on some form of media, but invariably, quaternions of quidnuncs would appear to bedizen the room with their sublime skepticism, and so the efforts were thwarted and in some cases destroyed.

This was also an experiment set against the payola driven radios which think we need to hear the exact same words every fifteen seconds to do the opposite and see exactly how long we could say as many separate ideas as possible in entirely different words, or a "no-repeat" motif. It was successfully performed for over seven years. Same ideas may have surfaced, but entirely different words from several different angles. If payola drove art galleries, we would see the exact same picture in every frame since those are the most popular.

Names and some details were changed in the story to protect the guilty and also the false charge of guilty on those who are actually innocent, since this projection is now a modern, socially acceptable habit. Some details may appear changed or new, but they aren't. They were present the entire time, known only to those who knew how to ask questions, or were kept dark until this work due to behavior soon to be outlined in full detail. The real names were kept secret even from the author, so in some cases the change is unavoidable. Therefore, the actual culprits, when speaking generally, aren't known, since names weren't recorded in all cases. The events described are real however and happened somewhere on the planet in some form or fashion more or less as described. So, since things aren't exactly as they appear in the text, calling any police or lawyers will be met with confusion since they'll have no idea what any caller is talking about. The people who can actually help use higher and more effective methods anyway.

The writing for this began around 2001 and ended this year, 2018. The difficulty in dealing with the various aspects of the subject matter being the largest contributing factor to the delay, but hospitals and hurricanes didn't help either. It's amazing given the events of the first story that anything which followed, including itself, was even possible.

Some elements that others may recall won't be here detailed if it can be determined that this would allow any repetition of the crimes, to the extent that this method of prevention is possible. Some stories are a relation more than an entertainment of any kind. The others which will follow in a third book are more for entertainment, but may shine exclusive light on some areas for those familiar with the case. Other elements will be described in detail for the same reason, that by illustrating the gross ignorance and stupidity, the crime will embarrass itself out of existence.

If we find we don't appreciate everything detailed in these accounts, we may remember how all the sitting around doing nothing enabled virtually all of it to happen, which has wound the book up in your hands as it now is.

It was attempted to sort every idea to its own category, but some seem to fit three or more, and were either left unsorted or placed where they seemed to fit more than another.

The polemic arguments contained in the work are not absolute laws and can possibly be refuted with sufficient proof. However, flapping lips, no matter how furiously they flap and no matter how violently popular this method of disproving anything is today, do *not* amount to proof. A study of what does amount to proof may be needed before receiving any audience. After sitting in the open and unchallenged by anything but silence for more than seven years, it appears they're as solid as they need to be. But as we'll soon discover, this may not be true.

Any subsequent questions won't be recognized if it is remotely likely or if even the slightest hint is detected that the questioner has no clue or concern for the meaning of "null hypothesis" or "prima facie." Since much of this may require further exploration, some are merely pretentious, they are certainly not cut in rigidity (unless they are). Since these aren't dogmatic dictums of democracy, but notions which either are covered in greater detail in other books or secret colleges with bad advertising agents, or are nowhere to be found on the earth, the fixed impression they may seem to provide is only illusory. They are what perhaps should be being discussed in many places, but strangely aren't.

Examples for anything here have been, for the most part, left out. One can easily look in any direction for three seconds and find over seven hundred and fifty-three trillion of them. However, for some things it is possible that a story will follow expanding the original idea into something illustrative.

What is here written is mostly based on this: The solution to any of our problems won't come from examining the same collections of words we've already seen hundreds of times. If at all, it will come from examining hundreds of times a different collection of words that no one has ever seen. This is from the repeated discovery that the solution is usually something we have never seen. An English professor at University of Houston accurately said that no one has ever seen all possible word combinations of any dictionary. But instead of these notions, we gravitate towards what we feel.

If we're all equal, everything here applies to everyone, since these are thoughts of everyone else, as equals. If we're not, then we need to think and act as if we are not. Far more will be possible this way than trying to shove everyone into a mold.

Much gratitude and thanks to the hundreds in this case who were able to help us all get to this point and prevent more people from dying than actually have already. There are too many to list and they know who they are, but they should know they are very much appreciated by us and will remain fondly remembered for their efforts, faith, and love.

Lastly, none of the following requires credence anymore than the sun needs faith to produce light and heat from hydrogen. Unless there is videotape evidence disproving what is said here, this stands as the truth till such evidence is produced. Asking the same question till the "correct" answer is heard disproves nothing.

- Jawn Chaemyl, December 17, 2018

1. THE BLINDER

Dedicated to all who helped put these four permanently behind bars. Written with hopes of further crime dissolution, ignorance prevention, and solution to this case. Much of the text has been available online since 2002, when the web page containing The Blinder was created on July 7 - Sunday.

Prologue

The first thing noticeable is the lack of skill. The second should be the height of the ideas. The third, the intense enormity of the crimes. Most of the time, justice does happen or there would be a greater evidence of chaos than we now see on the streets. Most of the time, everyone does their job just fine, especially when they are there for more than the money and actually care about the work involved. But nothing is entirely flawless. What we discuss here and elsewhere is an effort to approach the nearly unattainable goal of perfection while usually not reaching it, though sometimes we do. Perfection is as possible as its qualifiers. When something is as good as we can expect under the circumstances, it is, for all intents and purposes, perfect. The following real case is a glaring exception.

Far more than is here recorded actually happened. If it's here, it doesn't mean it's more important than what isn't. If it's not here, it doesn't mean it wasn't remembered, wasn't a crime, wasn't noteworthy, was a part which has been solved, or should not actually be included with the rest of the events described. It's here because it is or it isn't.

A few events occurred prior to Chapter One that may shed light on why certain events of a criminal nature took place seemingly authorized by God himself, when in reality no such authority was granted. They may explain why any of this ever happened at all. These may or may not be explained later, depending on ultimate relevance to anything other than that they occurred. Other events weren't described since the memories of them were either dim or non-existent, so other people may remember more or less of the events than are here recorded. What is written is what could be remembered and verified as much as is possible given what happened to cause the events to be forgotten in the first place.

Why were they forgotten in the first place? Other than the natural habit of the mind to block traumatic events to prevent further trauma, with a strong enough dose of societal conditioning in any of its various forms, a mind can begin to believe that real crimes never occur. This forms a false, invisible, imaginary barrier against both responsibility and dealing with criminals. Then it can also believe that pretending crimes don't occur or didn't happen is healthy. With enough of this, it can be used to hypnotize others to believe similarly, or force them to give up since fighting the world isn't possible. However, insanity begins instantly whenever we take any part of reality and call it fantasy.

This can be seen in situations where criminals become rapturous to find out that person "x" is a child molester, since then it seems to give them an excuse to commit rape and murder. The problem is that there is no such excuse in any reality or any dimension, on earth or in heaven.

This, then, was compiled to expose the criminals and their accomplices and provide a record of what occurred fifty years ago. Anyone who emphatically likes what is stated shouldn't have sat around for fifty years and let it all happen. Fifty years of sitting around letting it work the criminal's way is fifty years of wasted time which will receive its own reward in due course.

This is a relation of events in no particular order. Some things are explained to ensure the prevention of them in the future, others aren't for the same reason.

What is presented may seem to rail against a seemingly unchangeable fate. Hopefully, someone, either now or later, will arrive, see these things, and know precisely who and what is at fault and exactly what to do about it. We can think anything, most believe anything and everything; we call this faith. But with reality, the correct belief will often change it. The outcome has already been seen and decided, otherwise nothing would have been started and no arrests would ever have been made, but they were. From here, not much is left but to wait and accept.

Crime victims do not have very many benefits from their experience that are of any value. A possible one is that, from their perspective, they can see precisely what is *not* being considered, about which no one cares, and for which nothing or little is ever done. This is positive because once a concern rises to a certain level, something actually is done about it eventually. As a negative example, the victims of crimes are never proven to be liars, even though the burden of proof is always on the accuser. This allows the victims to see both who the criminals are, and those who are helping them. This is a restricted perspective, since if more had it, more would discover themselves to have not gotten away with the crimes, since more could clearly see who the real criminals are and deception would finally take the back seat more often.

The entire piece stands before God and all as both a testimony and a rebuke for what was allowed to happen to two three-year-olds as well as others in the 60s. May God lead us to stop lying to ourselves and do the right thing, whosoever we may be.

1. Under the Table

Thomas raced back home from a day's work remembering for the first time again the conversation he once had with two strange men on the then deserted street of his home on Tarpin Road in an urban community of Clabber, Texas.

"We're tired of God's people always finding out where we are, busting in our joints and ruining our business. Yeah, we hate God, but that's just a side issue. We're just tired of it, really. We want to see what happens if we can finish our work unhindered by His Majesty's finest," Fred Steiner told him while standing in the middle of Tarpin Road just before the two men stormed into the house and raped all within its silent, dark brown, wood-paneled walls.

"Yeah, we've had enough proving we know how to get around the law. They know they can't do anything to us really, so it's kinda boring watching them try it time after time. We just want a rest, kid. Can you help us out?" Bobby Raven asked Thomas, who was only about six at the time.

He knew if he didn't help them, or at least convince them he would, they would kill him on the spot. And what we know is how we go. He had seen them and their work before in another town before his family moved him here in a futile attempt to protect Thomas and his sister from them. He knew they didn't care about life, could kill anyone they wanted and no one would ever touch them. The courts, merely sluggishly, lackadaisically, with great ennui performed the formality of the law, and thus never seriously tried to prosecute them, for whatever reasons they thought they had for so doing, which was contrary to their oaths of position.

Thomas knew that allowing them to kill him would be the equivalent of giving up and letting them have his family -- a thing he would never, could never do in any lifetime. His family was his, not anyone else's; and he would never go without a massive fight -- a war waged with every atom in his physical composition. So, finally, after about two minutes of thought, he agreed to let the men build the Machine on his father's property.

This was the only part he agreed to do, since it made no sense. He knew that if God was God, it wouldn't make any difference in the end anyway. The two men, and whoever helped them get away with it, would spend all eternity burning in hell for their actions -- which, considering all the actions, wasn't quite enough of a punishment really.

Later, in some unknown church, behind a pulpit set on a turquoise, elevated platform, a hand disappeared holding a wad of green bills. From behind the same pulpit on the other side, another hand emerged holding the same wad of bills over which unknown words were exchanged. Whether either actually worked at the church wasn't known. One was a doctor, but which took and which gave? And was the doctor being paid to take or give? Or both? This exchange was reenacted a few times to ensure Thomas would remember it much later.

Before this, in a smoke-filled room, three to ten men were discussing how to "make them pay."

"They won't get away with this, and after we're done, most of us will be dead anyway, so no one will be able to stop it." All in the room agreed.

2. The Accessories

Once the family (at least those who weren't at work at the time) had been thoroughly raped, and the two men carted off in squad cars, only to be soon thereafter let off on technicalities, Thomas began wondering what they had meant about this "Machine." Thinking back on it, he passed an oak tree whose branch had been cut off. Where it was severed was now overgrown with new bark. The bark resembled the twisted face of a gargoyle overlooking the street, guarding one side of the property where a few feet further down the street to the east the Machine lie, droning - buzzing - humming. It stood towering several stories up into a blank, white, cloud-carpeted ceiling, sealing in its secrecy. Its main function seemed to lie in lying, keeping the executors of justice from seeing exactly what they needed to do to stop the group of men from their large, profligate business of repeatedly raping hundreds of children.

The Kinsey Report, published sometime in the mid-50's, gave some of the details of their work, of which Kinsey is not known to be connected, but this went way beyond Kinsey's sickest dreams. Fred called one of his agents and requested help with Thomas' family, a man named Tayler Garrist, pediatrician, M.D., B.A., PhD., and M.A. in psychiatry, psychology, hypnotism, and anatomical research. Certainly quite an unfair match for a six-year-old to be warring against.

But who cares about what's fair when raping children for decades is all one is obsessed about? Who cares when seeing how long one can get away with even murdering the child's father is the primary goal? Who cares when too many family members can be conscripted to fulfill all one's aims in the matter? Who cares when you can kill someone, then rape his children, then rape the children's children and get away with it? Who cares if everyone sits around and lets it happen? Life isn't fair anyway, so this is all acceptable.

This was the motivating plan behind the hypnosis conducted over an uncountable number of sessions that ensured every one of these questions seemed at the least plausible, if not fully enforced with great stricture. This will be elaborated more fully by the end of this work, with insights and glimpses of how it was effected. Despite the desire of some, no specific plans will be laid out for how to do this so that the crime, if repeated elsewhere, won't have come from this. But with everyone fully cooperating with demons and doing their every command, no manual is really needed.

3. The Checkup

As Cynthia and Thomas entered Dr. Garrist's office, shoved into it by their irate father who screamed, "Fix them!" and slammed the door to the sound-proof room behind them, they both knew they couldn't win this. They only wondered when it would stop, and who would stop it. This was after Fred and Bobby forced actions from them both in the church bathroom both together and solo, ending with the doctor using a scalpel and grinning from ear to ear as he left. The blood in the underwear was explained away with enough violent threats to ensure silence on the part of those who saw it, so nothing was done to him until later. This was all to prepare for what he and the rest were going to do later.

Their father's mind was ruined by Dr. Garrist previously, drawn to the office by an ad in the local paper exclaiming that smoking could be cured by this hypnosis. The mother's mind was also destroyed by a similar ad to help with diabetes and diet control. Both were replacement guardians since the first father was shot and the mother's whereabouts are still unknown to this day. Both allowed the hypnosis and were never the same again for the rest of their lives, since their free-will had been removed.

Dr. Garrist smiled cruelly at them back in his sound proof examination room and said, "Ok, first, you two are going to be separated because of what you did. But don't worry, I have some good replacements for you, so you won't be lonely."

Thomas and Cynthia both looked at each other, wondering what they had done that would require for them to be separated. It was only thirty-three years later they would find out all they had done was merely pose a threat to a business that had no right to operate in the first place. Other than that, they were innocent of all charges which Fred and Bobby had leveled against them in the "court of justice." (Any court biased in favor of criminals cannot logically be a court of justice.)

False accusations of collusion, confusion, obsessions with each other, only bought the rapists the time they needed to finish working on their machine, blinding God (only apparently) and the courts (most certainly) to the truth of what they were doing to the children of humanity. It bought them time to experience a life which the court judge had once promised Thomas would be cut off by execution "no matter what," so he said.

Here is an exact transcript of the statements:

Thomas said on the witness stand, "They shot my father and he died." Ralene's testimony was the same. After the jury returned with a guilty verdict, the court judge said, "Based on your testimony they will be executed."
Thomas: "Do you promise?"
Judge: "I promise."
Thomas: "Cross your heart and hope to die?"
Judge: "Cross my heart and hope to die."
Thomas: "Swear on the bible?"
Judge: (takes a bible and swears on it to the Lord)
Thomas: "No ifs ands or buts?"
Judge: "No ifs ands or buts."
Thomas: "No exceptions?"
Judge: "No exceptions."
Thomas: "Do you swear to God?"
Judge: "I swear to God they will be executed."
Thomas: "No matter what?"
Judge: "No matter what."

To clarify: The stipulation "no ifs, ands or buts" just mentioned didn't just apply to the judge's statement, but the entire case. This is obvious since we have all heard this from our parents. What isn't allowed by parents has no place in a court of law, or there would be urine, dirty diapers, used chewing gum, and toys scattered all over the courtroom. This is another primary reason for the case's failure. The defense used "but" almost exclusively without ever getting near an "if" or "and." Any judge worth their salt wouldn't have allowed one "but" to pass unslammed back into the trash can it came from. Why "no ifs, ands, or buts?" Because anyone of sufficient intelligence can apply one of these to almost anything, resulting in neither verdict, sentence, nor justice. There has to be some cutoff point, which should be fairly covered in at least one of the billions of books lining every law shelf in the entire universe.

But no matter what, thirty-four years later, there was still no execution. And no matter what, the children had been forced against their wills to live lives they gave no one any permission to force them to endure. And no matter what, by refusing to keep his word, the judge perjured himself, but refused to step down and let someone who knew how to keep their word do the job. There were false allegations that the testimony changed. Here's a repeat of the testimony -

Thomas: "They shot my father in his own home and it killed him and he died." Ralene's testimony was exactly the same.

If anyone notices this testimony changing by itself, please alert the author. The testimony, after having been observed on a website since 2002, has never changed, it has always been written down just this way in the court records from the first trial for over fifty years now. After sixteen years of careful observation, the words have not rearranged themselves on the page, so the testimony didn't change by itself. It is believed that lawyers who think that testimony has changed when in fact it has not are delusional, or are being bribed by the defendant to lie and say that it has when it obviously hasn't.

After an hour or so where much was added to the children's experience regarding the confusion Fred and Bobby accused them of in court, Dr. Garrist called their father to come pick up his two children. When Leon Hapsberg arrived at the office, he inquired as to why they were both crying uncontrollably. "Oh, it's nothing, I just gave them a checkup and a shot," Tayler replied casually, but didn't look Mr. Hapsberg in the eyes.

A checkup??? Thomas thought. Well, this was true after a fashion. The doctor had needlessly checked up every hole in their bodies, in some cases repeatedly -- and in most cases with the wrong kind of instrument.

4. The Testimony Changed?

Further Evidence of Societal Psychosis

A recent experience has possibly shed some light on this false accusation. It is possible that this is what they meant:

If the stenographer wrote down something other than what Thomas stated, as is exactly what happened in a recent phone hearing, then yes, anyone reading the testimony would be fooled into thinking the testimony had changed. If Thomas said, "I saw a murder, here is where it happened, here is who did it, here is how they did it, and you are helping them get away with it, so thank you so much for nothing," then the stenographer writes down, "The witness saw nothing and has nothing to say," then yes, anyone not in the courtroom at the time would be fooled into thinking the testimony had changed.

We might be inclined not to believe this possible, but on a recent phone hearing with the state of Texas (where this murder occurred fifty-one years ago) it was stated that harassment had occurred on a job. The hearing judge wrote down on the paper "The client stated harassment occurred on the job, but failed to give an example." An example was given, but since this would have destroyed the case the judge had been payed by the company to win for them, she then conveniently ignored both written and verbal evidence which didn't further her case. Does anyone need a legal background to know that this is illegal? Does anyone need to be a lawyer to say, "This is wrong as hell!"? Any blind dog could aver the same thing with *no* legal background.

We can take the lack of communique over the last sixteen years stating that any words have rearranged themselves as evidence that the testimony did *not* change. So, since this is the case, why have the criminals *not been executed yet*? What more is needed?

Thomas logged in his journal:

> *"On behalf of the innocent in this country, we thank you for wasting our time - time no one gave you any permission to waste - time no one has - waste no one gave you permission to enforce. May the Lord reward you according to your works - since you decided to forget what I have said, may the Lord forget your name forever. You don't care about who I am, then may the Lord reward you accordingly by forgetting who you are. I hope you enjoy the future you have made for yourself. If you don't like this, then change it and do what you said and execute these murderers. May you and the world both be saved by so doing."*

The testimony never changed.

5. The Machine

"Ok, you have to help us, we can't do this without you," Fred Steiner told Thomas and Ralene, the one prior to Cynthia, as they stood on the selected property on Tarpin Road in Clabber. Not that they had been given any choice about it, and not that either of them knew exactly what Fred was talking about. So far, the only thing that fighting against it had done was to give them more trips to the doctor's office and a shed in the back, mentioned in Shelled Soul, without the doctor even, and they'd had quite enough of that. So they began using their abilities to generate the Machine after Fred used the usual threat method and ranting hate spews to force them to perform.

It wasn't visible to the naked eye, they weren't even sure if it was real or not, only that what they created together was usually never questioned. It looked real since they could both see it. Looking down from above (as God would normally have to do according to the majority opinion) it appeared as a twisted, quite complicated morass of metal, pipes, and wires, interwoven, lattice-like, with occasional blocks where motors were housed. The only ones who could see it were those who had the unique ability to view what was truly there, and not just what appeared to be there. It even had a soothing, mellifluous sound, which normally would drown out the cries of the children being tortured beneath its massive, complicated structure. It didn't do anything, even in the invisible world, but produce soothing emanations. It only appeared to do something useful, because anything that looks that complex has to be useful for something, everyone knew that. Here's part of how they built it:

Most are familiar with the phrase - "For every action, there's an equal and opposite reaction." So, they would take a object and spin it around for a while. Since this did nothing visibly, it had to be doing something in the invisible world based on the phrase, where spinning nothing becomes something either spinning or not. So, after a time, they would stop and look at what was really there, and sure enough, a section of the massive structure had been created. It wasn't mere imaginations either, for the two would stop ever so often and compare notes only to discover they both saw the same structure in front of them with the same colors, the same parts, and taking up the same space on the property of their now dead father's house. All this was done with no prior descriptions of what was there being communicated in any form or fashion between them. By this means, and after much spinning, a huge, misshapen structure, surreal and almost vast, was stretched out before them when they looked into it. It made them as proud as it gave them horror, realizing what torturous memories this made for hundreds of children tormented beneath its massive, titanium frame.

During a break in their work, Thomas looked at Ralene through eyes of fear to see if she saw the same things as he did, hoping that none of this was real. She walked back from near the tree line, grabbed his upper arm and said, "Yes, it's there." She did this twice so he would remember it later. The monotonous droning and calming effect that the Machine had nearly put them to sleep several times, so they had to break and return after a short reviving period. It didn't take long before the construction was enough for the satisfaction of all the sadists surrounding them, so they indicated to stop building and everyone left. It was never returned to later, since its existence was all that was necessary for the abusers to continue with their plan.

Did Thomas or Ralene feel guilty about any of it? No, they weren't the ones forcing them to do it, they weren't the ones who let two criminals out of jail repeatedly, nor were they the ones sitting around letting it happen when it so easily could have been stopped at any time.

7. Colluding With Gaslights?

Chapter 6 was lost.

It was said accusations of collusion and gaslighting on the part of Thomas, Ralene, and Cynthia flew largely around the court room spouted from the murderous mouths of men promised by the court judge to have been executed "no matter what" after having been found guilty beyond reasonable doubt. Based on the sisters' unexcused thirty-four year absence, a select few seem to have no clue as to whether Thomas confessed guilt in regards to collusion and if so, why.

First, let's discuss why Fred did what he did.

Thomas' family was of German descent; Fred's alleged genealogy was Jewish/Hebrew. Fred was in recurrent habits of yelling plots of vengeance against all Germans, regardless of where they were at the time on the planet, for having committed the Holocaust. This is still a horrifyingly popular practice even today. The fact that all Germans didn't commit the Holocaust didn't seem to matter to biased Fred. This was the sole crime Thomas' father committed: He was German, although born in America.

Thomas wrote the following down in his journal:
Item A:

> *7. My interest in horror writing began as a child, when*
> *I saw my father shot to death by two men that walked*
> *into the house and sat down in the recliner chair next to*

his bed. And as his son struggled in vain to run over and grab the gun out of the killer's hand, as he pulled it out of the side pocket of the chair, before it could launch the fatal bullet that killed someone that, to the son, was more important than John F. Kennedy. Now thirty-three years later, nothing has been done against these men who killed his father. The men run free in the streets, flaunting justice, playing games with the courts of law: reason unknown.

Item B:

Since God does everything for a reason, God must have not done justice to these men to prove some kind of purpose beyond our understanding. God must have let these men rape children time after time as much as they wanted to their hearts content for some kind of divine purpose. That God allows children to be raped repeatedly must be some kind of divine reason that's beyond our comprehension.

Now if God isn't responsible for not executing justice in this case, then that leaves only one other culprit. The stronger belief is with the latter reason - That there is no divine purpose for any of this; that there is nothing beyond our understanding when it comes to executing justice on murderers and rapists. This will be proven later. Which leaves only one culprit that is truly responsible, and shall pay in full when the collectors arrive at the door and ask for their debt to be paid -- That culprit is modern man.

Questions:

If Thomas colluded with Cynthia against Fred for being a Jew, and Bobby for being who knows whatever he is, then why is there no mention of race in the above two journal quotes, or anywhere in the journal for that matter? No racist hate spew that flew out of Fred's mouth like feces from a pig every twenty-five seconds is contained anywhere in it.

How would anyone under ten know how to go about doing any of that anyway?

Who let this happen and for what reason?

What kind of "officer of justice" is it that believes lies wholesale without proving them first?

Why do they still have jobs?

If Thomas did admit to collusion, it is doubtful any six-year-old has any grasp on what that is, regardless of any programmed hypnotically induced behavior to the contrary. This is the first point.

The second is that if the killers were present in the room at the time of the questioning, and no one had prevented them from doing whatever they wanted to Thomas and his family, even now thirty-four years later, then this also explains why he would say what he did.

He knew his statements could wind other members of his family up very cold and dead later on, since no one felt motivated to stop Fred and Bobby from doing what they love to do. He knew that one day, other members could fill the four foot grave Fred dug for Thomas' father in the back yard in the northeast corner of the yard. He knew other members would have their dead bodies spat on, defecated on, urinated on, and whatever else Fred felt like doing out of his deep-rooted hatred for Germans. So if Thomas did whatever it took to keep his family alive, how is he then guilty of colluding against anyone? Not to mention that no one under ten would have any motive to do anything to two jerks they met in the middle of a street or at some unknown convention center. To this date, no one has offered any explanation to this question that makes a lick of sense. Most of the time, no explanation is ever given. Yet, Thomas' family is still illegally separated.

Before this issue arises again, none of this is about race in reality. Sadly, as in many other areas of the world, it's only used as a tool of extortion for either money, child sex, or to excuse volumes of other crimes which in reality there is no excuse for. Thomas' family was attacked by pedophiles and their sycophantic doctors and via the aid of hypnosis was led to appear as if they were racist to amass sufficient opprobrium, greasing the skids for the years-long plans crafted by sick minds. For this, there is no race that can be said to excel over any other since there are many in each race who have sick minds in dire need of psychiatric treatment or execution.

Since collude means *"to act together through a secret understanding,"*[1] all lawyers collude with their clients. The understanding is secret since everyone has secrets. The secret is what to say and what not to say. In this sense, collude is no different than cooperation, so yes, we cooperate/collude with lawyers to keep murderers off the street. Saying this is the case proves nothing about a murder, either for or against. This is just a mere waste of time since we still haven't asked the dumbest question: The one that wasn't asked. In this event, the dumbest question is the one that will solve the case. Instead we have people with degrees dining on red herring for fifty years.

Gaslighting didn't happen either, though this was the standard practice of Fred, Bobby, and Dr. Garrist. If Thomas ever afterward imitated this behavior, it's due to the extreme love affair everyone seemed to have with the criminals, so he was only giving the audience more of the cherished behavior that only seemed to produce worship when the criminals performed it, indicating a strong bias which he already knew existed. It also was pointing directly to the absence of any type of actions regarding the sentence which was issued. Any action other than performing the sentence was a deliberate waste of time and did nothing to help anyone: justice, victims, or anyone else. It did wonders for the criminals though, and is still being used to this day to provide them with luxuries they removed from Thomas' family. Any step in any direction other than performing the sworn sentence will be thwarted, otherwise why even have a trial in the first place? And it should even be further thwarted by something far more than gaslighting, while remaining within the bounds of the law. Because otherwise, we're condoning what we claim to hate and rewarding pedophiles and murderers with a free pass they most definitely don't deserve. By ignoring the sentence, we're actually colluding with the criminals to help them get away with everything they did or will do in the future.

8. The Torture Chamber

Without going into useless, sadistic detail, after Fred shot Thomas' and Ralene's father, Bobby took the gun, wrapped Thomas' tiny hand around the pistol grip, and squeezed off two shots, blowing most of Ralene's knees into pieces, which later resulted in having to amputate both legs below the knees. The entire scene from the father arriving home to the kneecapping was reenacted using different people for the "father" with various outcomes to confuse the testimony later, which evidently everyone swallowed wholesale again, even though it was carefully explained that the entire scene was redone about ten to twenty times.

Thomas and Ralene were then hung up on hooks on the east wall of the west back room and repeatedly molested till they were driven to a furious rage and forced to fight each other. Then, treated to a game of "Hide and go seek" which wound Ralene up in an army duffel bag in the closet for three days and Thomas up in the refrigerator till near death. Thomas could hear the police outside looking for him for a while before one finally decided to open the refrigerator and look.

Even after all this, the criminals were not able to remain in a prison cell long enough to prevent them from their continued attacks and abuse against this family. It was this, among many other things outside of this case, that caused Thomas to wonder what exactly does constitute a crime? Is it reality, or our individual decisions alone about whether or not any crime has even occurred? Do crimes really become erased from existence because we decided they never happened?

9. What Happened to the Backyard?

Prior to the day of the murder, or the two strange men approaching Thomas in the middle of his home street, Fred and Bobby hired a doctor to put both children under hypnosis, ostensibly for bed-wetting problems (a common excuse among pedophile hypnotists to get their foot into the door of the child's mind), but in reality, to install almost irreversible programming involving various spots in the backyard which would lead both children to their untimely deaths, unless someone intervened to stop it. Some of the programming involved tying Ralene up to a large, central tree in the backyard and abusing her for hours, then after convincing her Thomas was responsible for the abuse, releasing her to beat the fire out of Thomas. Ultimately, it was to cover the location of the body, which still hasn't been recovered by police. The only way to prevent the murder/suicide of the two children was to get rid of the place where they were programmed to commit the crimes or reverse the hypnosis entirely, a skill which our advanced age has yet to learn and which would have proved to be an invaluable life-saving implement later on. So, in 1970, a large warehouse was erected wiping out the entire backyard.

The warehouse was standing, till someone who wanted to further destroy evidence razed it and built homes over the entire lot. The body of the children's father was relocated a few times and now rests in a spot known only to one man. It is believed that when the two children are reunited after an illegal separation of fifty years, he will disclose the location of the body. The reason the body keeps moving is because

Fred and Bobby both know that with no body, the testimony of the two children, which should be sufficient for conviction, but isn't for whatever reason, there's no way they can be executed for the death of the hated German, who fought in WWII on the American side. So, in the process of destroying evidence, Fred and Bobby successfully destroyed the backyard, have tried to steal and destroy the body numerous times, and even tried to destroy the house where the murder occurred originally. They also sent a harassment team to attempt to destroy the second house where more crimes were allowed. It still stands.

Why this is being allowed to happen is still a mystery. Whatever it is everyone is waiting for is also unclear.

10. Do You Need Some Help?

Of the several people assigned to help Thomas recover from this excessively traumatic event, two key figures became "overdogs" and are still busying themselves with not actually helping at all, but destroying as much as they can by wasting time and preventing Thomas and Ralene from enjoying lives they should have been allowed to have. Here's one of the ways they did this.

Every time they would ask Thomas if he needed some help, instead of actually helping him, they would run over and molest him, foolishly thinking this would "help" him. To date, they have yet to actually do anything which literally helps reverse the large amount of damage performed by Fred, Bobby, and their band of sadistic, pedophile doctors. Two of the overdogs fell in love with each other, and in order to prevent discovery, are helping keep Thomas and Ralene separated, knowing or presuming that this will end their secret relationship. Certainly it would end their reign of control over both children's lives, and will disclose several unpermitted, inexcusable illegal activities which over thirty-four years amounts to quite a large number of offenses.

Their plan is to never allow the two children back together and thus prevent themselves from being incarcerated for illegally stealing at least one of Ralene's children and no telling how many more as the lies stack higher by the second. Both overdogs have made sure they were given plenty of money to educate themselves thoroughly in psychology and psychiatry which they use as a primary manipulative weapon against Thomas and Ralene and to this day have succeeded in maintaining the illegal, unpermitted separation.

How these two imagine their fate will be in any way different from that of the murderers is still a mystery, since it obviously will be no different at all four hundred seventy-five million years from today. How Thomas, Ralene, and Cynthia escaped being cured from the extensive damage which Dr. "Rape-the-World" Garrist did to all of them is also a mystery, since this cure has been requested several thousand times, and has yet to be successfully performed. Payoff, bribery, overt sadism, and extortion are suspected, but nothing yet proven, other than the use of psychology to maintain illusions in the minds of certain people about the behavioral motives for the two children, which results in the maintenance of the separation. However, these illusions have never worked on Thomas and the children of Cynthia, if there are any, are still paying the excessive price of never knowing their parents. Thomas wonders what any of the children did to deserve all of this.

So, in short, later in their lives, the overdogs made up bogus excuses to steal Cynthia's children, fulfilling the wishes of Fred, Bobby, and their band of sick and twisted, and did only God knows what to them in the 12-17 year period where she wasn't allowed to raise her own children.

Does this really "pay Hitler back" for his war crimes? If so, it will have to be proven, but nothing has been proven yet, since Thomas and Ralene's grandparents were in America since 1901 and had nothing to do with Hitler. When all one cares about is how to get away for fifty years with abusing children, and get literally everyone to help do it, who really cares about the facts? So long as the children get abused for their entire lives, everything else is irrelevant to a mind that is solely obsessed with child abuse. Eventually, this sick excuse will be seen for what it is.

11. The Backwards Jackass Project

Ralene is replaced with Cynthia and Thomas is forced to watch more abuse performed by Dr. Garrist to a second victim and more than three others while no one lifts a finger to stop it.

At this stage, a recurring theme seems to have emerged. It seems some person or group thinks all this abusing of children will pay someone back for a a prior offense. There is some nefarious plan to push this project through to the end regardless of who gets hurt or killed in the process. Yet at odd moments throughout Thomas' long life several Jews and Hebrews (all Hebrews may not necessarily practice Judaism and conversely) told him that they weren't behind this project and didn't see any reason for it to be en force, which Thomas believed to be true, and still does.

So, why has no one in an authority position payed any attention?

Number 1 reason: They have no clue who God is.

2. They think they're Jesus Christ and can walk around and do whatever they please with no consequences.

3. They are overt sadists and do not discriminate between age or sex when distributing their retardation and pain.

4. They are both blind and deaf.

5. They find logic in the torture of people for decades not even related to Hitler and think this makes things even.

6. They imagine Hitler was not an Austrian.

7. They imagine Hitler was not a Catholic.

8. They imagine Mussolini was German.

Thankfully, every Jewish person doesn't have the mind set of Fred Steiner, this is assuming that Fred is even a Jew to begin with and didn't lie about it just to see his sick, perverted whims fulfilled with the help of a large group of idiots. For all anyone knows, he could be Antarctican. Regardless of nationality, raping children won't be excused no matter what prior real or imaginary crimes were committed. If they are, then we're no longer dealing with real justice officials, despite the name plaque on their door.

12. "You're Obsessed!" - The Accusation That Always Works

It didn't take long, with the aid of doctor administered hypnosis, to convince over five girls (all under ten years of age) in the project that Thomas was obsessed with them. Not only him, but also every other male on the face of the planet. They believed it and still do, after making sure the idea was sufficiently planted in everyone around them for their comfort. They spend days putting on makeup, then go out and hide like mice from invisible fears and opinion-generated obsessions that don't exist. Of course because of this, separations were in order - *exactly* what the criminals wanted! When everyone is lying about who exists and who doesn't, it makes testifying against them impossible. So the courts once again play into the hands of the murderers.

Thomas was separated from his sisters and friends without any permission from God Almighty and none have returned to this day with news of their release from the bondage of hypnotically-induced obsessions or apologies for the inconvenience of the lies. At this point, an apology would make no difference anyway.

There were false rumors that Thomas' dad had done something to warrant this abuse, but this was already disproven. Odd to punish only one family for that, or punish anyone in the country for which they were fighting for defending it. But lies and rumor provide far more fodder for pedophiles than the truth even in other cases. Too much responsibility is involved with promoting the truth, or knowing how to find it to begin with, since that would involve asking questions.

To this end, Thomas ran a test: Before over 1,000 subjects, Thomas placed both truth and lies. In over 90% of the cases, the lies were clung to like long-lost children and the truth was shouted down even before the sentence was finished. Lies are easier to swallow and have less work involved. This does nothing for the victims of the lies, but our egos *must* be sated at all costs, or *else*!

Once a member of the court approached Thomas and stated, "You know, this is only going to work one way."

"Yeah, it's going to work the way I say it does," Thomas quickly replied, "because it's my life and I'm the witness to the murder. You weren't there, you know nothing other than what I tell you, and I'm telling the truth. The murderers *aren't* going to tell you the truth. To expect this indicates you're insane and expecting something that will never happen. That's how it's going to work.

"You will take my word for it, or you will take theirs, there isn't a third option. You already have sufficient evidence that I'm telling the truth, (age, missing person, blood on the carpet, more than five police reports, and more). Execute them so they can't get out of jail and kill more family members, which releases you have allowed to happen over three times, then you'll get more evidence once I'm assured my family is safe.

"'This' isn't going to work *any other way*. So, keep wasting time expecting something else to happen. You've perjured yourself too many times already for me to place any further trust in you. You allowed them out of jail twice to molest my sister and I in our own backyard and we placed trees to mark the spot so you can't lie and say it didn't happen like you've done countless times already.

"*Nothing* other than what I've said is going to happen. If you wait till you die, you go to hell. Whatever they're paying you isn't worth sending your soul to hell for eternity. I'd start to move if I were you, but again, truth has a weight of responsibility that your ego isn't willing to carry. We'll be watching to see what you do - *continued abuse*, or *justice*.

"It's *your* choice!"

1. THE BLINDER

The man smirked, smug in his liberal education and walked away. Thomas never saw him again. He is still waiting for the oath sworn to the Lord that the murderers would be executed and the evil removed from the land as ordered by the Lord when they blasphemed the Holy Spirit of God. As of now, it's not expected.

13. Botanical Markers

Several trees were planted along the roadside of Tarpin Road to mark the property and elsewhere along the fence line of a moderately sized curtilage which also contained a similar, yet opposite facing bungalow on Streetlight in another part of town. The trees marked various events - rendered of sufficient significance to inspire the planting of a tree. Some trees (mostly of oak) would serve as boundaries not to be crossed. When one was crossed, another tree would be planted to mark the new boundary. Other trees were to mark a place where a vital event took place - some of these being supposed initially to be wondrous and beautiful, but were later discovered only to hold as much of horror, disgust, and confusion in proportion as they initially were viewed to be wondrous and transportive.

The subsequent property owner of the Tarpin Road house, in a laughably vain attempt to lay down the law by ignoring it, set the boundaries marked by the oak trees, one of which had the gargoyle face grown over its lopped branch. He instructed Thomas not to cross these regions to see if he could follow instructions. But to follow directions of a known lawbreaker, who had sworn an oath to the living God and broken it, committing perjury in an American court of justice, would make Thomas equally guilty. At that young stage in his life, committing such an act would have allowed the evil to crawl into an unhealthy position of command, and once thus ensconced, would have become permanently affixed and unrecoverable by the time he at long length would remember it some thirty-four years later.

The reason for his forcibly manufactured memory loss was yet another of the endless train of insane dictums mandated by the covenant-breakers, secondary owners of the house, Thomas' father having been the initial owner, even after his death. Six such trees were planted at the Tarpin Road dwelling, marking as much as the enforcement of lawlessness as they did Thomas' disobedience - the latter merely in theory, not in practice or reality.

In the Streetlight house, a pecan tree marked the ineptitude of the jailors to contain Fred and Bobby, who would arrive daily to ensure Thomas was thoroughly molested. It was to be believed by all that this repaid some crime committed by the two children, but in fact was orchestrated using the hypnosis, not from any decision on the part of the assaulted family. How do we know all believed this? If not, the two would never have been allowed out of the prison. Exactly how this repayment was accomplished, even if any five-year-old had committed some alleged crime, absolutely no one has yet explained.

A bit further out, a pine tree marked the exact same event. Not just the ineptitude of the jailors, but where his sister would see the event take place from the back door.

"I saw what they did to you," she told him, trying to assure him that she was on his side. She hoped he would start believing her someday.

"You didn't see anything!" he replied in an undertone so as not to be overheard. "If you tell anyone, I'll kill you!"

This he said because Fred and Bobby had previously threatened to kill him and his whole family if he did anything to put them in jail. Only later would he wonder why this even mattered anyway since the prison seemed to have a perpetual revolving door; jail is nothing to these crabs scurrying indiscriminately in and right back out of it. So, he had promised not to say anything to anyone. It didn't matter much anyway, a psychic would know what Fred, Bobby, and the rest of them were up to. Surely it couldn't take too long for them to put them in jail permanently for murder and child molestation. And surely it couldn't take long to perform any execution after the sentence was passed by the judge and sworn to God to be done. Had he known judges and lawyers lie too often, he would have promised nothing after seeing such an example that they're actually all in the same group as the criminals.

He had no idea that most psychics were liars along with some in the police and justice system and that after they murdered his grandfather on his mother's side using a hypnosis trick, he would spend the next forty years being abused without the case ever coming to any semblance of rectitude.

A few other trees marked weddings that Thomas thought at the time were real, only to find out later that they were both wrong and illegal, thus rendering them both invalid, a waste of time, and further abuse perfectly orchestrated and form-fitting to the abuser's exact designs.

What followed all this was a slow crawl of forty years laced with further abuse, lack of self-defense ability, and forced statements garnered via hypnotic triggers, compounding the initial crime beyond the magnitude of measurement - and it didn't stop there.

14. Guilt Altering Reality

Courts imagine themselves, it appears, to have the power to alter facts. But guilt isn't determined by a courtroom proceeding, especially after the judge perjures himself by stating "they will be executed no matter what," then refusing to do so. Even had he said nothing, the verdict was guilty and the sentence was execution. So whatever he promised or whether such words are legal or not is irrelevant to the fact that the sentence was never carried out, which is illegal regardless of whoever doesn't like it. If the sentence fits the crime, not performing it is illegal.

Much the reverse - guilt is determined by the facts. Thomas, as an eyewitness, has the facts. The court only has lies though which it must sift, and a fifty year waste of time indicating that it has yet to do so. The court not only has no facts, but appears to have no interest in discovering them, since the scene of the primary crime (the murder) has now been destroyed, paved over, and topped with over-priced houses that are no more than two inches apart from each other.

Anyone even remotely familiar with the Bible knows that God, not man, is in control and doesn't require all the little "helpers" running around committing crimes in the name of God with the flimsy excuse of "righting wrongs," or whatever selfish confabulations they craft to condone their deleterious behavior.

When Thomas knew the court had been bought off was precisely when they asked him, who being an eyewitness *is* evidence himself, where the evidence is. When someone asks for something that is staring them in the face, it means one of two things:

    1.) We are talking to a crazy person, or
    2.) We are talking to someone who has been bought.

Further evidence of this fact:

Instead of executing the murderers, as stated by a court judge under oath, and determined by a sentence of execution after a guilty verdict was found by a jury in trial one, they wasted time using unqualified teachers to give Thomas a lesson about how to build a septic system correctly while using his property as a reservoir for nearly a decade with absolutely no permission.

To this day, for all anyone knows, no murderers have been executed and certainly no lesson about septic systems was asked for. The three trees in the yard were cut down when he was forty-five, in protest against any accusation of "preserving" the memories fondly. For Thomas, they were nothing close to fond.

On the other hand, if this was the desired result, we can rest assured Satan is extremely happy with the performance of the justice system in this case.

Children were raped, forced to watch their father executed, and were abused throughout the rest of their lives as much as possible. What more could slaves to an idiot who threw away paradise ask for?

15. Mock Trial

Since doing things in the reverse is the motif for Thomas' case, the reverse is exactly what was done from close to the very beginning. Since no criminals were executed after clearly stating they would be, the only possible logical conclusion is that people were talking in reverse, which only means one thing.

Namely, that the subsequent mock trial was the real, and what everyone supposed was the real trial was the mock.

Why?

One reason is that this wouldn't be the first time the "law officials" had placed Thomas or his family in jeopardy by ignoring rules of law merely for the sake of convenience. Such actions are ostensibly punishable by other rules, yet strangely enough, even alarmingly, not here. If we make a mockery of someone's life, they will mock us in turn, according to Newton's third law.

There was another reason.

There is a law in place, and ignoring this particular law for any reason could wind up killing the crime victim, and has already, otherwise the law would not exist.

The said law being that anyone present during hypnosis may not be present in the courtroom when the victim is giving testimony since this could both influence the testimony itself or as said previously, kill the victim. This was avoided by Dr. Garrist, since he knew that any death of either child would immediately get all three of them executed. Somehow murdering the father was acceptable to everyone and didn't require an execution.

This law is especially relevant when those present during hypnosis were using it to get away with repeatedly raping the victims after killing their father, even directly after many of the court sessions.

This is especially true also when those present during the illegal hypnosis (no permission was given, coercion doesn't equal a grant) are also the murderers, the accused, and the defendants.

Was this law followed? No. Reason? Irrelevant. It was all stated, understood, and written down in the first court case. If no one bothered to read that, the victims aren't responsible.

So, since everyone was busy following laws, or not following them, and no one was listening to what was being said (such as, "This is only going to work one way," "We will execute them no matter what," and "This is only going to be stated once,") then the reversal of the mock trial was the only way to convey the truth about the matter. Anyone paying attention would have noticed that anyway. Anyone studying the case (which should be done prior to calling witnesses) would have known Fred and Bobby paid doctors to use hypnosis way in advance of doing anything to the family, otherwise the crime would not have been performed. Stating whatever it was more than once had been programmed to cause a death of someone, so it was not possible to repeat. That person has either died as a result, or it was somehow prevented. The outcome of that isn't known, but the stupidity of asking for it to be repeated after knowing that it would kill someone can't be overstated.

There was another doctor prior to Dr. Garrist that laid the groundwork for the subsequent hypnosis sessions. By this and other means, they ensured there was no possible way they would be executed, so long as everyone was convinced of the appropriate ideas at pivotal moments. At the same time, they both knew that thinking about it would show there was no real reason *not* to execute them, that is if the law officers performed the oaths to which they had sworn, thus putting the responsibility entirely where it belongs and where it still remains: in the hands of the Justice system. This is how they escaped responsibility in their own heads, but not obviously in reality.

Saying, "it wasn't admitted into evidence" or "we didn't know" is the same as perjury, since all law officials swore an oath to protect the citizens of the United States of America. Refusing to allow truth into evidence is perjury since this is contrary to the oath of "stating the whole truth and nothing but the truth." Found is also implied since truth can't be stated until after it is found. Not studying "the whole truth and nothing but the truth" about the case is an admission of withholding critical case evidence and is an instance of Obstruction of Justice due to the irresponsibly of withholding critical, life-damning case evidence for no real reason.

Whosoever has done this has committed perjury by lying while under oath to perform their duty as judge or lawyer and has no real worth in this case. All decisions while made under perjury are null and void since the office is nothing after visibly sustained periods of lying.

What does this mean?

After so much has been proven to the contrary, some are still waiting for a body. But this request was made after the perjury. So, as said before, the body will show up *after* the execution - *not before*! Assuming it wasn't destroyed by someone already.

Why? "We will execute them no matter what." Body, or no body.

Why? Otherwise, another family member will die, after which God and myself included this time, will require it from their hands.

What purpose can there be even remotely connected to justice for having a trial, verdict, and sentence, then doing absolutely nothing for fifty years about any of it?

After saying, "We will execute them no matter what," then proceeding not to do so, they have committed perjury and no further decisions, judgments, or demands past that point will be recognized, as is clearly seen by understanding the words of the oath.

Thomas must live with what happened "no matter what." So must they.

Normally, truth is told in the real trial, lies are told in the mock (mockery of the truth) trial, otherwise the name "mock" doesn't mean mock. When things are reversed, the truth is told in the mock trial. We hope someone wrote it down, since we're only going to say this once. Whatever was said won't be repeated here either. It was the precise answer to the entire case, but memory of it wasn't allowed for the victims.

16. "You Set Me Up!"

Over the last fifty years there have been many who complain like infants with degrees about being set up. Let's ask ourselves why this could possibly be.

Thomas was initially asked by people posing as law enforcement to help keep someone in jail, which is a simple matter: don't let them out. Then we subsequently illegally, not legal by all moral and ethical laws, let people out of jail which set Thomas up and forced him to watch a murder of a family member for which we had no reason nor right to do. For some reason, we don't care about that, which is proven by the murderers still being alive, despite any laws or oaths.

So, what is it that is now expected, other than a pacifier required to stop the ignorance spilling out of our lives? For everything to go our way?

It will.

First stop is a lesson in what's wrong with killing someone; something with which, in all our lectures to Thomas about not molesting children, we neglected to explain why we have no qualms with letting people out of jail to kill someone, then molest their children for over fifty years.

The question is: How is this not obvious? There's only one possible answer to that question, which probably isn't obvious.

As is all too often the case, we only set ourselves up.

17. The God Haters

It may seem that by posing such complex issues, such as a team of doctors surrounding Thomas, asking, "What did he do?" after seeing several unfavorable results from the hypnosis he performed which bore negative effects on everyone, that Dr. Garrist was demonstrating how easy it is to deceive humans and how they should be born with more intelligence or survival instincts. This is what we are now to consider.

From the question, "What did he do?" after he had done an uncountable number of things, exposes the first problem with this question. It's not possible, even without the hypnosis, which deliberately clouds the mind, for any five year old to remember or count events past more than a few, of which there were more than a score per session. Since he was with Dr. Garrist for several days for twenty minutes to an hour each session, they knew there were more than a score, probably more than a hundred, maybe even several hundred.

Asking this question proves only that at *no* age do we have sufficient intelligence or survival instincts that are needed to face everything possible in our surroundings. Recording devices have been available since the late 1800s. Placing one of these in the rooms where the doctor performed his work would have told them precisely what he did. Asking a five year old what a doctor with even one degree did also demonstrates severe lack of intellect, or that those asking the dumb questions were working for him making sure the child couldn't remember what he did, allowing the avoidance of repercussions.

This may also seem to be a merciful aspect of the criminals, that they would request of God something that could potentially help us survive both encounters with murderous pedophiles as well as many other encounters we find in our travels through this jungle of sadism. This is how they want us to perceive them, so we don't.

After repeatedly forcing the children to blaspheme the Holy Ghost (which isn't possible, but they thought it was), repeatedly stating how they can't wait for the times when they can kill Christians in the streets like they used to do, and lying about whether or not they're Jews all lend to prove they have no merciful bone in their demonic frames. They have no love for God and repeatedly yelled the same as they were raping various children and as they forced the children to blaspheme God. Luckily, blasphemy is a decision, not something that can be forced.

"Fuck Christians! I can't wait till we can kill them in the streets the way we used to do!" Fred said more than three different times and on more than one occasion.

Therefore, love for God or acts of mercy isn't why they did any of this. Any who believe their feint have been grossly deceived, or sadistically don't care if they have.

Even with all this, they somehow still managed to gather a cadre of dutiful myrmidons that slavishly follow their every whim and hand them everything on a silver platter, whether it be rapes, murders, separations, refusing to perform results of prior court cases, or harassing the victims for over fifty years. These witting pawns can be found in every station in life, from family members to places in public office and police. This serves to further prove how very few there are who actually know Jesus Christ.

18. Anticipation Disorder

(A conversation between Thomas and the Perfect Prefect Fuga Speculum)

a. Initial Statements

7:15am

"Much of what you've said seems to indict everyone," said the Most Holy Prefect.

"Yes, it may seem that way," Thomas replied.

"Is it?"

"Depends on who's guilty. If everyone, then yes."

"You don't know?"

"Do you know who's lying and who isn't?" Thomas said, eying Fuga curiously.

"No," Fuga depressed into his chair slightly.

"Then neither do I."

"Then there's no way out?"

"No, there is a way out."

"We can't see one."

"I thought you said, 'We can do this any way you want.' What happened?

"There were alleged psychics just five houses down from where the murder occurred who claimed it was against their religion to get involved. When I involved them personally, suddenly their religion didn't have problems helping the police put the murderers behind bars. Either they are psychic, knew what was happening and didn't call the

46

police, or they're not and need to quit taking people's money. Either way, they could have told you a way out. Either way, they know which of my statements are true and which are false. If they don't tell you, they're guilty. So there's a blatantly obvious way out."

"Why would you say something false?"

"Good question. Why did you say you would execute them no matter what, then not do it? If I follow your example and you don't like it, why do you never blame yourself?"

"But all of this is already over and done a long time ago. Move on."

"Oh yeah? For you, maybe," Thomas said shaking his head.

"Glad you were able to enjoy your life at the expense of others," Thomas replied after a short pause. "But, there are people I know who, until they find out what really happened, which you'll never tell them, since it would point directly to your responsibility, for them, it never will be."

Thomas thought to himself, So, you told someone who saw a murder that you have no problems with murder? Sounds like you no longer want that relationship. Actually, sounds like we're pretty close to the end of it. If only this weren't the beginning.

b. The Actual Disruption of the Interruptions

7:25am

"You actually are responsible for what has been said," Thomas informed Mr. Speculum.

"We will prove this," he began.

"The fact is, it was said," Thomas placed one forefinger against another.

"Any investigator worth their salt would run through the five Ws to get the most information to go on.

"But you failed to ask *where* it was said.

"It was said in his mind. Had you asked, he would have told you, and what was said on top of that.

"Therefore, as I said, You are responsible for what was said, which wouldn't be true had a.) it not been said or b.) you were not in charge of investigating," he concluded.

"We're responsible even if we haven't heard what was said?" the Prefect exclaimed.

"Yes."

"Why?"

"The information was always available, you just didn't bother to ask. This will only be said once and said quickly since time is money. I said that on the witness stand of the mock trial, which was the real one.

"Reason: It's obvious and obvious facts don't necessarily require any statements about them.

"You would have gotten to this point fifty years ago had you not busied yourself interrupting the answers to questions you were asking. What college taught you that it's either respectable or reasonable to interrupt an answer to a question six milliseconds after you ask it? What are you covering and who paid you to protect the guilty by so doing? Why are you still a judge after covering, aiding, and abetting known murderers?" Thomas drove on as if a wall of steel were nothing before him.

"We don't know that they are murderers," Fuga hedged with the typical weasel-like dexterity.

"You know after you've been told, unless you're deaf," Thomas said.

"Fact: The murderer isn't guilty only after you say so," Thomas continued, "he is immediately guilty after one person has died by his hand. Your power doesn't extend to altering the fabric of reality. He is guilty at the point of the crime, not just because of your declaration. Your word, contrary to what your Jupiter-sized ego tells you, is not that damn powerful. The guilty are so because of their crime, not because of your almighty say so.

"Not recognizing these facts led to a forty-three year waste of time, for which you are responsible, guilty, and shall face subsequent punishment in an appropriate court of justice," Thomas summed up as he left the room for one of the many breaks needed to deal with this man-crafted insanity.

c. The Final Nails (Part 912)

7:18am

"So, you didn't see what you wanted to see?" Thomas inquired.

"No, we didn't," Prefect Speculum spat.

"That's good. You realize you could have though, right?"

"We don't see how that is."

"The first three words of that sentence explain exactly why that is. You see what you want to see. You always have and evidently that will never change," Thomas said, quietly gazing into a distant, unseen object.

"We don't think it's something we missed, we think it's something you're doing," Fuga accused defensively.

"You're right, it is something I'm doing. You keep trying to do things the wrong way, making things convenient for yourselves at the expense of everybody else and heedless of who it kills in the process. But when you're screwing up my life and wind up killing people that you obviously could care less about, you'll do things the right way whether you like it or not. You keep trying to have it both ways and that isn't going to happen. What I'm doing is making sure that specifically *that doesn't* happen; because if it does, more people will die. I know your concern is far elsewhere, but mine isn't."

"We don't believe that," Fuga deflected.

"Happily, this isn't based on what you believe," Thomas remarked without distrait. "You've had the answer spelled out for you several times, but instead of recognizing and admitting it, you just keep saying, 'No' till you get the answer you want, even though I'm fairly certain not even you know precisely what that is. But life or justice isn't an all you can eat buffet. The answer may occasionally be something you don't want. Also, I don't think you've ever understood the answer, you just think you do. The correct response to 'Is 2 + 2 = 4?' isn't 'No.' The correct response is, 'That's right.' Anything other than that response is just a deliberate waste of time. If you could have changed the outcome, you can't complain that you didn't see what you wanted to, since it was all your decision to begin with, and always has been."

"There are some things you don't know, some of which can kill you," Thomas said with caution, hoping some sign other than sociopath would suddenly start beaming from Fuga.

"Well, we've been wanting to tell you there are some things that you also don't know," Fuga replied.

"If you knew any of it, even a small part, it would change much of your thoughts and behavior."

"We could say the same to you."

"Aside from being irrelevant to your thoughts and behavior, I know. How do you think I had the idea in the first place?"

"How can you tell that the lawyers don't have the transcript of the first trial?" the Prefect asked with an obvious frantic shift of subject.

"Because they keep asking when no means yes or yes means no, and they always get it wrong."

"What does that have to do with the transcript?"

"If they had it, they wouldn't waste time asking, they would know. And if you don't know, you can't judge. And if you don't 'no,' you can't judge. So, you don't like what I'm saying?"

"No, we don't."

"Let me tell you how you can fix that."

"Enlighten us."

"Don't force a three-year-old to watch a murder, you sick, disgusting waste of air!!!"

d. Annalogue the Analyzer

8:20am

"What bothers me the most about this case? Finally, a nonobvious question. Well, that the people who didn't do anything wrong are being made to feel guilty while the actual murderers are being worshiped like gods and molly-coddled," Thomas began.

"That bothers you?" inquired Fuga rhetorically.

"You can sanely tell me that you would watch one of your friends being harassed when they didn't deliver the first strike and not be bothered? You have a problem remaining outside of the obvious, don't you?" Thomas shot back.

"So, what would you pass on were the world your audience?"

"After going through this useless hell, I would say, don't exactly pattern yourself after anyone else's behavior."

"Other than the obvious, why not?"

"Because what may work perfectly well for them can become a devastating disaster for you, as you said, because of the obvious.

"You let murderers live, then you want to prance around preaching to me about the law that you don't care about anyway? Your hypocrisy is speaking so loudly, I can't hear what you're saying. To me, you're just another Zero Sum Equation."

"You said he was a fake police officer?"

"Yeah. Anyone who doesn't follow the law of reason, logic, theology, or civility and especially can't be bothered with looking up every case leading up to the one he's investigating can't be properly termed an 'officer of the law.' He wants to pick and choose what he looks at instead of considering the entire set of facts merely because he thinks his race is better than every other can only be called a fake."

"He may have superior legal authority."

"If we find we're party to or directly responsible for harassing a rape victim, expect nothing from them ever, other than that we will never be trusted by them on any significant level. Even if they forgive us, it's impossible to trust anyone who decided to become part of the problem.

Mostly since condoning and extending the initial aggression indicates a deeper level of moral bankruptcy than the initial aggressor."

"The law doesn't necessarily require the trust of the public," Fuga hedged again.

"Well, let's review - If you don't 'no' = 'If you don't know when to stop' = 'If you don't know when enough is enough.' All of these are equivalent expressions and indicate the addressee has control issues and should receive appropriate treatment. This was also said in 1969, only a few short years ago.

"If you can't make something that doesn't break, what good is your degree? You throw people out on the street for not having one, but you can't make anything worth a damn yourself. Nice going! Sounds like you need to spend about five years in reassessment training," Thomas fumed.

"We should break and come back later," Fuga observed.

10:53am

"Why were two opposing statements issued during the trial?" Fuga inquired, adjusting the papers on the clipboard in front of him.

"Two opposing statements *weren't* issued *during* the trial. But there were two statements because you keep letting them out of jail. Your own actions are two opposing statements."

"That isn't our responsibility."

"When you keep causing your own problem, then pretend you have no responsibility, don't act surprised when no one trusts you - ever. When you stop letting them out, only one statement will be issued since no one will subsequently die from its utterance. If you can't actually defend the people, get out of the business and let someone who can. If you care nothing for the law, don't lie to others about what you are.

"So long as a statement is true, the following (contrary to popular myth) is irrelevant: Why it was said. Where it was said. When it was said. Or, who said it. If the statement implies a responsibility on any party, guilt is predicated with the party until their responsibility has been dispatched. So, only the '*what*' of the matter remains critical, otherwise nonsense has been distributed."

"So, where do you think things went wrong?"

"Aside from the obvious? During those hundreds of moments that are passed over with either no thought whatsoever or with thousands of excuses. Considering that, even our own behavior is pointing right to them."

Later, after he went home, Cynthia would sit with him on their favorite spot on a roof above the door of a small house in the yard.

"When do they realize their part in this?" asked Cynthia

"Most of the time? Never," Thomas' words followed fast on the heels of hers.

"How is this never seen?" Cynthia wondered.

"Because it's an illusion. They believe that sitting and doing nothing could never hurt anyone, since it's not an active, but a passive action. To them, it is 'logic' that no passive action could result in so much harm or even any. So, this lie coddles them to sleep every night," said Thomas, gritting his teeth in hate.

"How many have died from this so far?" asked Cynthia, her curiosity beginning to coalesce into fear.

"One is too many. And we've found far more than that so far," stated Thomas.

"What is one of the largest contributing factors in this?" Cynthia responded, not sure if her fears were merely growing or already beyond her control. She almost didn't want an answer.

"The choice of not arguing when they could, when it would do the most good, and require the least effort, or arguing when they shouldn't about what makes no difference, requires decades, and never arrives at any conclusion," said Thomas, with direction governing his motives. He also remembered the critical words of his friend: "With what measure ye mete."

Before falling asleep, after remembering some of the sessions with Dr. Garrist, Thomas was thinking of why it never occurred to people that telling someone whose head was crushed in three places with a railroad spike that our comprehension is slower than theirs is not believable. Unless we would like wearing a shirt that says, "I think slower than a person with a railroad-spike crushed head."

He also wondered why few realize that hypnotic programs are not directly intentional on the part of the victims, since they are a violation of the free-will contract established by nature. That is, they are not intended by the person in whom the program is running any more than the computer intends to show us what it does. In both cases, the person we're angry with is not in front of us. Becoming angry at the computer won't change the words the other person is typing into it. Actually, the computer doesn't care who we are at all. They are, however, directly intentional on the part of anyone who knows the triggers.

e. The Strength of Sin Is Ignorance

*"The strength of sin is the law:"*₂
Ignorance of the law is no excuse, but ignorance within the law is.
-Common behavior model.

8:10am

"When someone tells you that something is only going to be said once, why would you follow this with questions about a mock trial? What are the chances a mock trial will solve the case when something is only going to be said once?" Thomas inquired.

"Is this some of the promised help not arriving that you previously alluded to?" Fuga characteristically deflected once again.

"Yes, certainly wasn't expected that only the murderers would receive any."

"What would you have done?"

"Well, doesn't take a genius to know that as soon as you hear, 'This is only going to be said once' you damn well better turn on some kind of recording device. Either that or live the rest of your life knowing that you won't solve the case.

"I'm still having trouble understanding how exactly we're seeking the whole truth and nothing but the truth while we exclude evidence directly related to any case? It's logically and mathematically impossible to exclude any part of the whole and yet be seeking the whole. Unless you're insane, where you imagine things are happening that can't. This is why the bona fide mentally destabilized *aren't* the ones in the sanitariums. No, not by a country decade; you will find they hold many places of power and have for millennia."

"You have proof of this?" Fuga said, writing something on his clipboard.

"We argue in court over what's legal to enable criminals to roam the earth unpunished for doing what isn't."

"How can we correct this from here?" Fuga reclined slightly.

"What if everything in your life was based on one mistake made at the beginning?"

"Who made the mistake?"

"Many have mistakenly assumed my caprice indicates a lower intelligence. What it does indicate is that too often I see behavioral judgments assessed according to convenience rather than justice. Caprice forces judges to face the fact that they too often have no clue about what is directly in front of them. This is most clearly seen when we hear them ask for evidence of anything when sufficient evidence has overwhelmingly been supplied. When any eyewitness makes a statement, this is evidence. To ask for more evidence indicates we are ignoring the statement made by the witness. When we ignore evidence, we cannot also be looking for 'the whole truth.' Any ignoring or excluding of evidence is ignoring and excluding the truth, when the evidence is pointing directly at the truth. After this happens, we are guilty of perjury for swearing an oath to find the truth, then deliberately ignoring any of it," Thomas finished, nearly without a pause.

"Well, the children just don't communicate," Fuga muttered mechanically, looking away.

"Yes, because you've repeatedly done the wrong thing with everything that's been communicated so far, and 'the past is prologue.'"

"But that doesn't mean we'll do the wrong thing in the future."

"In your case, it does," Thomas replied with little effort, remembering again the fifth or so time Fred and Bobby showed up once more where he had repeatedly been moved to prevent them from finding him. The exact number of relocations is unknown.

f. How To Ask Questions

8:27am

"What else do you believe caused this case to fail?" Fuga began.

"It wouldn't have failed at all if not for this one element," Thomas said, growing weary with the much questioning and non-existent actions in response to any of the answers.

"Which?"

"Way too many people ostensibly involved with finding the truth turned out to not care at all about it."

"How do you know that?"

"I lost track of the number of times I heard the words 'I don't care' directly after providing critical information to solve the case. If you don't care, you have no business being anywhere near this case, and since you love the child molesters, as evidenced by the fact that you don't care, we'll let you get married to them before we execute them. Never tell a rape victim you don't care. They have a way of making sure that you do in the end," Thomas said, eyes riveted to a point on the wall.

"So, what are you waiting for now?"

"Other than the case to actually be solved? I'm waiting for the people who don't care to leave and for the people who do to show up. I had no idea it would take fifty years for this to happen."

g. Intended Damage

8:47am

Fuga brought in a helper with him today, a Gad Shillinger, expert in psychology, law, and evasion. Both sat opposite Thomas in the small room with only one door and no windows.

"So, you're ignoring a court order?" Fuga said, leaning into the table between them.

"Which order? The one made by the judge who had previously perjured himself and refused to admit it?" Thomas replied without moving.

"Everyone else is following the court orders to the letter."

"Yeah, and when they see who paid the court to cover this all up and what they stole from us, they will spend the rest of their short lives wishing they had ignored these orders made by a perjured judge harder and faster than I did."

"They're expecting you to help them recover."

"I was expecting that in 1995 also. The time to do that was in 1995. Now, I think I'll ignore them for the next fifty years instead."

"That may kill them with the depression."

"That was also true in 1995. Did they worry about that fact then?"

"What are they supposed to do then?"

"What anyone was supposed to do, in my observation, has never really been a major concern to anyone. They seem rather to just do whatever the hell they feel like doing, as long as it winds up destroying something," Thomas said, gritting his teeth again.

"So, now what?"

"Don't worry," Thomas smiled, "the murderous demons' butts your group has been slavishly breaking their necks to kiss will make sure you all have a nice cushy life ahead of you, I'm certain. But your money and bribes will have no effect on the throne of God Almighty. I think that's the only place in the universe that you won't be able to cover up the truth. I'll be there to see what your *real* answers are. And when the destruction you've set up for yourself finally hits you, I will laugh. I probably will have never laughed as hard in my entire existence."

"Why did you pretend to be the bad guy?" asked Gad Shillinger.

"Well, because even though they never wound up doing the right thing in the end, as they were informing me about right and wrong, the side result is that they had to listen themselves to what is right or wrong. So they heard their own responsibility from their own mouth. People who don't listen to themselves are insane. So in the end, they will be the ones who get locked up.

"One of the main purposes of reality is to hard code events for future review so no one can lie about what did or didn't happen. Like that doctor that told me when I was four, 'When anyone finds out what we did, I will be dead. It will be too late to do anything about it.' He is wrong," replied Thomas.

h. Sufficient Evidence

8:17am

"So, what's your point?" Fuga exclaimed in exasperation.

"You need to answer the same question after dragging a trial out for fifty years and pretending to offer justice," Thomas clarified.

"Our point is perfectly clear."

"To you? But I can say, my point is that you need to more quickly decide when you have sufficient evidence to make a decision. Two eyewitnesses telling you precisely what happened is sufficient. X-rays of a crushed skull, a wrist broken in two places with a pair of pliers, gun shot wounds to two knees that had to be amputated are sufficient evidence. Nine thousand police reports of men harassing one family, which you keep making excuses of not being able to find, yet I saw the police show up over twenty times personally, is sufficient evidence.

"After having enough, you ask for more, then make a charade of not knowing what to do only proves your incompetence. I noticed you left the entire blood-stained carpet in the northwest corner of the back bedroom untouched, not one strip removed, taken to the lab, or tested in any way, which I'm guessing your incompetence told you wasn't evidence. I think what everyone, God included, needs to know is: What in the hell precisely do you consider to be evidence?

"And don't say, 'a body.' Since you left the entire house and yard untouched by even one eyeball of an investigator, you also know where the body is and are only asking to find out if your secret is in any danger."

The prefect perfection dropped his clipboard on the floor and left the room.

i. No Palace in the Future

8:15am

"Why did you test the dual-task ability of most people you met?" Fuga wondered, as did several others in the case.

"So they could see first hand that they are incapable of adequately judging other people, so that when the time came for them to judge others their mind would tell them not to. Very few passed this test successfully. But every one of them judged us," Thomas replied without thinking long about it.

"How do you know they judged you?"

"Do you see us together now?" Thomas slapped the table, spilling Fuga's cup of ignorance sauce.

"Why do you think they did that?"

"Other than the primary reason of jealousy, the lethal subculture is too large for most people to either recognize or resist. But what the subculture doesn't recognize is when you take things this far, it gives your enemies every reason and right to do the same thing to you in the future in a time when you will be able to do nothing about it. Probably nothing less than that will show them the utter uselessness of their actions. But I'm pushing to make sure something does, because once those events unfold, they can't be reversed."

"But didn't one of your sisters tell you things would work out?"

"They saw the future, changed it, then expect the same future they saw to happen. It can't work that way, obviously. For some it works out. For most, not so much. Nothing close to what they expect anyway. It didn't work out at all for the ten or so people who are now dead," Thomas said, looking Fuga directly in the eye.

j. The Unbribable Investigator

8:37am

Thomas handed the prefect a piece of paper with the following on it:

"You don't feel guilty?" asked the officer.

"No, not if I can help it," Thomas replied.

"So, why don't you feel guilty?" said the officer who doesn't exist in reality.

"Because I don't believe everything I hear."

"You hear them telling you that you should feel guilty?"

"No, I see it in their actions."

"And they think you haven't remembered their actions previous to these?"

"Correct. I saw how events were manipulated - carefully arranged - in their favor, or so they thought. I also saw how they used hypnosis. Which is entirely the point: If you can use hypnosis to make the wrong things happen, then you could also have used it to make the *right* things happen - but you didn't."

"Seems they're asking you to feel guilty for their own decision."

"And why I never will. This is what they want. So, now who's the sociopath?"

Genuine Law Officer who hasn't shown up yet:

"What went through your mind all the thousands of times people in fake positions of authority asked you if you wanted to have sex with your sister or wanted to make a bomb?"

Me: "I always wonder where the real law officers are who will arrest these jerks for illegal solicitation to a crime."

Thomas then asked, "See anything different as far as direction?"

The prefect dropped his clipboard on the floor and fled out of the room as if he were on fire.

k. Qualified

8:27am

"Do you enjoy seeing the people around you suffer?" Fuga said, once more trying an obfuscation, frantically hoping for some other way than the path of responsibility.

"Why ask a question if you already know the answer? More importantly, were the people now suffering given a promise by you which, if done, would have avoided the suffering?"

"We didn't know what to do."

"Why do you keep saying things you and I both know aren't true? Trying to influence those not involved who can have no effect on the final outcome?"

"We couldn't be sure you weren't lying."

"This coming from people who can't stop lying. I wasn't, but it's only because you can't stop that you aren't sure. So, your college taught you to punish others for your own misconceptions? I need to know where this college is so I can make perfectly sure that the school is fast closed down - permanently."

"What should we do now?"

"Why do you need someone to draw you a picture of how to keep your own promise? And being in this condition, how did you ever get into a position of authority? I can tell you this: You are not now, and have never been qualified to be in authority over me. I have never recognized it, and never will. This can be changed, but not by me. It's possible, but you would first have to stop kissing the asses of murderers."

Once more, Fuga let the clipboard clap the floor with short echos as he ran out of the room leaving Thomas with both silence and hundreds of broken promises.

I. Mixed Results

8:47am

"Though you surely saw the great expansion of freedom, or at least its vibrant force, legality notwithstanding, during that all too short era which some have mercifully captured in various recordings?" Fuga said, attempting a different tack.

"Yes, though it remains that 'the dead sleep not alway,'" Thomas replied.

"True, yet initially, do you feel this freedom was due to the close occupation of the ones preventing it, giving millions a much needed breath of fresh air?"

"Maybe for you, but perhaps," Thomas conceded. It was obvious this line of inquiry was crafted by someone other than Fuga, so Thomas remained reticent.

m. Debriefing

8:53am

"You were already told that if I have to tell you the answer it changes. Knowing who made the problem, you also by that know the change won't be positive. This is how I know people who ask questions which they rather need to answer for themselves are only there to cause damage. Had they just done what they knew was right, ten people would be alive who are now dead," Thomas remonstrated.

"But they had to ask permission?" the prefect reminded in frantic despair.

"False: they didn't do that either. Is there never any point where you realize that none of your actions line up with any of your words?

"I was informed that you knew what you needed to know to help with this case. If you didn't, it's not my problem. If you get anything wrong, in the end, again, it's not my problem. As in greater cases, each agent will be evaluated based on what they knew and what they did. From my view, it appears to be a common thread: the least amount of effort which accomplished absolutely nothing. They're lucky I don't have the final say.

"I had said that because you have allowed these things to walk the earth that don't need to be here, you prevented changes that you yourself have wanted for this entire fifty year period.

"When you execute them, you will see the changes.

"Then everything that happened to me will happen to you.

"Then I will laugh.

"Then I will cry," Thomas concluded.

At this point, the clipboard was wondering if it wouldn't be easier to just glue itself to the floor.

n. What Did We Learn?

8:13am

"Why haven't we progressed further than we have as a whole?" Fuga asked with a cocked eyebrow.

"Too often when the devil gives any command, everyone just tells him, 'Yessa massa,'" Thomas retorted.

"Do you have any proof?"

"Sure, and so do you. When Fred and Bobby told everyone to keep my sister and I separated so we couldn't testify to the murder we both saw them commit over fifty years ago, everyone just said, 'Yessa massa.' Nothing like putting smiles on a murderous child molester's face. I'm sure the slaves are proud of themselves or are happy with whatever money they were paid for their cooperation."

"I don't think it's that simple," Fuga evaded once again. Fuga's characteristic deflections were almost a visible trench coat.

"I think it is. Justice is only hard if you say so. It's only as hard as the bribes you take to prevent it, or the degree of apathy with which you award it, or the number of excuses you use to extend its suppression."

Against any accusation of delusions of grandeur Fuga had been getting lately regarding Thomas' attitude, he asked him, "Do you believe this case couldn't have been solved without your extensive contributions?"

"Since it hasn't yet been solved, it's not possible to see that. And since every single clue and suggestion is being ignored, it's plain that absolutely no one considers them contributions. But I doubt any one person by themselves would be exclusively vital. Even though complicated situations can be and have been solved by the addition or subtraction of one critical element, it's never possible to see who, what, or where that is until the solution presents itself," Thomas surmised.

"Do you feel everything you say is right?" Fuga provoked.

"You obviously do, but no I don't. If anything I've said is wrong, I'm sure you or someone else will either let me know or prove it.

"People who have never been affected by a crime should never sit on a criminal jury: they have no scope for clear judgment. Their quiet lives don't afford them a disinterested view, but rather an extremely biased view against anything that disturbs their peace, is even a mild inconvenience to their sense of normalcy, or that they have no vested interest in considering," Thomas redirected.

"How can you arrive at that conclusion?" Fuga said aghast.

"How can you not? Have you even read anything about this case yet? That we're all considered a gross inconvenience to everyone is reflected in every word, act, and decision in this case so far. Come back after you have read *all five* trial transcripts, and stop wasting my time," Thomas yelled, dismissing Fuga's pretend shock.

o. So Now What? p.14,937

8:13am

"All distortions in critical communication will be dealt with when the time comes," Thomas launched.

"But you've done this yourself," Fuga surprisingly deflected.

"This is a misleading perception: I made *corrections* in critical communication or code because what they said was wrong," Thomas redeflected.

"Is this where you changed your answer when the question was repeated?" Fuga maintained his line of deflection.

"No, that was where I knew I was talking to an idiot who has no clue about what was just said, indicating either Fred or Bobby was speaking through them trying to get info for their schemata. It makes no difference what you say to an idiot since they don't remember anything anyway. The goal there, as always for any sane person when dealing with the insane, is to make sure they get *no* information for their schemata. But this is all of course highly obvious. We have stenographers and twenty people sitting around with notepads and pens. There's no reason to ask any question more than once if we're paying attention and taking notes. If our jobs are that boring that we need to ask questions eight hundred times, it's time to find another one," Thomas remarked.

"Now that the smoke has mostly cleared, why is it true that if we don't help the criminals stay out of jail they will kill more family members?" Fuga began once more.

"It isn't. It was made to be true," Thomas replied.

"How?"

"Because the first statement wasn't true: 'We need your help keeping them in jail.' You don't need help when all you have to do is not let them out. Ulterior motive was grossly evident from the beginning. And since they weren't in jail very often, they could easily kill more family members."

"Why did they do this?"

"Mostly because everyone let them. Also, it was a fantastic way to create more child porn to sell on the black market and pretend not to know about it. I always knew it was a scam though. Luckily, no porn was sold, so no one got rich from this mistake that I'm aware of anyway.

"Unfortunately, being surrounded by this much incompetence, there's no way I can help with the current human trafficking issues," Thomas said, gazing into the distance.

Fuga's face lost color as he once more dropped his battered and cracked clipboard to the cement floor with the red and grey tiles and vanished from the room as if he were sucked out by a large vacuum.

p. Transitional Sheering

10:57am

"It's not that I don't understand; I know why many things were done. I just don't understand why other things weren't," Thomas remarked.

"Maybe those things are in the future," the receptionist said as Thomas was leaving.

"Yes, I agree, many things would be best placed in the future. So then I should just clear my head to prepare for those days then?"

"Yes."

"It has already begun. One thing we always knew: It's impossible to begin too early to prepare for the future."

As he neared the door, the psychiatrist called him into his office for a final review upon release. So, Thomas ventured to ask, "We can do anything we put our mind to?"

"Yes"

"This is our life to live how we want."

"Yes"

"You don't need to have X and can live without it."

"No"

"Why not?"

"Cuz it's your fault and there's nothing we can do about it," the psychiatrist averred.

"So, you're not even going to try?"

"No. We don't *think* we can have any effect on X."

"But.... we can do anything we put our mind to."

"Yes."

"Really? I think I see the exact problem."

19. We Will Excuse Them No Matter What

If by now it hasn't been made sufficiently clear, Thomas doesn't need any lessons about what Dr. Garrist showed him when he was three or what's wrong with it. The paid shill taught both Thomas, Cynthia, Ralene, Evelyn, and about six others more than enough to not need added, unnecessary input or opinion. He also learned when he was three how people will say they're going to execute the criminals who did this to his family, then turn around and for over fifty years do nothing about what they swore to God to do and cough up twelve billion excuses for why. If anyone needs a lesson, it's not Thomas. We should make sure we understand this before attacking again.

No one cares about the excuses why, nor does Thomas need anymore lessons in how much anyone loves Dr. Garrist and enjoys keeping him alive. We should teach ourselves a lesson before instructing others.

"But natural consciousness, as long as it doesn't learn its lesson and retain its knowledge, isn't going to advance."[3]

This is why Thomas will always question a wholesale dismissal of the past. Many who do this want precisely that: for nothing to change. They want criminals to continue to live unpunished, they want the crimes they performed to continue since they're obviously making money or some other benefit as a result, they want nothing to be learned from the victims, they want the victims to continue suffering through never seeing justice. All this done to increase the amount of doubt applied to

God Himself, which is whom their main argument is with. They can do whatever they please; Thomas will continue to study the past and learn how to make sure executions take place when they are both commanded by verdict and sentence as well as sworn to God to occur.

If actions have consequences, we're not seeing it in too many cases or at all. Maybe it's because we actually believe that words speak louder than actions. After taking the body, urinating on it, defecating into the mouth then hiding it in multiple areas, Thomas saw nearly everyone still protecting the people who did it. The consequences, therefore, must be unimaginable and devastating. Thomas was just glad he was not part of whatever this is. Maybe saying that oral testimony isn't evidence is something we should stop believing, or at least stop acting as though we don't.

He is still running into people who don't seem to remember the arrangement. Until this is done, nothing can move forward. Any time anyone feels like doing what they swore to God to do, they may easily let him know and he'll be happy to move on with his life. If they wait till after we all die to do this, they'll be spending eternity with the molesters. We're all waiting. This was the sentence of the first court case, so it isn't optional. Unless we're intending to say that all court decisions are optional, which is precisely how it appears.

It would be both telling and revealing to examine what percentage of current sex traffickers are ex-cons. Yet we have on record the judge's statement that "we will execute them no matter what." Maybe they should have, then the traffick problem wouldn't be as large, even if it was just one less. But knowing their kind, they probably released or supported the release or life extension of way more than one. Not really justice for the victims whose lives they took. Doesn't flagrant disregard for the life of other people make them an anti-social sociopath? How then can they still be a judge? Why are so many judges doing this?

Thomas can suppose that based on the amount of harassment he has received, that he was directed to recommend never identifying murderers after they commit the crime. It does seem sometimes that the trouble identifying brings isn't worth going through, since people manufacture an inflated, artificial cost which they apply constantly over a fifty year period. He even thought about saying he would not recommend identifying them after seeing the murderers show up at his job as applicants in November 2003 after being told in 1968 that they would be "executed no matter what." However, he won't say that. He will say that he's glad everyone that actually helped and didn't stand in the way actually did what it took to put them in jail so they can't murder anyone else, even though allowing them to live doesn't guarantee this result.

He was glad it wasn't him that allowed them to live. He was glad he's not kissing their ass by letting them continue to breathe air. And he would recommend doing the same thing to any who may find themselves in this sad situation. Since there's no greater way to say you love people who kill fathers in front of their children than to let them live, lie to the victims, and convince yourself God is behind you when you swore the following oath, but did nothing about it or the court results: "We will execute them no matter what."

Did we discover that we hate something in Thomas' behavior? This is good. Not doing what we swore is directly responsible for everything everyone hates about his behavior. If we had a part in this, then Thomas is not our biggest problem in life. He's very much looking forward to the difference this makes. The first thing will be to leave very far behind everyone who didn't do this. No, he will never miss them at all for the rest of eternity.

At some point during the waiting period, he changed his mind. Previously he had said he doesn't think Dr. Garrist should get the death penalty, since he didn't kill anyone. But after making the connection that he covered up for those who did, he thinks all four of them should.

The earth mourns the passing of real investigators. These had courage enough to only ask questions to which they didn't know the answers. They had the honesty to only search for the real truth. They were educated and highly skilled in logic, collecting all statements and evidence from multiple trials and sources. Pooling information and delving with great strength to locate any truth of every matter. They knew how to use calculators. They followed facts, not opinions and negative spin. They had the responsibility to do whatever it took to close

74

cases correctly and perform justice. They will be sorely missed as the earth tailspins into oblivion. Today, too often we have only pretenders who worship treacle, sentimentality, negativity, slander, sex trafficking, and mammon.

20. Public Evidence

The murder of Abel illustrates the fact that a crime can be committed while there is no existing law on the books. Therefore no laws are needed in any books for a crime to have occurred in reality, nor a trial, verdict, or sentence. Moses, who carried the stones with the first laws written by the finger of God, was over 1000 years past the time of that murder. The modern, highly educated justice system has not only forgotten this, but imagines itself to have the power to assign both guilt or innocence where neither existed previously. But while ignoring both this point and eyewitness testimony and contending they're only interested in hearing the truth only proves that one power they do have is the power to ignore and renders any assignation from this agency less powerful than it would be if they would stop.

When it was clearly stated that something will only be said once and anyone asks to hear it again, this indicates many things, none positive about the inquisitor. In either case, all we need is either a recording or transcript of the initial statement and we're done. If we couldn't provide this, then at that particular point our degree became useless.

Oral testimony *is* evidence. When anyone asks for evidence directly after giving them oral testimony, we know repeating the sentence to a deaf person will just be a waste of time. And that since they've indicated they're deaf, they won't be part of the solution.

While murderers are allowed to roam in and out of jail at their leisure, having children with whomever they want (two so far from Dr. Garrist alone, Cathy and Saundra), there will be no damning testimony against them. This would endanger the lives of those few of us remaining and none of us are interested in committing that type of suicide. However, this will change instantly the second the revolving door of the prison is permanently uninstalled.

21. This Is Only Going To Go One Way

"Why I occasionally never stated precisely how things happened is because, with sufficient study and information, the process is capable of duplication. If I tell you what they did, this will become a blueprint for how to do this to someone else and it will ruin fifty years of someone else's time. You may not care about that other person, but I do. Keep waiting for me to hand you a blueprint that you can give to the person who paid you to get it - wait another fifty years, wait for eternity. I'll wait for the person who actually does have the right to judge others, which isn't you."

- portion of Thomas' testimony from the 1969 case

Why do we discuss so much about paybacks? At which times are paybacks right or wrong and what are the consequences? Several other questions may be posited in this lifelong quest many have conscripted themselves to enforce. Apart from the majority, who believe all paybacks are always right, many of the things in Thomas' life, both what we know about and what we don't, are the result of several groups of people trying to pay him back for what they perceive to have happened, while ignoring what actually did.

What actually did happen, which they'll never tell you, is that they made a promise to do something, which also by law they were commanded to do. They were told exactly what would happen if they didn't, so did the oath they swore when they began their law career. They were told at the very beginning that things would become worse and worse until they kept their promise. They wound up breaking that promise and have yet to keep it, and things got worse and worse, exactly as they were told, which they chose at the time not to believe. Now, and at various points in time since then, they put complicated systems of paybacks into his family's life for no reason, since he's not the one who broke the promise. We're all waiting for them to do what they said. Until then, things will continue to get worse and worse, as previously stated and set up by the doctor administered hypnosis sessions that were allowed to progress past the point of repair. We can fight gravity and not believe it exists, but this only proves our insanity and in the end, gravity wins.

There will eventually be positive changes, but they will be non-violent, or we will make sure they fail. Keeping people alive that murder fathers in front of their children does *not* count as non-violent since there's a repeated history of letting them out of jail to continue committing crimes.

The sentence of trial one was execution. Attempting trial two while refusing to perform the sentence of trial one will logically always fail. This is due to that fact that "doing the exact same thing and expecting a different result is insanity." Trial 3, 4, 5 to infinity will fail for the same reason. It will go the right way whether anyone likes it or not.

22. The Doubtful Journal

a. Spewl Pool

While waiting for even one person to keep their word and do what they claimed they would do, Thomas wrote a few things down over the fifty year period. Some excerpts from this journal are presented here in no particular order.

Ug-Oust 43rd, 1971

In 2007, they handed me a trick question. So in 1969 I handed them the same trick question. I was shunned and ignored. In 2008, they handed me a sliding floor. So in 1969, I handed them a sliding floor. I was slapped, told I was crazy, and ignored. In 2009, they handed me a double meaning. So in 1969, I handed them a double meaning. I was told to be serious and ignored. In 2010, they handed me a catch-22. So in 1969, I handed them the exact same catch-22. I was told I ruined the case and was ignored. In 2011, they handed me victim-blaming. So in 1969, I handed them blaming the actual people responsible. I was called a liar and ignored. In 2012, they handed me a trick bag. So in 1969, I handed them the same trick bag. I was separated from my family, shunned, and ignored.

Since authority is authority, what does this mean for the pretenders according to current methods of projection used by the educational field? By the admission of the actions of court judges, they should be slapped, told their crazy, not serious, informed that they have ruined the case of people's lives, called liars, separated from their families, then be shunned, and ignored.

- I Didn't Start It, But I Will Finish It

Slipt-Ember 21ˢᵗ, 2012

In 1968, a group of people set me up and blamed me for the outcome. In 1969, I set the same group up who then got blamed for the outcome. In 2006, the same group set me up multiple times and blamed me for the outcome. Looks like the bottom half of round two is coming up.

- I Am the Mirror

NoRemember 13ᵗʰ, 1971

"Afraid? No way. We laugh at slew foot and it's hard not to. His brain is highly distractive and he teaches his children likewise. You can know them by the fact that they interrupt everyone eight hundred times a minute and rarely listen when people talk. Well, he has to distract his mind from the fact that he had everything and threw it all away.

So fear? Rather we laugh at the deserving."

Febrilary 38ᵗʰ, 2018

It's now on the table whether to release these that have been in prison this last fifty years. After all the whining I've heard about it I'm considering just letting them out into the public. You won't be able to get them back in again, nor stop them from doing whatever they want. What they want isn't going to be what you want. But at least everyone (except the initial set of victims) will be happy. If they show up at your front door, you were warned. But the final decision is in the future.

- "Release Barabbas" (Give the Audience What They Want)

Maynot 48ᵗʰ, 1971

Most of the time, when anyone asks a question it is because they already know the answer. This is due to the fear of responsibility. So, when someone asks you to swear to God, your first response should be "no," since swearing is both proscribed and incurs the greatest responsibility. If you say "yes," and then perform a swear, you are responsible for carrying out the sworn duty. Especially if the conditional qualifier was added, "No matter what." If this is stated, then with or without "eye contact," with or without any special dances, procedures, statements or any other activity you think you need to shift the burden of responsibility to someone else, the sworn duty will still be performed. This is why when people call or knock at the door and preach about the law or what is or isn't appropriate, yet they haven't performed the sworn duty which they swore to God "no matter what" to perform, I ignore them.

Your words are wasted until you do what you swore to do "no matter what."

When rape victims are harassed, this is precisely what the rapists want. When victims of pedophiles are harassed, tortured, and forced to watch murders, this is precisely what the pedophiles and murderers want. The four we put in the state prison before 1969 wanted me to say to everyone who has done this: "Thank you for helping us."

What can we say that's positive from this otherwise useless experiment? I can say without thinking twice that when anyone uses hypnosis to mask off any part of anyone's mind from them, regardless of the reason or what is being hidden, believe whatever the hell you want, they are no longer the same person.

- The Iconoclastic Call

Slipt-Ember 111th, 2003

Remembering more conversations from the trials when lawyers said, "We don't have time for games." Keeping in mind they speak backwards since they said they would execute the murderers, then proceeded not to do it, I told them. "I know you do, but you wouldn't listen." Decoding this, when no means yes since they talk backwards, they actually said, "We do have time for games" flaunting the behavior they are still exhibiting. My reply should have been heard, "I know you don't, but you wouldn't listen." Anyone knows no doesn't always mean yes. This is also because for them, not listening is a constant.

- Extrapolate (How Do We Interpret English?)

Umbral 108th, 1971

If everything is relative, then everything is relevant, since whatever is related is relevant to whatever else it's related to, otherwise it's not related, and thus irrelevant. Among the pertinent issues of relevance is this fact: guilty or not guilty, which was decided during Court Case #1. The verdict was guilty. This is definitely relevant to everything.

Ignore everything that stands in the way of progress. This will ensure a faster enforcement of the delayed, denied justice. E.g., when people say they will execute a murderer, ignore everything else they say other than things or steps leading directly to the execution. Otherwise, tell them what they want to hear since nothing is more important than progress, especially in this area.

I'm never sure how to react to people who won't execute three men known to have committed murder, child molestation, and rape, but seem to think they're invested with the God-given right to harass every one of their victims. I'm not really sure I can guarantee civility if I continue to see this happen when there is no excuse for any of it. I keep waiting for the real police to show up and the fake ones to go to hell. So far, this hasn't worked.

Only idiots argue with an eyewitness.

Remembered more about the trials. Wasn't trying to. Was trying to turn off anger (succeeded) about something else, and trial info emerged. Without long details, what was said in the first trial can't be repeated. If it is, it will cost someone their life. After that came trials 2-5 where idiots keep asking what was said, instead of reading the court documents, tempting fate, and proving they're murderers by requesting to see someone die from any of trial 1 being repeated.

"Well, we don't know that someone would die...." was their oft-heard reply.

That's right: *you don't know*! And thanks to me not being a complete stupid ass and answering your jackassy questions, you never will!

- "Without First Counting the Cost"

Julousy 28th, 2002

Sadists seek positions of high authority so they may more easily extend their field of abuse. Their tissue-thin papers force courts to more quickly take their word over anyone else's, regardless of any overwhelming evidence to the contrary. The trained eye sees through any facade. The earmark of most sadists is this: They have absolutely no sense of humor whatsoever.

- Worship the Liars

Julousy 83rd, 2002

False accusations never land on anyone who didn't start them to begin with. They can be an example of what *not* to do in a court of law. If someone is telling the truth, don't falsely accuse them of lying while excluding evidence that proves they were telling the truth such as blood on a carpet in sufficient amounts to prove that no one could have survived losing that much which has yet to be tested for DNA, meanwhile lying to everyone by saying they're "looking for the whole truth and nothing but the truth." When such victims later falsely accuse them, is this a surprise? Not since everyone knows "what you give is what you get."

Umbral 412th, 2016

The climate of debates has always had some element of this to it, which isn't at all either useful or comforting, but lately they've grown nearly to the same level as they were in the courtroom in which I sat in the 60s. In that setting, not only the defendants and their lawyers, but even the judges would interrupt any answer not even three words past the beginning of the sentence given to questions they asked themselves. Yelling was common, which also was common as the murderers and their hired hands were raping us to make sure we understood we deserved to be raped and why. The voice heard wasn't the one with the facts, presented by the eyewitnesses, but the loudest opinion, typically lies about hating Jews, whereas neither Ralene nor I had any idea what in holy frog piss a Jew even was. Or typically whoever could interrupt anyone the greatest number of times, and this all ostensibly being called "justice in a court of law." Being reminded of any of this can happen any time listening doesn't or interruptions flow like Niagara Falls, but has reached an all time high lately and doesn't show any signs of doing anything but increasing.

This is why I hate lies and will sacrifice anything to expose them. Taking sides will only increase the number of lies you swallow due to name-flipping and subversion. But just like then, when lies are swallowed willingly, people are paid nice sums of cash to spread them, and still too many think it's all just a game and you'll win if you stick to your team. When listening, facts, and logic are not allowed anywhere, then there's only one way to win. Partly described in the book everyone hates that starts with the words, *"I also will laugh..."*[4]

- Tell The Truth By Interrupting It

Divember 405th, 2015

It is regrettable that not liking things the way they are offends anyone since "accept the changes" seems ready at all lips, but something else has once again appeared to need discussion.

Many diagnoses have been found to hold one characteristic. It begins from the fact that the people sent to help us on occasion have never experienced the things that we have. Take my case: A person who saw a murder is judged and evaluated by a thousand or so people who haven't, certainly not at age three or four. Their overall thrust has one characteristic, which is not so much to help, but rather to keep the entire issue away from them so they don't have too much face time with their responsibility of dealing directly with something they allow in society.

This applies more to the "armchair quarterback" and "talk show" type therapists and doctors as well as the ones seen prior to 1980 than the ones I see today.

Some things have changed for the better. So here's the sped up version: We allow murderers back out onto the street, but want to spend either zero time or as little as possible with their victims and want nothing to do with cleaning up the messes they leave in people's lives. Again, it's entirely unclear which of these three groups needs more therapy: the enablers for enabling, the murderers for chain murdering, or the victims with messes and shattered lives. As these things spread into time, it will be impossible to leave all of these conditions the way they are now. Eventually, they will directly affect every person on the planet. It is hoped we never get to that point.

Morchuary 53rd, 2015

If you care about the well-being of criminals, then you could care less about their victims. I'll continue to care less about you.

If you refuse to punish the criminal, you have punished the victims.
- Like It Or Not

Genuinary 1st, 2002

So, there's a giant blood stain on the back bedroom floor exactly where I said the shooting occurred, the owner of the house is missing with no one else in that neighborhood missing, both kids are saying they saw their dad shot in front of their face, two pedophiles who keep mysteriously getting out of jail are standing in the front yard with grins on their faces, but we're stuck on needing a body to prove something happened? I don't think the biggest problem here is the pedos. To whoever they're paying to do this, I think we can easily arrange to have more than three executions. This can occur either before or after we all die.

Genuinary 33rd, 2002

When you see the men who shot your dad in front of your face at age three walk into your job in November of 2003, you aren't really worried about optics. You don't really give one damn about rumors. And you can see every lie told over the last thirty-five years, who said them, and why. Then you have to reassess the motives of the liars, which till then you didn't think were any problem, since you were unaware of the actual degree of the lies. So if I'm not dancing to your lies the way you want me to, you can see why I really don't care anymore. You can also see what's about to happen.

Divember 38th, 1971

If what you believe separates me from my family, I could care less about either what you believe or you. And I'm fairly sure you won't be prepared for the response.

Umbral 71st, 1994

When I hear people say they wish everything were equal, I think back to the time when someone was about four years old getting their head crushed with the blunt end of a railroad spike. I'm fairly sure most of these "equality" whiners never had that experience and evidently aren't thankful that they didn't. If there were a way, we actually could take these babies back to age four and crush their heads with railroad spikes, then everything would actually be equal. I know for a fact that they really *don't* want things to be equal. I was very lucky to have survived that experience and I'm very glad that others don't have to.

- "Would a Foot in Your Crotch Make Things Equal?"

October 19th, 1971

Whenever those who are protecting the demon ask anything, alway shew by pure reflexion the face of the demon to them as accurately as possible. This way, they always know exactly what they're protecting, as well as that this informs them that you know precisely who they are and what they're doing.

- "We Don't Like What We See"

Julousy 57th, 1970

Feelings aren't provable. This seems to be an underlying cause for most sadistic behavior; not so much to cause feelings in the victims, but to try to cause a connective link to them with hopes of sparking feelings in themselves. They took us away from everyone we wanted to be with. They took us away from everyone who wanted us to be with them. There is a critical question concerning this. I am now trying to determine that if this is all for some kind of purpose, then I need to know where is the line between when proving something stops and the torture begins.

Umbral 7th, 2018

When they said they would execute them no matter what, then didn't, I realized they hear words backwards. When this happens, you can't use normal language, but have to speak in reverse. I don't have this problem, so speaking backwards to me does nothing. So, when they asked if the railroad spike used to crush my head was rusty and had a fractured head, I said yes, since they speak in reverse this would mean the actual spike used is essentially new. They brought a rusty, fractured-headed spike to court and asked me if that was the one that was used, which of course didn't work since it was nothing like it. And since they love releasing criminals from jail, I wasn't interested in having that one used on top of the place where other one was hammered into three separate spots. Then I realized that no matter what is said, their questions are always arbitrary, the answers taken are also not what is stated, arbitrary over a wide range, and always tend in any negative direction. When this happens, it's best to say nothing, but I've seen them use even this to travel over fifty years in a wrong, negative direction. After considering all this, I always wonder the same thing: Whom are you serving?

Genuinary 75th, 1976

Courts can pretend, but sometimes absence is the presence of something you don't want. The presence of the missing person. It's the lies you have to believe to get through one day. It's the deep concern you have for the welfare of someone, or more than one, you'll never see for a long time to come. It's the hope that when you finally meet again, all the lost time will become as *nothing*! Because without them, that's what it is anyway.

Febrilary 33rd, 2017

It's good to review especially when comparing reality to itself because in doing so the light becomes brighter. We had before said, "There's a reason for everything." It was also said at some point over the last year, "Nothing is true all of the time." In light of last night's events, I think this qualifies as one of those times where the first phrase isn't true, since there is manifestly no reason for any of this. In looking back, I can only find a few times where I was left questioning my own existence to this degree that led to anything positive. I have never and will never argue for death or any who promote it outside of the justice system which has typically been instituted by hundreds of cultures to prevent idiots from killing who love nothing more than to spread death around as if it's nothing serious. I have felt since I was three that if you take a life, you no longer need to be here. People who love to spread death are no different than a virus which also kills people and should be treated exactly like a virus by killing the virus itself. Some viruses cannot be killed, however, and are only stopped by preventing their reproduction. Unfortunately, there is only one way to prevent a human's ideas from reproducing.

Maynot 147th, 2014

Speaking of conceit, due to the high level encountered in the majority of life, a personal account has been scheduled so that all payments are to be deferred until *after* we die. That way there can't be any dodging the bill, hedging of words, calling of lawyers, spreading of false rumors, espionage of the innocent, slaughter of the innocent to avoid punishments, blame-shifting, psychotic psychiatric manipulations performed by the sadistic damned, rearrangement of facts to suit a childish whim, or any other connivance or gross exercise of envy, anger, malice, or feigned ignorance of facts. After being forced to see a murder at age three, then seeing no one really giving a damn after the fact, I don't have time for those games. I'll wait for the real God to show up after all the pretend ones leave.

Umbral 18th, 2004

People who say, "Move on," when their actions are the precise reason that no one can move on are puzzling. People who say to forget about a problem is how to solve it have never taken a math class. Solving some problems (not all, some have no solution) is the *only* way to move on.

So, having the courage to face our own ignorance, look the problem in the face and try to arrive at a solution does far more healing than burying our head in the sand and ignoring it. We can ignore it, but our minds will bring it up again later until we face it. A few writers have said *"the mind abhors a vacuum,"*$_5$ it also seems to dislike unresolved conflicts, as seen by how often it keeps reminding us of them.

Incidentally, bringing known murderers to our job sites does nothing to help anyone move on. It also does nothing to help execute them no matter what.

- Move On To Yourself

Slipt-Ember 37th, 2010

On examining the vigintillions of tests various people thought was a good idea to give me, I noticed a common theme - If we fear that something will happen, most of the time this alone, not anything else (as some vainly imagine), is responsible for pulling fear into reality.

No-Remember 92nd, 2015

I'm not sure if "not forgiving" is the same as "stop loving," but I've always generally equated them. I've been told that someone made a mistake and that when they return they will need me to forgive them. And although how I feel about them can't change, to me, telling them they're forgiven seems both above my station and similar to telling them what they did is acceptable when it obviously isn't.

When anyone or anything dies as a result, whatever the cause, it can't be acceptable. Knowing this time was approaching, I pushed things to the limit to see who would forgive and who wouldn't. Only one person out of over twenty experiments passively offered any forgiveness. So, in spite of these results, I have an opportunity to visibly figure out how to forgive, not just this one person, but probably several others as well. Consequently, I won't be able to forgive them by myself. I don't even feel like it. Precisely and largely based on those results.

Morchuary 37th, 2015

So much has been said and so many things I signed in the hospital said, "May cause memory loss" and I know it did for some things. But, another typical mistake made by Biff Crumple was that he, as is the habit of very many who should know better, in the decades long process of harassing rape victims, keeps using "Either/Or" logic, allowing for only two outcomes. However, when presented with the logic puzzle of "No means Yes," he and the majority believe there can be only one outcome, and that is whoever believes this is a sexual predator, which is a lie.

Logic Failure: From both Boolean Algebra and Discrete Math, we know that there are four outcomes, not two. If we have A & B, and either one can be right or wrong, true or false, we obtain AB, AnotBnot, AnotB, and ABnot. The only reason to restrict the outcome to "either one person is right, or the other is right, in either case both opposites absolutely must be wrong" is either to exploit something, or done through ignorance. But given that we're dealing with a murder case, ignorance inside the law is also no excuse. If studying the case is too taxing, don't talk to me at all since you won't be solving it ever that way. If you're not aware of this difficulty, then you have no business being in either the law or the justice system. In the case of Biff, he's using it as an attempt to kill Evelyn. He is aware of this and so is everyone who is helping him. He can speculate as much as Socrates about why, but I had to stop answering his questions because they all had this tendency, which I'm not going to allow. Seeing one murder is enough. I'm not sure why I have to deal with fifty years of people I don't know on top of family members trying to make sure I see more of them.

Are murders really that wonderful that they have to continually be recreated for whoever the hell is getting off on them? They are going to change what they are doing - I never will.

- What You Say Can Kill People

Maynot 1273rd, 2012

The emotional roller coaster that led to the hospital in '97 is pretty avoidable now. Control the emotions, don't allow extremes, nothing happens that shouldn't. But from noticing that hypnosis prevented many memories of people and events, good and bad, I see people who haven't been hypnotized imagining their memory doesn't suffer similarly. But behind something we either don't want to or can't look at is something we don't remember. Not facing or not believing it blocks the memory exactly like hypnosis, but without the doctor involved in the process of blocking reality from our minds and allowing it to be dealt with. Something bringing it to our attention can remind us of it or we can force it to appear. Evidently, given the modern rising levels of insanity, this doesn't happen very often.

Julousy 154th, 1975

Having your skull crushed in three places with a railroad spike before you were five means you have to work twice as hard or more to get your brain to work on very many occasions. So forgive me if I take a dim view to anyone who appears that they're not even trying.

No-Remember 83rd, 2005

There are certain things that won't be on these pages and it will stay that way. I won't give air time to the undeserving. And, call it selfish all you want, until Fred, Bobby, Dr. Garrist, and Pax have been executed, there are far worse things than politics that can walk into your house after being released from prison for bogus reasons that will destroy your entire family. No, even after they're executed I won't shut up about it, so you should know what to expect. Had they been in 1970 as promised probably by now I would have. So you made your bed, have fun sleeping in it.

- What You Won't See

b. Sometimes the Law is Illegal

October 39th, 2007

Lying under oath is illegal, but believing any lie under oath is legal. This happens when anyone lies under oath, yet every person in hearing distance believes it and acts upon it, regardless of whether they know that a lie is being told or not. But reality quickly shows us that believing a lie is illegal.

This is yet another reason neither Fred, Bobby, nor Dr. Garrist have been executed. Everyone knows what they did, but we're all going to sit around and pretend we don't know and hope God is fooled by it.

c. If You Have To Be Told

October 40th, 2005

What did I learn? That if you're going to hypnotize anyone to forget random things to make your life more convenient, then later expect them to forcibly recall things you deleted from memory, then get upset when they don't, first put the entire idea through a computer to make sure you didn't create any programing errors such as endless loops or null strings, etc. Also remember that computers and humans don't process data entirely the same way. Know well that this particular patient had a skull crushed in three places, so everything may not work the way you wish it would for the sake of Almighty Convenience. Any investigator worth their salt would have done this before any hypnosis ever took place. Now things are different, because if you have to be told, it's not the same.

d. Retrospect

Ug-Oust 32nd, 1971

I do remember how the arrangement changed, but it was still funny to see how a problem was set up to *only* be solved one way, then see everyone blindly attempt to solve it in the way that was most convenient for them with a complete disregard for the actual solution. If things have changed, even if they haven't, I'm not sure I now know what the answer is. I can say that so far, no one has found it. There are certain things that will happen immediately when anyone does. Most of the clues for the answer are obvious: You can't ask the wrong person at the wrong time what it is. You can't *fail* to ask the 5Ws for any attempt at gaining an answer. E.g., if you ask What was said, but don't find out Who said it, you will head widely into the wrong direction, hence the last fifty years. And so forth.

e. Does God Have An Authority Complex?

Slipt-Ember 13th, 2018

Hours of entertainment are provided by watching people who fund the existence of child molesters who kill the parents in front of the children try to give me lectures about life and what can and can't be done to whom. I always wonder if they know how they look to other people as they preach about what's appropriate.

Buffet style of the application of justice, taking some laws while ignoring others, is precisely what Christ objected to with the Pharisees, and today's public is no different.

Using hypocrisy to keep ourselves safe while others die because of continued prisoner release means it's time to find another job. Change something at least.

Finney said, *"Arbitrary legislation is invalid legislation."* [6]
This is obvious.

Any lawyer or judge who takes any case, while refusing to closely study the twenty cases related to and preceding the one in question probably isn't a lawyer or judge, at least should be one no further, or has been bought.

Proof: Harassing rape victims with impunity was confirmed by eyewitness testimony.

Who does this? Everyone not involved in executing the murderers no matter what.

Proof: We have over 1.57 billion counts of not executing the murderers no matter what, so this is 1.57 billion affirmations that those in power believe we need child-molesting murderers in the world. Since this is the case, I don't need anyone preaching morality to me. (50 years = ~1.57 billion seconds)

How is this proof? There are one of two explanations why anyone would harass a rape victim:

a.) They've been bought, or

b.) Severe mental retardation or some kind of mental disorder. Anyone who can add 2+2 knows whether harassing a rape victim is appropriate, therefore the likely and most probable answer is (a).

While we await the promised execution, we know that the ones who promised to do so while not performing the act exist under a condition of perjury and are liable to future punishment.

Proof: a. A lie is the opposite of the truth.

b. Both judges and lawyers swore to God that they would "execute them no matter what."

c. No execution of criminals identified by eyewitnesses to have committed murder prior to 1968 at Tarpin Road has yet been performed.

d. Both judges and lawyers have perjured themselves by lying under the oath of their respective offices to uphold justice.

e. Only a punishment can await those who perform not only these acts, but also framing the victims and survivors of the murder with over fifty years of false allegations which do nothing about the execution and only add crime to crime.

I keep hearing requests for evidence. Here's what this means in light of the overwhelming evidence already present in this case:

Sadists request evidence when enough has already been supplied so they can set up to film additional crimes happening to sell the pictures (moving and stills) on the black market. They already burned down my apartment to find non-existent films to sell on the black market, so their desire for this has no known limit.

We have two eyewitnesses to the murder at Tarpin Road prior to 1968. Blood all over a carpet in sufficient amounts to prove a death happened on that spot. DNA testing would prove the identity. We have no evidence to the contrary. There is no reason to not execute the guilty after the sentence was pronounced.

From what I've noticed, the people who complain the loudest about no one communicating with them are the ones who have their ears closed. I first noted this when I was three or five years old when lawyers kept asking questions in trial five that had been sufficiently answered in trial one. All they needed to do was read the transcript of the trial and not waste further time asking questions they already had answers to, instead of asking questions that would give them answers they didn't have. This gross oversight wound up killing a lot of people over the last fifty years, some of whom would otherwise be with us today, which was also accurately predicted if no scheduled executions had taken place. Let their blood be on the heads of the liars.

So, while people spread lies and spin for their sanctimoniously infallible party's platform, there remain tens of millions outside of this seven party system we've constructed whose views go unrepresented. Their lives are long and dark, unfrequented by even the shadow of any opinion that represents them. Too often, separation creates fear and hatred. Too often, fear and hatred create death. Too often, the sadist, applauding and using every available tool to create unnecessary separations, could care less.

Evidently, separation is god.

f. How to Extend Torture Beyond the Initial Crime

No-Remember 29th, 2013

Remembered again the room where my dad died. Not sure why the memory chooses certain times to visit with unusual clarity. The house isn't there anymore. Not sure why anyone is so intent on covering up all the evidence they can get their hands on. When anyone is possessed, worshiping the demons that possess them by doing everything they tell you will never work the way you imagine.

g. Legerdemain

Divember 17th, 1993

"We have to watch you because of what you said."

"No you don't," I always told them.

"Yes, we do."

This same dialog has repeated so many times I lost count.

Here's proof that they don't:

If your job is to find the truth, you should know the truth before you find it, otherwise how would you recognize it? You should know what is in front of you, otherwise you are admitting you have no idea what you're looking at. If this isn't the case, your position needs to be filled by someone who does. More specifically, if your character assessment skills are that pathetically low, you then have no business holding any title even remotely connected to an officer of the law. If you lack these skills, then you will fail entirely when asked to assess a situation where people are taking advantage of what no one can see.

h. Why Did This Fail?

October 4th, 1971

Just remembered another reason why this case has failed so far. Countless times this has happened.

Someone comes up to me and says, "We're going to do what you say."

Then I tell them, "Ok, no means yes, and yes means no."

They say, "We're not going to use that."

Then I tell them, "Then how are you doing what I say?"

That's why this is going nowhere fast. The children need to get off the positions of power and let someone handle the case that doesn't have their head up their rectal cavity.

Someone asked, "What if their answer is the reverse of what they meant, meaning that they *will* use what you said, since 'no means yes,' then 'not going to' means 'are going to?'"

Answer: Their behavior indicates not only that they didn't use the reversal method that we find in reality, but that they have no intention of ever doing so. Their consistently applied method is to cause the most damage possible with the futile hope that God can't see what they're doing and that there will never be any consequences for any of their actions. They say they're using "yes means yes," yet they said, "yes we'll execute" then turned around and didn't do it; so obviously yes means no. If yes means no, then no means yes, otherwise there's no way to say "yes." If they can confuse a "yes," then they can confuse a "no" answer, which murderers and pedophiles love. So this then proves the judges and lawyers in this case are both murderers and pedophiles.

Since I was three I've asked people to not believe everything they hear. They did this mostly by arguing with everything I said, which is good. I don't want people auto-believing every thing I say since it's impossible for anyone to be right 100% of the time. I'd rather have people going through their lives making their own, good, quality decisions rather than blind faith. How is blind faith bad for religion, but good in politics or football? It's either bad or it's good, it can't be both.

What I never saw is the main point (commonly missed in most communication) I was making. Challenge your own beliefs - argue with yourself. I've never seen anyone question anything that comes out of their mouth. Given all the crap I've heard, I should have at least heard this once. People seem locked into auto-believing that everything they say is right 100% of the time, which is impossible.

"But you do think people feel guilty; isn't this proof they question themselves?"

Normally this is only about what others say is wrong with them, usually not something they've discovered themselves. And I've never seen anyone question themselves when telling me I'm wrong. This seems clearer and truer in their minds than anything even God Almighty ever said. But I question this. Why?

i. Death Is Unnecessary

Umbral 26th, 1997

I think people say "death is a part of life" in a feeble effort to justify the unnecessary number of murders, whether by commission or omission (letting criminals out of jail is by omission), which they feel compelled to perform for some invisible, unknown master. They coddle themselves with this notion so they can continue to perform as many murders as they like while feeling nothing. This gives them a false sense of security about whether they will ever face consequences either now or later.

They can say this till they die. I'll continue to believe that death is unnecessary.

I am strong.

I saw death too early and know how to move past the pain to deal with the question of "How do we now move on from here?"

When to turn off the tears and use them when no one will be saddened by them. No one will take the intended damage caused by my pain.

I will keep this from you since I see it as giving people who hate us exactly what they want. My pain becomes their smile. They won't feed on me.

It's one of my earliest reactions, so it has more training.

I am weak.

I was never taught, conditioned, or controlled to think I had to accept death as a part of life before I saw it shoved in front of my face and in front of Ralene's face.

I have a hatred for it that you will never know.

I have said I am weaker because of this, but maybe this also is a strength?

The weakness could only be a false appearance, a misread difference from the norm, fueling the hatred of the sadists who love to misjudge the universe for points.

One thing I can say for now is that as far as I can see, my view on this won't change. I will always feel, think, and know that death is unnecessary.

j. I'm Not Going Anywhere

Maynot 3rd, 1971

True religion is largely undiscovered and lies isolated, undisturbed by any company, while a sham facsimile constructed by each person occupies the place it would normally hold. This structure in turn is the object of the largest volley of assaults which can be mustered against it, as they try to wipe it from the face of reality, never realizing it's their own creation.

One of the many reasons people enjoy hating their own concept of religion is that they want to bully, harm, steal from, or perform any other sadistic rituals on others while feeling no guilt in the process. The only problem with this is: They can destroy all religion, pure or false, if it were possible, but I will still be here to enjoy letting them know I can see them doing these things to others. I will enjoy reminding them about how to "execute them no matter what." I will enjoy arguing with people who think they have a right to do these things to others. I will enjoy burning the fabrications and lies of the history revisers who think they can't be seen. So destroy anything you like, it changes nothing because I'm not going anywhere.

k. Redefine Yourself

Maynot 23rd, 1972

I think it's interesting how sometimes people redefine or re-codify what I've said after which it bears no resemblance to what I originally stated. E.g., I say "murder," they say "delusional" or I say "they harmed my sister," they say "obsessed." After a short time (three seconds) it gets boring talking to them, so I just tell them what they want to hear. They say, "obsessed," I say, "yes." But in my mind, the actual statement is "obsessed with making sure the criminals are executed no matter what." This works since any psychic will immediately know the truth and the rest aren't listening anyway. They wouldn't hear the rest of the sentence even if it were printed or stated, put on a billboard, or plastered on their front doors.

l. The Psychopath

Junior 7th, 1971

People who kill someone right in front of your face enjoy making you uncertain about what you've seen. They're addicted to gaslighting.

The people who help them are not your friends, no matter what they say. Judges who exclude evidence that help them get away with this are not concerned with justice. People who make excuses for any of this are psychopaths.

If you say the right thing while doing the wrong thing, the words are irrelevant. If you say you care about the victims of crimes while either abusing them every possible way or doing nothing to actually punish the criminals, you have no actual, visible, provable feelings about the issue. If you say you feel for the victims while continuing a fifty year streak of releasing the criminals from jail, you have no actual feelings about it or anything else, more than likely. Having feelings for criminals is the same thing as having no feelings at all. When all of your questions only relieve you from responsibility and do nothing to solve the crime, it's difficult to say exactly what any feelings are really doing for you, if they even exist.

Since this was obvious from the start, on the deepest levels, I was never fooled by it. Regardless of how many letters follow your name, station, or title, you, everyone you pay or are paid by to cover up, who continue this way with no thoughts at all about it, are the only ones who may truly be said to have richly earned the name: The Psychopath.

m. I Will Laugh

Genuinary 27th, 2015

When something happens on a repeated basis, I think about and weigh the merits of doing the same thing to the people who are attacking me. For things that don't matter one way or the other and are a creative response, sure. But to go so far as the attackers themselves (heated screws applied to skin, pliers to break my sister's nose, needless destruction of property such as apartment fires deliberately set, fake needs for medical procedures that destroy the pancreas, etc. ad infinitum) I find I can't go this far to prove a point even if just thinking about it.

This contradicts the theory that the abused become the abusers and may be seen by others as a sign of weakness. But I choose to see it as a sign that I refuse to become like either the criminals or those who are in love with them and continue to protect them to this day. You can repeat the mantra "abused become the abusers" all your life, but I will never fit into your fabricated boxes since this idea isn't a constant anyway. One thing I can say is that when their protectors are finally married to the criminals and thrown away with them, I will laugh.

n. Fear Intelligence

Slipt-Ember 1ˢᵗ, 1977

I can see now this case is being viewed as a potential "Pandora's Box" to allow other crimes to be passed over. But if we take all the events together, there is no other case like it. So the actual fault for this particular fear lies with a system that routinely performs the logical error of narrow sampling by trying to force every act into being driven by just one motive. When reality repeatedly shows us that there is never just one motive for any act. A complex reality means every motive is complex. Also, motive flagrantly ignores dominating environmental factors such as someone holding a gun to your head.

o. Keep Waiting

Maynot 3ʳᵈ, 2018

Having so many things happen before you're five makes their return a not so necessarily sought after exercise as many believe, but more of a random resurfacing of things forgotten that many times I wish would stay that way. Among these though, I recall that the arrangement of hypnotic programming was crafted such that the verbal recounting of it would cause it to reoccur. This could be used advantageously but obviously wasn't. Meaning that if I recited the exact words they used to do this, the last fifty years would happen all over again in exact detail. There is a group of people who think I'm going to explain exactly how they did this. Only two things to say to this idea:

a. I waited fifty years so far and haven't explained it and I can wait fifty more.

b. If you think I'm giving you the keys to do this to anyone else so you can make a profit in the black market selling various items to more pedo doctors, I have only two words for you: keep waiting.

p. Errors Overbalance

Divember 25th, 1973
Remembering events leading up to the removal
Of people who are no longer here.
They were removed around this time of year.
The more I focus, the more becomes clear.

I try to remember his last words and practice them whenever I can. The purpose of solving a murder isn't what I keep hearing in movie or TV scripts "to bring them back." To forget what happened and ignore our past is to sign the permission slip for its recurrence. The purpose of justice is to restore the balance that was lost when the crime occurred. But till any previously issued sentence is carried out, there can be no justice while errors overbalance.

q. Three Words You Never Say To A Rape Victim

Octember 80th, 2009
In math, there are variables: x, k, c, etc. In language, there are also variables when the meaning is unclear. On the subatomic level this happens in every sentence, since each person has their own unique definition and atmosphere for every word. We only share a tacit agreement that we all understand each other. One variable which I've mentioned previously is the phrase "I don't care."
It could mean, "I don't care if what I believe kills people."
Or "I don't care if what you believe kills people."
"I don't care if what I don't know kills either me or you."

"I don't care if you're innocent, I will punish you anyway since we all know we're guilty till proven innocent."

"I don't care if the guilty remain in an unpunished state, as long as it doesn't affect me personally."

"I don't care if the things that I think are harmless actually aren't."

"I don't care if my own actions bring harm to me or those around me."

"I don't care if what I believe is why I don't have more money."

"I don't even care enough to question what the hell it is I actually believe."

All this and more runs through my mind when I hear those simple three words you never say to a rape victim.

r. Equal & Opposite Reaction

Febrilary 82nd, 2011

For those waiting for me to say something further about Fred, Bobby, or Tayler: Why? The verdict of the first court case was - Guilty. Do I need to say that again? Just read the court case (which every subsequent lawyer should have done before proceeding with any other case). Also, why is there so much need for repetition? How many times do you need to hear something before you do something about it? Do I need to say the sentence again for you? Ok - Death Penalty for both Fred, Bobby, Dr. Garrist, and Pax. I don't see anything else that needs to be said about it. So you were waiting for fifty years for me to say what exactly? Something you already know? 1. Why? 2. Is that your version of justice for the murder? Luckily for all crime victims there is an equal and opposite reaction. I'll be there, it won't be performed by my hand or doings, and you *won't* like it.

s. Song & Dance

Morchuary 14th, 1973

It makes no difference what any narrative is when everyone knows what happened. Taking a specific case: we know two children saw their father murdered in front of their faces. It doesn't matter what either child said under threat of future murders; it doesn't matter how many judges and lawyers were paid to throw the case; everyone knows what happened. Then it's the responsibility of those in power to perform the previously decided sentence of execution. I'm not sure who is trying to fool who when no one is fooled in reality. Another name for narrative, other than "complete waste of time" is song and dance.

t. "We Don't Know" Won't Save You

Maynot 60th, 1985

Similar to this are the ones who enjoy saying, "We didn't know," when in fact they either *do* know, or could have. Among the many things that happened before I was five, I remember being interrupted while speaking in court after having been asked a question. Before too long, I stopped answering after the interruption. I realized that whoever interrupts is responsible for every word of the unfinished sentence. Then it didn't matter if I answered it or not. I lost count of the number of times this happened and don't remember exactly what they lost by interrupting, nor do I care.

How can I say that? How can they be responsible? The fact that they're interrupting indicates they know the answer and are attempting to hide the facts or cover their own responsibility in the matter. Whatever they didn't do still needs to be done regardless of the answer and isn't my concern. Secondly, if they hadn't interrupted, they would have the answer, but they decided that to interrupt and yell after asking a question was supremely intelligent. So again, the fact they don't have the answer isn't my concern. This wasn't just a few questions. I estimate over twenty times per court appearance, of which there were over thirty, probably more since after about five or six disruptions, I stopped counting. I just considered it to be more abuse from the abusers. Therefore, sadly for them, "We don't know" won't save you.

u. Faces of Love and Concern

Maynot 12th, 1973

"This has been going on for a long time and there isn't anything you or anyone else can do to stop it," Fred told me once while standing in a gathering of many of his friends who also enjoyed raping children.

"I'll stop you," I told him.

He laughed. So did Bobby. In 2003, Bobby was still laughing. Sure, if they get out again now, they can still go into any men's restroom and kidnap any boy. But soon, they can dress up and go into any woman's restroom and steal girls also for their favorite meal - mated pairs. Most are for this, so long as it's not their son or daughter who gets forced into sex or raped - who really cares - that's someone else's problem. Then move off to delude themselves about their deep-seated compassion and open-mindedness for humanity. It will be fun to see their reaction as they watch Fred, Bobby, and Dr. Garrist's smiles growing wider as this new scam becomes a law. It will also be fun to see their face when they realize what these things really are.

v. Missing Pieces

Morchuary 7th, 2014

Remembering over the last week more about the first trial regarding Fred and Bobby. None of it is good. I can only pray somehow the records were preserved that were destroyed by the other criminals (their friends of course) who entered the courtroom after the sentence was pronounced. Possibly explains why the future lawyers didn't know the verdict and sentence of the first trial. Doesn't explain how you avoid trying the same person twice for murder if the records are somehow destroyed. You should always have a backup. I think someone did know this could happen and did hide copies of the proceedings, just haven't remembered that far yet.

(In case any are wondering why this is happening so late, with hypnosis, the memories come back when they choose on their own schedule, or as the FBI likes to say, "We have our own clock." Or in my case, by repeated wondering and demanding to know what actually happened and why. Even with this, it still has its own clock.)

w. Vengeance Isn't Mine

Maynot 62nd, 2012

What is the line between revenge and justice? How do you get justice for those who use the justice system to exact revenge on your family because of their race? For those who believe (very close to 99%) that two wrongs make a right, how do we see whether this is revenge or justice? Can two wrongs make four rights? For those who don't care, will doing nothing provide either revenge or justice?

Without having applied much study to the subject, though I wish I had the time to, the biggest difference I can see between vengeance and justice (and there are probably many others) is this:

Vengeance wants to spread the misery, justice wants to end it.

Vengeance wants the criminal to suffer to the maximum, justice wants only to both punish within the bounds of reason and prevent further crimes.

Vengeance wants to continue the chains of pain, Justice wants to break the chain, severe the link, and end the violence.

To prove my position on this: I don't want Fred, Bobby, or Dr. Garrist to suffer and actually have taken steps to make sure they don't encounter any prison rapes. Two crimes isn't better than one. But since I know they will kill again and have already done so, execution is the only way to make sure there are no future murders, which if they are allowed to live and the people worshiping them have their way, there will be. And not just one either.

If vengeance is only due to jealousy that someone "got away" with a crime that we wish we could commit, any punishment we give them *won't* receive any blessing, has *nothing* to do with justice, and won't be credited as any righteous act, even though the majority may think otherwise.

107

How can we tell? When the anger displayed is actually covering the real desire, it's visible to some. Also, forgiveness is entirely absent in cases where anger decides the punishment. Expected fears only realized by acting them out in reverse is noticeable much of the time. It only creates two problems where at first there was only one, and as such, solves just nothing.

Julousy 10ᵗʰ 2005

Among the many tenets of the Anti-Justice league is their oft-repeated mantra of "that won't bring them back" found in very many forms of media communication today. Even though it's true that what this is intended to prevent isn't at all a desirable outcome, what is forgotten, unaddressed, untreated, and not prevented is satisfactorily ensuring that the original crime isn't repeated.

Justice isn't about vengeance; it's supposed to stop the crime from happening a second or trillionth time. Often the effluvium surrounding the issue causes this to fail. Assuming the person seeking justice is engaged in vengeance or "trying to bring back the dead" does nothing to make sure the original offender stops their reckless train of the decimation of human life, time, and memories. Releasing criminals into the public, as we've seen happen using various methods recently in the political spectrum, or personally seen criminals released to visit me where I live three times and on my job once, does absolutely nothing to keep any criminal from re-offending. In fact, it ensures that they will; if not absolutely, then they are provided a 360° field of opportunity to do so.

Amusing who we decide can't change and who can and the characteristic traits of each. Thanks to all involved for making sure that we're safe in the knowledge that we never know when the next visit will occur. The dead may or may not come back, but what exactly does leaving murderers alive bring back? I think by now we all know.

For all those who feel that the karmic god has anointed them to be the dispenser of equality and justice, remember that playing god is the precise thing that caused Satan to be kicked out, and *as lightning fall from heaven.*[7] *"Vengeance is mine"*[8] has become their personal mantra.

Since too many today are busying themselves doing nothing but filling the self-appointed role of God's little helpers, no wonder they don't like the bible and recommend against reading it, since it removes the one of the few toys they have to play with their reality.

x. Diarrhea of the Mouth

Junior 6th, 1987

No one other than the eyewitness saw the crime. People who weren't there have no clue what actually happened, regardless of how many billions of pieces of evidence are collected, not counting video or audio tape. Guilt isn't proven by a court; it's proven by what actually happened, which the eyewitness saw first hand, and no one else did. Yes, that means the criminal is also an eyewitness. You say, "we don't know what happened" while asking questions of the eyewitness then (not joking) two words into the answer you interrupt with who cares what, since in finding the truth, answering whatever question is being asked is the only way to find the truth of the event. Four words explain the exact problem and the solution to this.

While not addressing this problem, you will never see the truth and you will pretend to never know why, even though we all know exactly why you don't know. Pretending you know more than the eyewitness when you weren't there won't solve anything either. If you suddenly realize you don't really know the person you thought you did, these four words are the reason. Yes, I speak from experience and my experience tells me that it isn't necessary. While the following remains untreated, you will continue to know less and less until you know absolutely nothing. Sitting in a position of justice or any position of authority doesn't provide either a license, currency, or excuse for these four words. If you discover this can't be treated in your case, it is recommended you resign and stay away from any authoritative position until this mental problem is under control. You will never see the truth about anything while you have diarrhea of the mouth.

y. No Matter What

Slipt-Ember 21st, 1973

If you don't get more than my word for anything, this is why. If my word is valueless, then so are you. If you don't know how to interpret the words, that's not my problem.

Many seem confused about the meaning of the words "no matter what." It would pay to spend a year or so studying this based on the negative effects of not understanding it. In short, the action or avoidance will happen regardless of actions or statements made by anyone else ever. There are no ifs, ands, or buts once "no matter what" has been established. And the action or avoidance will occur regardless of whether it seems possible or not. If this can't be done, then it shouldn't be said to begin with. Once anyone swears to God to do something no matter what, it will happen or any consequences won't be avoidable and should always be expected.

z. Repeat the Lesson

Februlary 14th, 2016

One day, God showed us what happens to people who harass rape victims. It's unimaginable and I don't wish it for anyone. Then He asked us does He need to repeat the lesson for those who may have forgotten? I was waiting to give Him an answer because it's not something to take lightly. So I've now waited over fifty years. But based on the love affair some people seem to have with Fred, Bobby, Dr. Garrist, and everyone like them, I don't have any choice but to say, "repeat the lesson."

It isn't pretty, it's devastating, and after it's over there won't be any questions. Short list of what the people involved may not say:
* We didn't know
* We had no idea
* No one told us it was wrong
* We thought we were doing the right thing
* The law is on our side
* God could never do this.

What God actually did *not* do is give anyone permission to harass any rape victim at any point in their lives for any reason whatsoever and if you think the law is on your side, either you or the law is wrong. A lesson demonstrating this is on the way. I'm very glad I won't be in their party when God begins to repeat the lesson.

Over the past fifty years, I've offered several people an opportunity for payback. The ones who didn't take the offer will be the ones who will have no regrets.

al. You Were Told

Ug-Oust 38th, 2004

In 1993, a few men stood behind me at my job off Haverly and said they would give my mom a stroke. In 1995 she had one. I don't believe this is a coincidence, but those who are in love with Fred, Bobby, and Dr. Garrist can believe it if they want to. I tried to turn to see who said it, but couldn't for some reason; probably the "took took kind" nonsense that people are so in love with. I hope that all the ones in love with Fred, Bobby, and Tayler find their lovers to be worth all the deaths they've caused, even after warning everyone that others would die if they weren't executed. It's fine, you don't need to listen to me, but when God tells you they weren't worth all the deaths they caused, don't try to say you didn't know or weren't told, even though I know you will try to say this. I will laugh in your face.

bl. Liars On Top Of Us

Divember 52nd, 2017

If you're ever around me and you hear me say to someone, "You're one of those stupid jerks that believe everything they hear?" If they say anything other than, "You're right", you're staring at the reason this took over fifty years to solve. You're also looking at someone being paid by a murderer to obstruct justice.

It has been said that the judge wouldn't have punished me and that I punished myself. Both of these are false. (This will be over when the liars finally admit to themselves the truth about who and what they are, not before. Their punishment hasn't happened yet.)

Proof: Separation is a punishment that I didn't award myself.

c1. Flashback Further

Slipt-Ember 22nd, 2017

Only now, around twenty years after I started to remember what happened, are the details between the first and second court cases beginning to become clear. The first ended very badly, after the correct verdict and sentence were established. I heard that things may not be as bad as I thought after the criminal's friends entered the courtroom and held everyone at gunpoint. But so far, I have no visible proof of this, but I do believe the rumor is true. The second court case, still not sure how that ended. The third everyone knows about and believes it to be the first. This is not the case.

d1. Retribution Recipe

October 71st, 1995

I keep seeing things mostly in movies or TV, not usually in written stories, where people keep thinking they're responsible for something happening, then feeling guilty about it. It appears strange to me since I never see this happening in real life, even when it should. I typically see it used as a deflection for what they should be concerned about, but never, as keeps happening in show after show, for something for which they're actually responsible.

"They tried to do the right thing, but something's wrong and they couldn't," Cynthia said once.

I might believe that, if I didn't remember back to before anything happened where conversations took place outside of my dad's presence before they shot him. Tons of anti-German spew about how they were going to "make us pay." Then everything that followed, none of which actually paid for anything and didn't teach anyone a lesson, since the people who thought they were, actually *weren't* qualified to teach. The five court cases that followed, where numbers two through five only had to perform the law laid out in the first, where the law was entirely ignored for no reason, also paid for nothing in reality. No, seeing all this, looks to me like the people who actually are responsible aren't trying to do anything at all other than make sure their lives are convenient and comfortable while not really giving a damn if anyone else's are or not.

el. The Last Dilemma

Slipt-Ember 51st, 2018

The problem now with this case is the same as it was fifty years ago. Waiting around for no reason, as we might expect, didn't change anything. I could easily execute Fred, Bobby, and Tayler since no one else seems capable or up to the task of keeping their word and obeying the law, if ever afforded the opportunity. But this will necessarily and immediately curse and damn every person who previously swore to God to execute them and then didn't do it. So, there is a very high probability that more than three people will be getting executed when the first three are executed in chain reaction format.

This is entirely up to the Lord Jesus Christ and there isn't anything anyone can do to change it. You waited for nothing, now live with it, if you can. This makes the weight of the matter even greater than it was already. This was calculated and foreknown by all three criminals and everyone did exactly as they expected they would. In this case, laws have made people's behavior predictable. When this happens, the demonically possessed will necessarily take advantage and exploit it. At one of my previous jobs, a non-case-related group said something that also applies here, "We are going to use your own laws to destroy you."

They are not lying or joking about this. To expect anything else is a form of self-delusion. Whenever anyone gets tired of being a puppet, we can move on with the rest of our lives.

"Well, what do you want us to do?"

Given your job, position, and experience, this question indicates you need to return to kindergarten and start all over again. Perform the law, is the obvious answer. The verdict and the sentence of the first trial haven't changed in over fifty years. I doubt they ever will. When someone will ever do anything about it is still a large unknown.

Many people are uptight because they don't know what my final decision will be. However, since my decision is primarily based on theirs, they already know what I'm going to decide, which may or may not make them more uptight.

f1. Kissing Criminal's Asses (We're Always Right)

Febrilary 14th, 2004

Anyone that's for murder has a mental problem. Any who pretend not to notice may want to consider what type of problem they may have. Any pretenders won't be part of a solution. Nor will they be in the future.

While waiting to pull together the rest of the details of this case, let's consider the excuses for Saundra. It appears her mother is the daughter of one of Dr. Garrist's victims and Dr. Garrist himself. I'm way beyond caring about why at this late stage in the process of execution. Not sure why an execution for someone who broke my wrist and Cynthia's nose with a pair of pliers and crushed my head in three places with a railroad spike would ever take more than one day in a land of justice, but we're still waiting. Not only not executed, but for who cares what reason, is allowed to leave prison to impregnate the daughter of one of his victims.

It really doesn't matter what prayers or what church anyone is attending who does this and allows it; their future is 180 degrees from whatever they think it is. Whatever reasons they think they have to do this are equally wrong and equally irrelevant. Sending her to my front door sometime between 1998 and 2003 was also a bad decision. The front door didn't open then and it never will. Coughing up any excuses for this and continuing to attack me won't save you either. Actually, I would burn whatever book is telling you that you have some right to attack any victim of a pedophile before it tells you something else that brings harm to someone else that never asked to be subjected to your opinions and pernicious judgment.

Those innocent of judging others habitually don't need to be tested. The judges do, otherwise they will never see themselves failing the test. Makes me laugh to see people who are still busy judging me come apply a test as if they're in some position of authority, which they would have been, if they had ever stopped judging. Now they never will be.

gl. Ignore the Threat

No-remember 37th, 2017

While any threat remains, the behavior, either some of it or all, of the threatened will remain unchanged. This means that moving on, in way too many respects, is impossible. Saying to move on while not removing the obstacle preventing it makes the person saying to move on part of the threat. Most of these obvious statements are answers to questions people asked me over the years. Usually, since the answer is clear, I don't respond, since a question that we already know the answer to is really a very bad question. There's no point in asking a question to which we know the answer to when asking one that we don't will be more likely to yield a long term or permanent solution. Documenting these thousands of things that were known but ignored allows those not familiar with the case to see the unbelievable degree to which the problem extends and that it doesn't just exist on the side of the criminals. Can it be called justice or law that ignores so many things that are readily apparent, or asks so many questions while pretending to have no clue about the obvious?

hl. Homicidal Tendencies

Slipt-Ember 25th, 2006

Where I used to work in 2004, some people there thought that raping a three-year-old was justifiable since the rapist had been called a name. Some there even thought they were psychic. It remains unclear how to deal with this type of insanity. Too bad there's no phone number we can call to lock these types permanently away because since they think like that, the chance that some future crimes will be justified because of them is almost 100%.

il. The Mind Wipers

Julousy 74th, 1985

Our problems would have been reduced by 90% if they had not let me forget the things I needed to know. Since our mind automatically forgets useful information, a process developed by evolution that guarantees a greater survival rate by helping us forget about things that kill us, since our mind is not healthy unless it has fully processed all available information, and healthy or not, the person is the sum total of their known/processed experiences, we are never fully seeing or realizing any person standing in front of us. This illusion is increased by using any device to mask any part of the mind from itself.

Some have used these same precision devices to eliminate their conscience. No one has been known to have returned after their conscience was thus severed. The purposes they gave for so doing were also found to be of no moment, since the knowledge they sought can be found via other, less final methods. In severing their own conscience, it seems they also severed anyone else's conscience regarding them. No one cares what they've done or where they're going. I haven't heard their name in over forty years. Now, I don't think anyone even remembers.

jl. Forced Reality

Divember 12th 1976

If we don't want an answer to a question, it's better not to ask it.

"But I don't want to get a surprise."

You will. The surprise is: If you had never asked the question, nothing bad would have ever happened. I've seen over 1000 things

116

forced into reality that shouldn't exist due to bad questions. If we don't want the "yes" or "no" part of any question, why waste time and add to the things in our life that we would rather not have? We would have been better off studying basket weaving.

kl. Death Leaves Nothing Positive

Maynot 77th, 2014

While still grieving the loss, I was realizing: There's no way to replace the friends we lose or family who have left us. If there were, they wouldn't be as valuable since we could just throw down another disposable pet, friend, or family member. I had already said "and the future, no, not any part of it, will ever see their like or kind again." Even we ourselves would lose our own value since we could so easily be replaced, if it were possible.

But we're far more valuable as we are: unique, irreplaceable, rare. This is true for those of us who have chosen not to be carbon copies of everyone else, at any rate. But even these, due to their potential, are valuable. Others may attempt to defend it all they like, but I'll still say there's nothing positive about death and death leaves nothing positive.

ll. Parthian Shot

Divember 24th, 2018

In memory of my dad, his last words as he died in my sister's arms were, "Don't let them blame you. If they blame you, they win." I misunderstood his final facial expressions, since I was young at the time. But I understand them now. All I can say is that I tried.

Another realization: If you demand more than my word for anything, you aren't taking my word. If you don't take my word, you're calling me a liar. If you call me a liar, you can't be on my side of the argument. If you aren't on my side of the argument, you can't claim you are and you have no further rights to question me about anything.

"This is only going to go one way."

23. The Halls of the Fear Slaves

Some people's fears are so large and consuming, they refuse reality and choose their fear instead. There is no reasoning with them. Nodding and saying, "yes" is the only way to deal with them. They bend reality to suit their fear. They hide behind pseudo-intellectualism and refuse to answer questions about the evolution of space, electricity, gravity, love, or time. They hypnotize victims into living out their projected fears, then blame the victim, failing to realize that when the hypnosis wears off, *everyone* knows what really happened.

"We can't allow you to have your free will, since we're consumed with the fear of what you'll do when you get it back," they are often heard to say in varying forms of expression.

The only crime was being afraid of anything to begin with. We can only hope that they destroy their fear before they kill what they fear and take someone's life along with it. People can be killed without guns. Thomas and his sisters could have had a life together, but due to fear, the life they could have had was killed and they were forced to live fifty wasted years spent in fulfilling the ignorant wishes of the fearful. His sister's minds are still slaves to many fears, dutifully kept alive by the people they call their friends.

No one is sure what the sisters' reactions will be when they see that their lives were just wasted by people who don't care about them, whose every action only serves to cover their father's murder brought about by the exact same people using false allegations, fear, and the worship of money.

24. Why You Can't See Your Future

The largest underestimation when dealing with covert demonic possession (those familiar, especially the demons, know that covert works better than overt) comes from the fact that we never really know who is listening, who we're talking to, or who is speaking. We can't address the victim of a possession the same as we do the thing which possesses them without severe consequences. Any punishment of the innocent has repercussions that are unimaginable. They take full advantage of this. People treating any of these cases indiscriminately, thoughtlessly, or with little to no experience do more harm than the demons themselves. Once again, they take full advantage of this. There is much less work when you can get someone else to do your job for you. People who don't believe this happens do more harm than anyone.

If we don't believe thieves are in our house, they will take our entire house and we'll still stupidly believe we have one. Demons use unbelief as a battery to power most of their operations. This is why is it written, *"So we see that they could not enter in* (to the promised land) *because of unbelief."*₉ The up side is that for those who enable so much harm to occur, the day will be when they won't believe the future they have even after it hits them as they're standing in it, but they won't be able to do anything about it either. And the people they harmed, slighted, and ignored with their unbelief and irresponsibility will tell them the self-same words heard for scores of years from the mouths of the blind: "We don't believe there's a problem."

For every second past January 1, 1995 that passes without the execution of Fred, Bobby, Dr. Garrist, and Pax, there will be a different and sizable punishment that will fit that type of crime of selfish negligence and condoning of child molesters who shoot fathers in front of their children. They are condoned by granting them life when they don't care anything about it.

Thomas knew, after receiving a few questions making sure that he understood that there is a reason for everything, that some things were arranged from the beginning to continue going in the wrong direction by the illegal use of hypnosis. Some tried to assure him that everything that could be done to prevent the damage from this had been tried.

He couldn't disagree more.

That there is a reason for everything doesn't mean everything has to permanently be the way that it is, since this would override the experience that we all have a free will and that changes happen every day, many times when it's entirely unnecessary. It only points to the balance and justice that is built into the universe. Thomas will continue to point to areas that haven't been explored and things that haven't been tried until we all know beyond a shadow of a doubt that there aren't any.

Maybe the dividing line isn't where we thought it was? Maybe there are no connections where we have been hypnotized to believe there are? Maybe there are no dangers where our overly worshiped, overly mollycoddled fears have told us there are? Maybe the one thing that has never been tried is completely getting rid of every fear and paranoia, no, not even to allow it to exist in so much as a thought. Thomas can say from his view: That's one thing he's never seen tried, discussed, or even barely mentioned for one second in this case.

25. The Game Changer

Another secret disclosed, which was obvious the entire time, so in reality it never was a secret: When asking a child if they have lied about anyone hated by criminals, we need to be certain they are not an eyewitness to a murder prior to the event in question. No child who ever witnessed a murder would ever wish to repeat the experience, regardless of the dealing hand. If we decide to push this through and ask them anyway, here is the thought chain:

"Did you lie about person x having committed any crime?"

"(They know I saw a murder previously, they know I want nothing to do with death. So, the only reason they can possibly be asking is that they are not in their right mind and are channeling the murderers of the first one, who have no trouble getting out of jail any time they please and forcing me to watch another one. So, I better say what they want me to say and that is...) Yes.

"Any person who knows what I saw will know that the opposite is the truth and will know what to do about it. If they don't know, then they can't judge."

So, here again, Yes can mean No. Here again, Yes may not only mean they are not guilty, but that *the questioner is* by aiding and abetting known criminals, known to eyewitnesses for what they are, from whom they cannot hide. And now they know that the questioner is also a criminal. No person in their right mind would ever ask a child who saw their father shot in front of their face if they would like commit any crime. They would not ever ask this for any reason ever at any point in time.

Now we know who they are - Now we know what to do about it.

26. What You Don't Know Can Kill You

We either punish the criminal or the victim. A person who didn't commit a crime, but gets punished anyway is a victim. Those who illegally punish the innocent are criminals. Not punishing the criminal punishes the innocent, as previously described. Since this is logically correct and unavoidable, the only thing we should fear is *not exclusively* concerned with punishing the innocent, but in failing to identify and punish the criminals.

Through fear of punishing the innocent, we fail to punish the true criminals, which punishes the victims, which punish the innocent. No person or group of people who illegally punish the innocent will have a very happy meeting when they finally figure out who God is and meet with Him. These are all foreign concepts.

"We will execute them no matter what."
Some have said that this is illegal to say. It isn't.

Proof: a. Freedom of speech.
b. If the sentence has already been passed and states that there will be an execution, we may not only say it, but we either do it or *we* will be illegal. Unless it's written somewhere that we may have a sentence, then sit around for fifty years doing nothing about it and call it legal.

When person A exists under a threat and person B does not, imitating person A's behavior won't ever be a solution. Especially when removing the threat is as easy as performing the sentence of the first and only valid trial.

Worrying about what we say instead of watching what we do is suicidal. Why even have a sentence or a verdict when no one is going to do anything about either one and just do whatever they please? For the sake of saying something was done when it actually wasn't? What is actually illegal is to have a sentence, then sit around and refuse to perform it for fabricated reasons. As the bodies pile higher, the "reasons" fade into obscurity.

27. Cannot Remember the Past

Unforgiveness: Expecting others to have greater concern or guilt for lesser, petty criminal acts while glossing over or completely ignoring larger, inescapable ones. Courts do this when they ignore events which led up to a crime which they failed to remove, thus extracting themselves (only in their minds) from the chain of events and proceeding as if this is either just or logical. Failing to note every cause which led up to the crime in question will cause something to happen, but whatever it is *won't* be justice. Justice is in these cases not only blind, but unforgiving.

28. This Won't Change

If it has been proven that two people are possessed by the devil, any who allow them to live or don't perform an exorcism will be treated as both accomplices and mouthpieces of the possessed. This affects all questions they ask and consequently the answers given to them. Rarely will straight or correct answers be given to them since this has only proven to result in more harm to self or family members. Execution is the only thing that can alter this, otherwise this won't change.

29. What Objections Occasionally Reveal

If the witness is bound under oath to tell the truth, then so is everyone else, otherwise what is produced won't be the truth.

Assume that it isn't the case. Then this happens:

"I have seen this event," says Witness A.

"The witness has stated that they have NOT seen the event, let the record reflect this," says Lawyer Z.

"Let the record so reflect the witness has NOT seen this event," says Judge B.

From then on, the record reflects only an imaginary event that is false with regards to reality.

This is what happens when judges and lawyers aren't also required to tell the truth. It's also a way to see when either of them have been bought off. Therefore, they *are* under oath to tell the truth.

Judges and lawyers both take oaths when they are sworn into office. If the oath doesn't include telling and finding "the whole truth and nothing but the truth," it is useless, since they are then not bound to not lie, thus providing a wide possibility of producing no truth and reams of erroneous records, as just demonstrated.

When an eyewitness is giving testimony directly observed at a crime scene where only the witness and the murderers were actually there at the scene, interrupting both the thought processes and flow of testimony with 12,000 objections per sentence establishes that the truth is not being sought. Saying what did or didn't happen at the time when one wasn't present is a clear drive to obfuscate the truth. If one wasn't there, what ground does one have to say anything about what did or didn't happen? Only hearsay regarding the events of the case. Hearsay is not evidence in this instance, especially not from the mouths of murderers.

So, we interrupt solid evidence with objections which produce no evidence, only hearsay, and this is legal? Proving that the guilt the truth brings with it is what is being avoided by preventing the direct eyewitness testimony from reaching the ears of anyone or being recorded.

Thus, the objector and the judge who allow this are guilty of perjury by lying under their respective oaths they swore to locate and produce the truth, yet instead, stand directly in the way of it ever being entered into the record for study.

We can't have it both ways. At some point we must realize saying one thing while doing another doesn't fool anyone, save possibly ourselves.

30. You Can Stop This At Any Time

Characters in the apathetic charade:
   Judge
   Azuman Guedley
(Names changed to incriminate the guilty)

J: "You say you saw this happen?"

A: "Yes. The doctor hypnotized her and told her to do all kinds of stupid and useless stuff."

J: "Why would he do that?"

A: "For the same reason you just asked that question - none."

J: "I'm asking the questions."

A: "Then try something that you *don't* already know the answer to."

J: "So, where exactly is she, this Evelyn, on this list of programming we found in his office?"

A: "Probably near the end."

J: "How much of this did she wind up doing."

A: "Nearly all of it, but that wouldn't have happened without all the 'doubting Thomases.'"

J: "Say what?"

A: "You idiots that keep telling her 'We don't believe that.' What do you think the command is that triggers the next step in the list? Fools! You've been doing this yourselves the whole time. So, as I said, she's innocent.

"'Dining from my brains again, sir?' she was once heard to say."

31. Quick Recap of the Last Fifty Years

When statement A is true, but B through K are false, everyone pretending not to know what to do about A doesn't fool anyone. "Paying the person back" for lying about B through K (when there is no command anywhere authorizing any paybacks) while refusing to address A also doesn't fool anyone. The greater the amount of time while A remains unaddressed necessarily increases the consequences exponentially based on universal laws which apply equally to emotional, psychological, and spiritual levels as anyone with eyes can see. B through K being false doesn't make A false. The critical failure caused by resting on this assumption won't always be recoverable.

32. What You Don't Read

There were five court cases. Case 1 succeeded completely and is the law. Case 2 also succeeded completely, but due to case 1 was entirely unnecessary. It was believed that men with guns, friends hired by Fred and Bobby, who believed their lies, where the child molesters/murderers were viewed as the victims instead of the factual event, came into the courtroom after the sentence was read and stole the court records then destroyed them, necessitating a second case. This didn't happen. Meaning that all the records weren't destroyed and exist somewhere to this day. Why the sentence still hasn't been carried out yet remains an inexcusable mystery.

33. 1996 - ? Antithesis of Reason

It remains unclear what type of mind could ever equate any murderer with any one of their victims who never committed one. Moreover, it's unclear how that any of these same minds would imagine they're somehow any facsimile of even the dimmest semblance of the law. It is also unclear why they would never use the law to do anything other than the will of the murderers when it comes to harassing the victims. It is not just this particular case that is being referred to here, though it may seem so. If all of this is happening here, it's very likely also happening somewhere else. Were humanity free of habits or predictability, we couldn't say that.

34. Murder the Victims

Whether or not any legal actions are possible for an attempted murder case is irrelevant since God weighs the *"thoughts and intents of the heart"*[10] and all three will be discussed after death. If we have the opportunity to execute criminals, then proceed to spend over fifty years not doing so, it only proves the following:

    a. We are in love with the criminals and want to marry them.
    b. We enjoy seeing what they did.
    c. We are hoping they get out of jail so we can watch it again or make money from the audio/video media they create from their crimes, both past, present, or future.

There is no other explanation or possible reasons that can fully explain the behavior of every person involved. If we are busying about not executing them and acting as if what they did offends us in any way, we are pretending, since it is in our power to execute them and our bad acting isn't fooling anyone. If we in sincerity don't approve of any of their actions, there is one way always available for us to prove it.

"This is only going to go one way," obviously means that this will be true only if the right things happen. So far, only the wrong things are happening. And just as equally, while everyone is thinking life is a big joke and a game, so long as things are not being done the right way, "this is only going to go the other way."

Having seen first hand some of what that other way is, Thomas can guarantee that absolutely no one would want to see it. To any still convinced that they're right about this, we can't say that we're right after having a sentence of execution, then proceeding not to do so. This is neither allowed nor appropriate. But a few comically keep preaching about what is or isn't appropriate.

35. Devolution: It's Not Just For This Century Anymore

Today, few typically consider eye-witness testimony to be any kind of evidence that amounts to anything other than something to be ignored, interrupted, talked over, or shouted down; since all of these forms of argument are valid and far heavier than any known type of evidence anywhere in the universe.

Sadly, there are no more minds who are anywhere persuaded by oral testimony in either public or private cases or conversations. It's doubtful if we can, as a civilization, ever be as advanced as some societies were over 2500 years ago in accepting and recognizing oral testimony as a valid kind of evidence. Billions of questions of "where is the evidence?" after any oral statements are given is proof that we no longer have this advancement and will most likely die without it. If this fails to cause a self-extinction, we will most likely devolve into a society that has absolutely no form of justice in it whatsoever, assuming that we are not now in this state presently, which, lacking any physical evidence to the contrary, cannot now be proven.

36. Not the End of the Show

While the hoards of lost dead whined about not knowing what to do or how to perform law while preaching about appropriateness to a group of victims who never asked for the job, Pax borrowed Thomas through some blackmailed arrangement for a while and took him to a dark room where he would molest and rape him at will, then sit down to watch TV. If Thomas cried, he would rape him again. He had been placed in some type of seat on a counter where he couldn't move or get off of it. Ever so often, someone would show up at the door behind which bright sunlight streamed past the silhouette of the answerer and asked if he were done or ready to come home. How this ended isn't clear, but eventually it did.

Later also, Fred insisted that both Thomas and Cynthia, not Ralene, go to the local parish and ask the priest to molest them. He refused. Cynthia was against it and tried to talk Thomas out of it as they passed by the stairs up to the choir loft, but Thomas didn't think they had a choice. There were far too many people kissing the murderer's asses to take a chance.

Mercifully, Thomas avoided one of the doctor ordered arrangements of trying to kill himself, since if he were dead, this would keep testimony from damaging the beloved murderers. Mareth and Cynthia both worked hard to prevent this, only resulting in one broken window and were successfully able to stave off any further attempts for the rest of his life. May their work be blessed and remembered. Thomas will never forget it.

37. Closing Arguments

What do we know? We know criminals get out of jail whenever they want to harass the victims.

Proof: Maren is the daughter of Nevil and Evelyn. Saundra is the daughter of Dr. Garrist & Maren. Cathy is possibly the second daughter of Dr. Garrist and Maren. None of these relationships were done with permission from anyone. If prisoners are in jail, then they do need permission, or the full penalty applies. Dr. Garrist was supposed to have been in the state penitentiary for the last fifty years; but due to the fact that he has two kids, possibly more, we know this isn't the truth.

A police officer told Thomas at the time, "We know what you're doing."

Thomas thought to himself, 'I doubt it, otherwise you wouldn't be helping criminals since I'm going to put you both either in jail or hell - preferably both. If you knew that, you certainly wouldn't be helping them. So, you may think you know what I'm doing, but more importantly: *I KNOW WHAT YOU'RE DOING AND WHAT TO DO ABOUT IT.*

'If you notice that you're soliciting a crime from a rape victim, it's time to retire - you're a fake cop!'

When communications are being monitored by people who get out of jail whenever they please and hire agents to harass the victims, understandably then we must speak in code. If what Thomas said was due to the fact the criminals were alive and not executed in 1969 when they should have been, all we need to do to know the truth is either invert the statements he made, or know the person he identified *after*

Fred, Bobby, Dr. Garrist, and Pax are not correct, but in fact, point most of the time to someone else, or no one. None if regarding the nonsensical badgering questions which Thomas has received at the minimum of yearly for no reason which typically only precede more illegal or incorrect things being done by people who should know better.

Since this is the case, everyone knows what they need to know, all answers to all questions, what to do in this situation, and no further testimony is needed from anyone. It says in the book we swear on when taking an oath, *"To him that knoweth to do good and doeth it not, to him it is sin."*[11] While we sit in the halls of justice and do nothing when we know what we need to do, we deserve to be in jail with the criminals or somewhere other than hearing criminal cases or in any public office. But in no event do we need any further to be practicing law, nor can we believe our hands are clean in a matter while we point fingers at everything but the mirror and shirk our responsibilities when we know precisely what needs to be done since "this is only going to work one way."

Yes, criminals attempt to find ways to make law officials pay, and this may have had no small part in what they did, but Thomas believes that with the billions of people on earth who have degrees, this case and others like it could be handled far more skillfully, effectively, and efficiently than anything that's been done so far.

38. Aftermath Coagulant

Once anyone has witnessed a crime, then watches everyone systematically remove the punishment phase, the world doesn't look the same anymore. Yet, everyone seems to expect this growing number to see the world like everyone else does. This expectation, however, is unrealistic. The universe has forever been changed for them, and even had punishment been enforced, the world will never be the same.

When nearly everyone is kissing the butts of people they saw commit a murder, following this, they tend to behave in such a way as to keep everyone else as far away as possible until the cessation of all the fawning admiration due more to people that love life than those who hate it.

Sometimes demons speak through other people, and by this is meant people other than the ones whom they possess. This is done very much in ventriloquist fashion and even over great distances. We know this by the kinds of questions they ask. No one in their right mind would ask a rape victim if they want to see a crime; so by this we may know a demon is speaking through that person. We could just tell the demon mouth-piece what they want to hear and wait for the police to arrest them for soliciting a crime; but this rarely happens.

By this we may know there are no real investigators left in the known universe. All of this happens because instead of either exorcizing or executing the demon possessed, we allow them to live and spew their nonsense to other inmates, allowing them to reproduce their mentality unhindered throughout the world. This isn't the wisest approach, which is why Jesus often commanded the demons not to speak; and it's also why it's never recommended.

"The past is already gone. We ruined your life and got away with it." Maybe. But this deliberately ignores the presence of eternity. It is often said we can't comprehend what an infinite being could compose in reality. This is unprovable, but we can start to understand an infinite number of things about it (it being both eternity, the infinite being, and His compositions) if we start to believe what He has already said and showed us about it. From this, several wonderful and harsh realities can be revealed.

-The Other Shoe.

Imagination, while offering speculations on the seemingly impossible, lies at the fringes of reality and guides us in its direction. Through its window, we see the vast possibilities and can make any choice we want. Via this process, we can see that any limit is an illusion.

Arguments are not attempted when there is little to no chance of persuasion. Eventually, all of Thomas' audiences would just be told what they wanted to hear, then abandoned. This also happens with people who ask the same question twice. The definition of insanity and coercion explains why.

Sometimes when someone is crying, they don't need us to stop them. The oceans could be filled to overflowing with the tears caused by injustice. Processing through the deep waters is ofttimes required before it becomes clear what can be done about it. Or considered another way, the dark pond must be drained before the shape of the statue at the bottom becomes visible.

For any who think anything said here is merely a reaction to what happened prior to 1968, *the* reaction hasn't happened yet. It will be a planned one, not knee-jerked. It will happen when the time is appropriate. Some of the reactions forming the whole have been decided, some haven't; nothing has been finalized. People who haven't yet arrived will be involved in the final decisions. And when it happens, it won't be avoidable and it will be devastating to everyone who either committed or enabled that crime to both happen and go unpunished for over fifty years. Not believing any of this won't change the outcome.

"The crime can't be solved in the manner the criminal describes," some say.

Under the correct conditions, maybe it can be solved *exactly* the way they describe it. In fact, sometimes it's the *only* solution. Otherwise, we will sadly discover that we have been revolving one decision over fifty years, which was just seen.

Many are surprised when they find lust at the bottom of their anger. Much anger is only jealousy that another person actually did what they secretly wanted to do. It is saying, "If I can't have my lust, neither can you." Many will be coping with this idea for days and decades if they ever decide to face themselves. Even anger at this idea lends proof to its truth.

People tend to try to kill whatever makes them responsible, if they can't dismiss it some other way, either by victim-blaming or ignoratio elenchi. This is why anger is not justice and killing what makes us angry does *not* break the cycle of violence. It only moves it over to *us*.

Allowing character assassination to have bearing on a statement is not only an open admission that we have a complete lack of discernment, but it is also the avenue childish excuses take to prevent justice.

While any case remains unsolved, everyone involved is under oath. Otherwise, we are granting wood, stone, and other construction material the power of sentience which they don't have.

Q: What do you call people who beg for evidence after sufficient evidence has already been presented?
A: Criminals
Q: What can we say about them?
A: They are being paid by, or are the originators of the crime.
Q: What can we tell them?
A: The opposite of the truth, or what they want to hear.
Q: Why?
A: Because if you don't, they'll kill another member of your family.

Sadists are brought beyond ecstatic pleasure when the innocent suffer. So the laws are constituted to make sure they have what they need.

Sometimes yes means no and no means yes.
If you don't know, you can't judge.
If you don't "no," you can't judge.
If you can't tell which is which,
you must resign you silly witch.
- Clue from 1969

Here is an example of when yes means no: When in a court room asking an eyewitness to a murder that is under five years old if they were lying about their statements, yet we haven't performed the promised execution and the murderers have threatened to kill more family members if the eyewitness doesn't lie about what happened and they say "yes," then yes means no. Pretending a known threat isn't real does nothing. This is when we have said "yes" a real existing threat means "no" isn't real, when the opposite is the whole truth and nothing but the truth. When it is said, "whatever happens is up to you" - those words mean exactly what they say. This will be lost on a world that never says what they mean.

Punishing the innocent on the outside chance that they're guilty is a suicidal thought pattern.

Proof: Once their innocence is proven and our motives are fully revealed, the only alternative at that late stage in the game is a death sentence that will last for eternity. Yet here we are fifty years later. If we imagine any three-year-old can be guilty of anything based solely on their race, we have immediately removed ourselves from having any power of judgment over them for the rest of their lives. And in case this is the first time we've heard any objections to the concept of race qualifying everyone within it for death, since we've also added the insane conditional of punishing a three-year-old solely on the basis of their race, our opinion is thereafter worth nothing precisely due to the existence of that belief, and in the end it will only kill us.

- What You Believe Can Kill You

A requirement for death isn't always due to vengeance, anger, or retribution. It could, and should be more often, due to a desire to not see more people murdered or raped than have been by the criminal already since there are so many that are released back into the public to murder again to their heart's content till they're caught again. This is the purpose of executions. Fake justice releases them back to the public to murder hundreds more, using the excuses of anger, vengeance, retribution, or the fake fear of punishing the innocent to coax the unwitting into not punishing them. True justice prevents death.

- Fake Justice

In anything (especially politics), if we want the truth, we ignore the words and examine the behavior. If we don't find a balance in any aspect, e.g., one side defends the other while the other remains silent, the side supplying the deficiency is guilty of removing balance. When one side can take the other and well defend it while the other doesn't, the side that doesn't is guilty since they have by deficiency removed the balance of actions. In a court, regardless of the words, the side removing the balance is guilty. This is the solution to whole case in 1968.

"So, you arranged all of those subsequent crimes to cover the fact that you allowed four men who raped a three-year-old after they shot his dad in front of his face and shot his sister's legs in the knees to live for forty years after the murder/rape? Then you want the three-year-old to feel guilty when he turns thirty-two and again at thirty-six?" Thomas replied to the men who were paid to harass him and lie about the facts of the case for fifty years.

"My God!" he continued, "I really don't think there's anything I can say to a mind that is that sick and has that capacity for insanity. Actually, if I had my way, you would get executed right beside them after we marry you to them. Since you're that in love with them, go to hell beside them!"

Since we know there is balance, this means that if the judgments we pronounce have effects that are sharp and burdensome, then later when we are judged, the effect will be sharp and burdensome to precisely the exact same degree - the exact same kind - the exact same measure. So if we, after knowing all this and hearing it since we were children, judge a three-year-old later in his life with an effect that is life threatening for something he did under the threat of a violent, racist, murderous criminal, we know that the effect when we're later judged for this will be mind-blowing and devastating. If any recovery is even possible, it will be an extremely large miracle. The treatment for this type of insanity will immediately ensue after the judgment.

Since mouths can be fired just like a gun and do way more damage, we need gun control for people's mouths more than anything else in the world.

Mouths can be fired off, killing an innumerable number of people while leaving no traces at all behind to prove who fired the deadly shots. They can leave scar tissue behind that can't be proven since no one can see the bleeding, the pain, the scars, or prove where any of them came from. That the majority blatantly takes full advantage of all this today is now so patently obvious that too many treat it as if it's a kid's game. Generally speaking "words can never hurt," but false accusations are prohibited repeatedly for clear and real reasons, otherwise nothing about them would ever have been mentioned either in the ten commandments or repeatedly elsewhere and also in several other books besides. It also constitutes lying under oath by definition since false and true are opposites.

That criminals also take full advantage of the nowadays play-toy that false accusations have become is what this case with which we're all now familiar is partly about. If what is flying from mouths is actually provable, (the fact that something came from someone's mouth doesn't amount to proof, even though the majority thinks that it does), backed up by evidence, not bare opinions, wishes, whims, or criminal intent, only then have we actually achieved [Mouth Control]. Therefore, we can clearly see there are an innumerable number of mouths in need of [Mouth Control].

Thomas had previously behaved in such a way as to put forward the idea by way of explicit example and copious amounts of explanation, which he still believes is true, that "reasonable doubt" as defined by law, can be brought to bear on any event, idea, noun, or verb in existence. He is still waiting for the rebuttal and definition of when reasonable doubt cannot apply. This has to be the case, otherwise anyone can use reasonable doubt to obstruct any and all forward movement as we have just seen, thereby using false reasoning to provide an unreasonable situation. He wonders if he should wait another fifty years for this. All the while he's being told to move on. Upon the arrival of the answer to this question, he'll be happy to do so. The entire case hangs on this and a few other critical points we have yet to discuss. We actually do have eternity to arrive at some conclusion to this.

He realized the other day he only knew the person he hasn't seen in over fifty years for little more than two to four years before they were shot in front of his face. No one can say whether he would have grown to love or hate that person later. In spite of this, he still misses them sometimes. He wonders about his character and personality. The main thing he recalls is that he was very often worried about the safety of his children. In the end, he didn't have either. There are more laws that protect the criminals than the victims while we pretend we care about the innocents.

After waiting this long for an execution that was scheduled to happen in 1969, it doesn't really make much difference anymore. The people who committed the murder got to live full lives, didn't have to work for fifty years, got all the sex they wanted to have, got in and out of jail as much as they wanted to, and had three square meals a day while the person they killed didn't live past 1967. There are no reasonable explanations to be found when considering why we reward murderers this way, but those are the facts of this case. We can take comfort with the fact that we paid for it with our tax money.

Major changes today. The report was sent in. The response is on its way. Since the report didn't have what was desired inside it, it's assured the response from God isn't going to be what anyone wants. But, we can't expect otherwise when people worship child-molesting murderers for fifty years and reward them with life they don't deserve to have. When justice is denied, don't expect any blessings.

Just for the record, here's the time they had to perform the execution the judge "swore to God" would happen: They had more than 18,212 days, or 50 years, or 1,573,516,800 seconds, or 26,225,280 minutes, or 437,088 hours, or 2600 weeks. Plenty of time to perform four executions which should only take one week in a state that performs over 15.5 on average a year.

The ones who care little for life praise those who take the most kills. They enshrine them in prisons and keep them alive, treating them better than any kings or rulers of the earth. Imagining that if they worship these gods of death, their lives will be spared later, failing to see that any god of death doesn't care whose death it is. This is how we know them. They are the true kings of ignorance

39. Summary

Under the Table were found The Accessories who entirely enabled The Checkup. It was only after this checkup when anyone began to ask, "Has The Testimony Changed?" which led to the doubt, space, and ability needed to construct The Machine. The emanations generated by the machine prompted further questions, such as Colluding with Gaslights? which was believed and led fairly rapidly to The Torture Chamber. These activities spread into the curtilage surrounding the houses where they were performed, prompting further questions such as What Happened to the Backyard? and Do You Need Some Help?

Quick to the rescue, The Backwards Jackass Project was dispatched to clean up the errors which obsessively and necessarily required several people to yell You're Obsessed - The Accusation That Always Works and provided several Botanical Markers in order to stave off any possibility of Guilt Altering Reality.

Since the Mock Trial was entirely misapprehended, more accusations flew, among which was heard You Set Me Up! The God Haters soon followed to produce complete Anticipation Disorder suppressing any Initial Statements which then blossomed into The Actual Disruption of the Interruptions, ultimately bringing about The Final Nails (Part 912).

All attempts to Annalogue the Analyzer were also stifled since The Strength of Sin is Ignorance and the book on How to Ask Questions was trammeled, while the book on Intended Damage was instead preferred. After a review, there was Sufficient Evidence to reveal that for some there is No Palace in the Future and that The Unbribable Investigator or anyone Qualified either doesn't exist at all, or yielded Mixed Results.

During the Debriefing, several were heard to exclaim, "What Did We Learn?" or "So Now What? p.14,937," leading to a Transitional Sheering after which it was determined an official ruling that We Will Excuse Them No Matter What when enough Public Evidence was amassed to clearly see that This is Only Going to Go One Way.

The Doubtful Journal, found near the Spewl Pool, helped to discover that Sometimes the Law is Illegal. If You Have To Be Told in Retrospect that asking Does God Have an Authority Complex? is a bad question, you will only discover instead How to Extend Torture Beyond the Initial Crime using doses of Legerdemain.

Why Did This Fail? was another question posed by the journal, to which Death is Unnecessary was only one of the possible answers. Even after being asked to relocate somewhere else literally everywhere they moved, Thomas' usual reply to the incessant goading was, "I'm Not Going Anywhere until after you Redefine Yourself as something other than The Psychopath. Continue not doing so, and I Will Laugh."

But instead the Project's staple prescription was to Fear Intelligence and Keep Waiting till it's too late and Errors Overbalance, especially with heaping dosages of Three Words You Never Say to a Rape Victim, ignoring the proven laws of Equal & Opposite Reaction, proffering numerous versions of their staid Song & Dance while forgetting that "We Don't Know" Won't Save You.

The many Faces of Love and Concern only added to the number of Missing Pieces, which faces repeatedly forgot that Vengeance Isn't Mine and never cured their chronic Diarrhea of the Mouth No Matter What any evidence in front of those same faces indicated. Choosing rather to Repeat the Lesson, in spite of having known they had already heard several times over the childhood admonishment, "You Were Told."

The many Liars On Top Of Us only caused the victims to have to Flashback Further as an ofttimes futile effort to concoct a Retribution Recipe, which after failing only pointed to the prodigious advent of The Last Dilemma, exacerbated by the incessant practice of Kissing Criminal's Asses (We're Always Right).

Choosing rather to Ignore the Threat posed by ignoring the voice of justice only confirmed the Homicidal Tendencies of The Mind Wipers as they trudged blindly forward into their Forced Reality forgetting that Death Leaves Nothing Positive regardless of to whom it reveals the Parthian Shot.

The Halls of the Fear Slaves, bedizened with rich tapestries, and from which few ever ventured far, did much to explain Why You Can't See Your Future and helped to find The Game Changer, when venturing merely a bit further out would have adequately revealed What You Don't Know Can Kill You or why we Cannot Remember the Past. In either case, This Won't Change. What Objections Occasionally Reveal regarding this was precisely how You Can Stop This At Any Time while providing an elucidating Quick Recap of the Last 50 years, but all of this is only What You Don't Read forming the record found in the files under 1996 - ? Antithesis of Reason.

The stock habits of the actions of far too many explained how to Murder the Victims and appear like God-ordained saints of time and eternity, but only lent further proof to support the growing fad of Devolution: It's Not Just For This Century Anymore.

But this is Not the End of the Show, there were some Closing Arguments which, when brewed sufficiently over a low fire, brought to the surface the richness of the Aftermath Coagulant, which was followed by a stern warning found in the Epilogue: Additionally Added Addendum, only added subsequently to the Summary.

40. Epilogue: Additionally Added Addendum

In considering the behaviors of the various characters in The Blinder from an inside position, what seems to have happened is that a screwdriver was used to commit a murder. Instead of punishing the murderers, the screwdriver was given a fifty year period of instructions about what is and isn't appropriate, had its carrying case burned to ashes, had its replacement case flooded and was never sharpened by any grindstone ever. Meanwhile, the actual murderers were almost completely ignored. All we can do is hope that this isn't what happens on average, and that this case is either an individual, or a replica of a smaller number than ten. Hopefully, for once, we can be right at least about this much.

> "Everyone loved the feeling and experience of being forgiven, but no one wanted to be the first one to forgive the victims."
>
> - *Epitaph on a tombstone found where the earth used to be at the end of time.*

2. THE OBFUSCATORY OBLIVION OF THE OBVIOUS

1. Why?

Many statements which we label "obvious" are only so *after* they have been stated, not usually before. Even then, they are not absolutely obvious, in that prior to being explained they are generally not universally understood or known. What usually occurs after these observations is a grand-scale dismissive sweep which wipes the idea in its entirety from memory. A grand-scale accounting of all diamonds, gold, and dust as equal and dissolving them all into an invisible powder. This emotionless sweep of thought-death is one of the greatest obstacles to progress and one of the greatest boons to ignorance known to mankind.

A society's largest blind spot creates the greatest deficiency in their collective reasoning. The largest blind spot happens with those things with which we are most familiar. What is familiar is obvious. Therefore, the obvious is the most difficult to understand, memorize, or process. This is why hiding things in plain sight works.

From this, a pool is formed into which most useful knowledge descends to never be seen again. However, with the tools provided here, it is possible that many things may be extracted and recovered from it. But without adroit assiduity and rabid tenacity, the most valuable knowledge will forever remain lost due to the high gravitational pull of the sepulchral pool of oblivion.

If a characteristic of geniuses is that they have a firm grasp of the obvious, then because of this, it is impossible to overstate the obvious.

2. Pellucidity

1. People who know the world is better than it looks can study problems that aren't.

2. Shibboleths are an enigma about which not much can be said.

3. Without limits, boundaries, or laws, it would be impossible for an atom to exist. These laws were not written until they were, yet were still in force.

4. Catch-22: If we're a victim of any crime, we're the least likely to be able to handle the stress involved in catching the criminals as a result of the trauma. But because of the crime we are the most interested in catching them and by comparison everyone else appears aloof, unconcerned, or apathetic, though this is usually an illusion. Sometimes it's not.

5. We use many smaller works in preparation for the larger.

6. Since time is a concept and a construct, it requires both design and planning, implying a designer and a planner - both would have to exist outside of time to be able to create it.

7. Reading other people's minds isn't always a picnic. Then we know when they hate us and we have to figure out how not to hate them back, which we may or may not feel like doing at that particular moment. Especially if we've just eaten explosive chili.
- Psychic Feedback Loop

8. The releasing of murderers back out onto the streets is killing any message of kindness and compassion anyone may otherwise be preaching. The message won't be heard. This behavior has a name.

9. Most never calculate the cost of being wrong. If we're wrong about God, *we* pay, not the church or the preacher we hate. If we're

wrong about politics, *we* pay, not the opposite party. If we're wrong about money, *we* pay, not the bank. If we're wrong about society, *we* pay, not the person we're arguing with about correct social structures. If we're wrong about electricity, *we* pay, not the wall socket. Too often, no one cares about what everyone takes for granted, which is the obvious.

10. By observing any government, it's easy to see that sometimes people's concept of balance and order in the universe completely screws to hell the balance and order of the universe.

11. To the two or three still addicted to interruptions, after hearing a recent interruption convention: People who interrupt are so afraid someone else's view will permanently change their behavior, as if they have no control whatsoever. However true that lack of control may be, they fail to see that by interrupting anyone, *they* are the ones changing other people's behavior by not letting the silenced opinions be heard and adding unnecessary frustration to the entire equation. So, by using fear and ignorance they become precisely what they hate in other people.

12. Just like in audio, where the ear tunes out sounds that have been heard too many times, it's highly likely that we do the same thing with the behavior of familiar people. Since this is the case, the fact that we know someone is the very thing that keeps us from knowing them.

13. Ignoring what people say and think as if they're our child until they behave the way we want them to is a way to show the love of Jesus Christ for the world. Everyone knows that it feels good to be ignored as if everything they're doing is wrong. We all know that judging others this way is a perfect and right way to behave and there will never be any punishment for it. Since having a superiority complex is popular, then it has to be right.

14. Some seem to believe we are to acquire our dreams in order to thereafter ignore the entire universe for the rest of our lives. This is false.

15. All theory requires faith until it becomes law. Most law requires no faith, but may be relied on to supply evidence for faith or to be able to see faith as evidence.

16. To: People who think they've gotten away with something.

Fact: We have eternity in *front* of us. This allows plenty of time for us to figure out exactly how to treat whatever they think they got away with.

17. Since greed has no emotions, it's possible that we may safely call people addicted to it disorder afflicted.

18. Aside from anything else, it has been sufficiently demonstrated that what may be obvious to some minds is not so to all, as per the previous warning. This is the other fatal mistake teachers make: assuming just because something is clear to a mind with 75 PhDs, B.A.s, D.D.s, MDAs, and ADHDs that it is equally clear to every student with barely a GED. It's difficult to fathom why this isn't a glaring red flag to a mind so ostensibly educated, but this only serves to prove its own point. I.e., when it isn't obvious to one that it isn't obvious to all, the one should realize that when it isn't obvious to one, it isn't something that may be assumed to be obvious to all.

19. When we see any bad example, we have three choices:

a. Assume nothing and don't follow the bad example at any point in the future.

b. Assume the person did this bad behavior deliberately and wants us to punish them; so we may pretend we're Jesus Christ and decide what punishment to give them since we know everything. Usually this takes the form of doing the same thing back to them years later, or even immediately.

c. Carefully study reality and see that there are two options when giving any example: 1. Show people what to do, or 2. Show people what *not* to do.

If we're interested in positive thinking, a bad example will translate as what *not* to do. This especially after such a question as: "Tell us what we need to know for this time period so we don't make a mistake."

If we know how to assume the positive, we will pick (c) when we have well developed logic, reasoning, and communication skills. We will pick (a) if we have no clue whatsoever, or just want to be safe. We will pick (b) if we are negative, worship Satan, and don't care at all about what God wrote in the bible or on the ground in the sand.

20. When we treat people we don't know as enemies, almost 100% of the time, this is precisely what made them one, regardless of whatever they were previously.

21. A correct definition of "explanation" would be: to adequately show someone how to do something. Many think flapping their lips is sufficient to "show," when lip flapping involves no demonstrations or hands on experience. This explains the near 99% level of ignorance in the known universe.

22. If the asking of a certain question is the cause of any wrong thing happening, it's beyond certain that it's past time to stop asking that question.

"But we're required by law to ask it."

If your asking causes harm or death to another person, you're required by an extremely critical, prodigiously higher moral law to *not* ask it.

23. In works of fiction, the author strives to make sure things make sense so everyone will believe the story. But the story is fiction. In real life, criminals make sure their crimes *don't* make sense so when they're reported, *no one* will believe them. Any servant of justice is wasting their time if trying to make sure all the facts and evidence make sense when this is very often the case; and this strategy has been the case for over 6,000 years.

They should first prove the criminal didn't arrange things to not make sense before arriving at any conclusions that put the victims in further danger by neither prosecuting nor punishing the criminal. This lesson has yet to be learned. Maybe in another 6,000 years someone can figure it out?

24. A criminal will always claim the evidence is insufficient to amount to any proof, or they will be heard to frequently say, "that proves nothing." So, when we hear this and we know enough evidence has been supplied to amount to proof, we know we are either talking to

　　a. the criminal,

　　b. someone being coerced or paid by the criminal, or

　　c. someone sympathetic to the criminal.

25. Any oath taken, with or without complex, involved, lengthy, or terse ceremony, has precisely the same weight, force, and meaning in every part of the universe. A second oath forced or coerced once a first has been ignored is irrelevant and holds no weight nor is it binding.

26. Too many believe they can use hypnosis to force words from people's mouths and that this binds them to those words. It does no such thing. One is too many and there are far more than one.

27. Any relationship crafted solely under the rules of one side isn't.

28. Ignoring the cause changes neither the effect nor the cause. It only changes our preparedness for the ramifications of the entire causal chain.

29. To ensure justice has no common field with vengeance, it is occupied with ensuring the same crime can't happen twice outside of punishing the criminal, which isn't a crime, but a response to the initial action. When it does not do this, it can't be called justice. Releasing criminals from prisons randomly, therefore, has no part with justice and very likely and often has more to do with seeking vengeance on the original victims of the crime.

30. Hypnosis is an abridgment of the freedom of speech. Discussing this will disclose a multiplicity of ramified evasions.

31. We don't look to justice as a means of bringing back the dead, but as a way to secure the means of the living for our future. When people incessantly repeat this false belief, it's as if they're saying, "Punishing criminals won't bring back the dead, so never punish anyone ever."

32. If we aren't balanced, the future will either shave or add something to what we are now.

   - Centrist Reflect

33. We spend gross and inordinate amounts of time particularizing our distinctions in order to force others to accept them, whereas if we accepted our own distinctions it would make no difference whether anyone else did or not. This is sometimes mistaken to be an inability to defend our position, but this is just an optical illusion.

34. For some reason, when people disagree with us, we take this opportunity to question our right to exist and try to kill the offender. It's amazing that minds capable of such unlimited potential can function this pathetically on such a basic level. People who do this aren't interested in solving any problems and as such will only create them.

35. People sometimes act like anyone who clearly illustrates any problem is like a baby crying who needs to be silenced for everyone's

sanity. Let's assume this incorrect analogy is actually a good one. The baby will cry far less when you actually solve the problem instead of throwing a Walmart supply of pacifiers at it. This they do while simultaneously whining like babies, far louder than the first, about something that is either contrived or a non-issue. This second type has never been possible to silence by any known means of pacification.

36. The only good thing about being judged, if this can even be said, is that we can immediately see what's wrong with it.

37. If the price is always > x and the paycheck is always < x, then this can only mean that the possible amount actually available to pay for anything will, on average, always be < price where x = either autonomous consumption or the cost of living. Since (price) > x > (paycheck).

Companies can't continue to underpay employees while overcharging customers and remain in business, where business = the US economy. Neither can they expect the employees to feel guilty about the debt created by the companies themselves. Let x = x and only charge x while paying x. Doing otherwise is an indication of a gross lack of awareness of one's surroundings, in which case we need to have neither companies nor employees, but should remain in therapy until the surroundings have been fully realized and accepted.

38. Asking the same question until we hear the answer we like doesn't mean

a. that we have the right answer,

b. that we're not guilty of coercion,

c. that we actually have an intended answer,

or d. that we have anything whatsoever.

39. Reality exists regardless of any human laws. A law then is merely a recognition or denial of reality. Our job is to align with reality and support it, or be classified as insane.

40. It has been noticed that no one really cares if anyone is offended when they constantly interrupt them. Since this happens daily in courts of law, there can't possibly ever be any legal reason to care about offending anyone.

41. When considering Euclid, he sometimes seems to over-explain what appears to be obvious. Since we find today most not only can't see

the obvious much less explain it, it is a good way to prove to ourselves that just because it's obvious doesn't mean we understand it, doesn't mean we can see it, doesn't mean we shouldn't spend time thinking about it, and doesn't mean we won't learn anything from it.

42. To a mind governed solely by emotions, there is no such thing as evidence. This is proven by these words: Accept This. Where non-acceptance is an indication that it is actually the case. It's also proof that we're not as emotional, thoughtful, benevolent, kind, caring, or compassionate as we thought, since we can now see how unacceptable we are.

43. Guilt is an unbearable weight that will always pull in the direction of the offending crime. Since those slinging it the most are too often the initial offenders, we can see the failure of the guilt-peddlers

44. Calling an eyewitness to a crime a liar makes the accuser an accessory to the crime. Not acting on their statements amounts to the same thing as calling them a liar.

45. What needs to be done is what was said would be and should have been, but wasn't. What doesn't need to be done is what was said would be done, should not have been done, but was anyway. We know our responsibility in each case. This may seem obvious, but in many critical cases it appears not to be at all.

46. We get what we expect. We may freely change what we expect if we don't like what we get.

47. If God were a tyrant, we would know about it.

48. The fuel of dense hatred doesn't require anything to be true.

49. It's always difficult to teach blind people since they can never see what you're saying.

50. We have obviously, quite recently, been discussing the obvious, sometimes as a joke, sometimes en serio. From this we can see that if it is this difficult to see the obvious, we cannot say it's impossible to see anything that is hidden since many great minds have revealed hidden truths for thousands of years now, but we can say that it will take far longer to see them.

If we're struggling this much to see the obvious, then those hidden things, the invisible worlds, the dark corners where absolutely no one is even the least concerned to shine the feeblest candle light, might not forever remain shrouded in black darkness, but will take centuries longer to locate. This would be required were it only to decide if further investigation is even worthwhile.

The upside is that through understanding, accepting, and recognizing the obvious, that which isn't can become more understandable. We can see this not only from "as above, so below," or "what is seen are merely pictures of the unseen,"$_{12}$ but also through logic. If we come to the point where we can actually see the invisible in any of its millions of facets, we are no longer viewing the unknown, but staring directly into the face of what has suddenly become the obvious.

- Ideas Are Far More Beautiful Than Any Diamond.

51. Hypocrisy has become among the foremost of modern day gods worshiped by a "profoundly sick society,"$_{13}$ sitting next to the gods of Convenience, Apathy, and Ignorance.

52. To the majority, God is an alien: A foreign entity with whom not even a remote acquaintance has either been established or attempted.

53. Plagiarism is funny, since in order for every film ever made to succeed, the actor has to plagiarize the idea of the writer and convince us that it was his or her own. Yes, here we aren't using the strict, legal sense of the term, but the looser one of simply "an idea borrowed from another whether paid to do so or not."

So we see here a clear example of how plagiarism is sometimes perfectly acceptable and so obvious that no one ever has thought about or discussed it. So now there's the question: What do we do after realizing that doublethink has been happening for a very long time now?

54. The churches teaching it's ok to kill people who don't agree with us, hospitalize them for their vote, or destroy their property due to some lie the church members believe, don't need to be taxed at all. The churches who teach that God will allow them into heaven after murdering anyone they feel deserves it and that baptism allows full benefits so we can do anything we wish at all and never fear the consequences don't need to be taxed at all. They need to be closed down.

55. Whoever characteristically avoids any and every confrontation or argument is fighting with unsharpened blades and will consequently lose any war they ever engage on every level.

56. It is clear that in the irresistible urge, stoked by unnamed sources that no one cares to trace or lift one speck of dust to detect their motives, to be as socially acceptable as possible, we imagine that by repeating ad infinitum the cornucopia of things we oppose, that this somehow defines who we are. The urge is so consuming that it seems nearly irresistible and takes on an almost hypnotic, perfunctory, quotidian automation, which, in order to maintain the godlike "acceptable" status, spreads exponentially like thoughts through a psychic.

Difficulty: When the outline decried of what we oppose is only fabrication, lies, and hate spew of a figure that doesn't exist, we only wind up becoming what doesn't exist.

Proof: The opposite of something that doesn't exist is only the negative form of something else that also doesn't exist.

Trying to exist as something that doesn't removes us from the center, from who we are to who we're not. When this happens, no one is fooled and the shift is obvious to everyone.

57. If we fear what we don't understand, a way to serve fear as a god is to never try to understand, never listen, never think, never study while harassing any who do. Then compound the issue by blaming anyone but ourselves for the fears we create by refusing to investigate, among other reasons. Then pretend that nothing can be done about this unsolvable problem, while to everyone all the time, everywhere, every part of this process we're simmering in, depending on the fear, is shadowed by the reckless villain, the obvious.

58. The largest problem in any misunderstanding is the misunderstanding.

59. Follow the methods of the mafia, and we'll be sleeping with them. It's not a question.

60. Any who think that two wrongs can ever make a right will discover there can actually be three wrongs, which should, according to their own belief, make things extremely right.

61. There is yet another pattern: We imagine we can do whatever we want while restricting speech on everyone but ourselves to imply that every person cannot say whatever they want, when in fact, the

opposite is the truth: We may *say* whatever we want, but we may not *do* whatever we want.

This behavior, mostly tacitly taught by example and lemming relationships, is a failed, overtly obvious attempt to cover the fact that in far too many instances, we never did what we said. We never felt like doing what we said; we never even thought about doing what we said even 0.8 seconds after saying it.

Next time, we should try not to make this obvious. Or, what is easier, just align with reality and make sure we have no vain imaginings that we can do whatever we want while restricting speech on everything but oxygen when the result is harm or death to others. Speech doesn't kill people, actions do, or the lack thereof. Pretending otherwise is laughable and hilarious, until someone is killed because of it.

62. The ones who know the most are the ones who know they don't.

63. When we meet any who love not answering questions, then assume a superior posture, remind them of this: People who cannot sufficiently explain anything aren't any improvement over those who can, and that believing otherwise only accentuates a super-inflated posterior.

64. The people who destroy us with their opinions probably won't be the ones who could ever save us.

65. Always dealing on someone else's terms isn't compromise, but is actually a form of slavery.

66. It is highly likely that the average divorce rate from responsibility is the same as the actual divorce rate.

67. If we hold anyone to a higher standard, then by the laws of math we are now using a double standard.

68. When the shoe is on the other foot, we quickly figure out how to remove it.

- The Rest of the Sentence

69. As also applied directly to this entire work, when the shoe fits, dance extravagantly in it.

70. An opinion that can be proven is no longer an opinion.

71. The Justice System makes a mockery of itself when it repeatedly refuses to perform it.

72. Outside courts of law, we ask questions to which we don't know the answers and expect an answer while ignoring things we already know and refuse to put them together to ask better questions. Inside courts of law, while ignoring things we don't know and refusing to find them out to put more things together to ask better questions, we ask questions to which we already know the answer and expect justice. We then pretend that we're dumbstruck when it doesn't happen. From this, we may clearly see the problem.

73. We are under no moral obligation to talk to anyone who is not listening.

74. It's far easier to hear what we say when everything we say isn't a shakedown for quick cash.

75. If it doesn't come from a point of objective observation, nothing has been observed.

76. If we see what we want to see, then we also don't see what we don't want to see. This includes reason, logic, and understanding.

77. Fear worshipers are a terrorist organization. (They have too many groups and names to list here.)

78. For those following along in Euclid, by now we see how the obvious has at least one, sometimes many, ways to prove that it actually is the case. End runs, block builder techniques, laws of cause and effect playing their expected roles to allow multiple paths of perception to unsully minds that were never built to easily comprehend three-dimensional objects in three-dimensional spacial delineations. This then lends the obvious a quality that it actually may not be quite so obvious as it was when it first entered the scene, which actually is the case to those who don't understand the issue.

79. While we're walking on eggshells to not offend, we can make sure not to offend the Truth by spreading or believing lies.

80. Given enough glossing over of the facts, we obtain a blurring of the lines. Given a sufficient number of blurred lines, we obtain a blurry picture. Given a sufficient number of "experts" explaining how the blurred picture is actually "scientific," "valid," "clear," "unmistakable," "accurate," or "credible," we obtain a mass extortion.

81. Regardless of any contrary arguments, there can never be any right to spread known lies.

82. It's rude to force people to not discuss whatever could remove anything that prevents them from understanding who we are.

83. People not having money is bad for any economy and whoever wishes they didn't hates the people they try to steal it from and are therefore thieves and murderers.

84. Many of the powers of self-reflection are denied to those forced into isolation, thus preventing their advancement in many directions. We should remember this when forcing anyone into exile while any vain imagination is held that their behavior will improve. It won't. It can't.

85. When we turn seventy-two, any purposefully short memory will return to remove our heads with a shovel.

86. Looking for an opportunity for someone to prove they are what we think they are only proves we have no thought control.

87. Self deceivers are of two kinds: willful and unwitting pawns.

88. Facts will never penetrate gross ignorance, and if they do, the ignorant won't even be aware of it.

89. People who refuse to take their own advice aren't worth hearing.

90. If we discover that we're delusional, and we see ourselves reflected in others as we all do, then this means that the others are also delusional.

91. If ourselves, our group, our crowd, or our team think we are the only ones who have something to say, we have nothing to say.

92. [Severe Reading Comprehension Disorder] is a preventable disease.

93. Constantly discussing what makes no difference at all prevents progress on everything that does.

94. This is true more often than anyone would expect: When we don't make a problem, then there isn't one.

95. When what we believe kills people, we can know for a fact that we have at least two enemies.

96. When everyone has their mind made up about what is and isn't the case, it's impossible to discuss the case.

97. If any judge a book by its cover, then we'll judge their book by that cover.

98. Just 622 years after Adam was created, Enoch was born. Some time after this he wrote his book. So any who say writing took billions of years to develop are lying.

99. *"Put not your trust in princes, nor in the son of man, in whom there is no help."* 14

Many think they know more than God and ignore this, saying the entire book is full of lies, then put their faith in some imaginary "perfect" man who doesn't exist whom they expect to at long last lead them all down a path of false security. Then, full of shock and bewilderment, they become murderous when they can't find him. Wildly careening through years, they print a litany of faults of every person who isn't perfect, as if this will somehow bring some perfect person into existence. Spending billions of hours, and blowing quadrillions of metric tons of CO_2 into the atmosphere in the process, discussing why various people, both famous and not, aren't perfect and how they could be if they would just do everything all the armchair quarterbacks tell them to do, as if they themselves are the personification of the perfect leaders they envision and how all should fall prostrate and bow to their sanctimonious advice.

It would save a lot of time, energy, atmospheric CO_2, and recording space to just do what this one verse says to begin with.

100. Ignorance can never see itself because of what it is.

101. Being constantly jealous over a non-sequitur *won't ever* make us equal.

102. The largest difficulty in trying to get dead people to understand anything is that they're dead.

103. When we leap into the air, we are no longer part of the earth - because we're not touching it.

104. We may achieve all our goals and objectives using this foolproof method: Don't have any.

105. If we were once told not to believe everything we hear, we may not logically thereafter accuse the same person who told us this of lying. If we believe everything we hear, we may only accuse ourselves.

106. What happens if the person we decided deserved to be paid back turns out to be innocent? The price for punishing or abusing the innocent is fairly high and isn't governed by any decision, but the laws

regarding it are built into the very laws of actions and reactions. It seems we're about to find out exactly what happens.

- Closely Attending the Oblivious

107. If there's a part of reality that we are refusing to hear, we know nothing about reality.

108. The author is both sender and receiver of the messages in their writing.

109. If we realize that we were a pawn, then we were. But remember, without pawns, one half of the chess game is missing.

110. If critics were as smart as they think they are, they would have given their information to the right person *before* it was too late, not *after*.

111. People who talk realize whether what they're saying is stupid or not. People who don't have yet to realize this.

112. "The Right to Not Be Offended" is an extremely offensive right, and can't exist since it cancels itself out.

113. Creating reasons to ignore an object doesn't affect the object and leaves us still ignorant of everything about it.

114. Some think naked is the be-all and end-all; but just like people, some ideas are *way* better with the clothes *on*.

- Naked Reality

115. People who only create doubt have only one father, and it isn't God.

116. Slippery slopes are fun, until we're standing on one.

117. People keep talking about root cellars, but roots don't need cellars to grow in, they grow in the ground.

118. There will always be people on the outer edges, otherwise when we say, "It takes all kinds," we're lying.

119. It's only a short road to becoming a *nondemocratic* society when people are punishable according to voting habits.

120. The ability to forgive distinguishes the real sensitive people from the fakes.

121. If homophobia is evil, then so is heterophobia, androphobia, and gynophobia. This is because

- You Can't Have It Both Ways

122. Since cement is a *"chemical combination of calcium, silicon, aluminum, iron and other ingredients,"*[15] "concrete" isn't precisely concrete, or a pure, unadulterated element, which the expression "concrete evidence" appears to claim that it is.

In fact, this truth about its nature is more concrete than concrete itself.

If pure truth were to reflect the actual nature of concrete, it would be a mixture of truth, lies, and plausible opinion. The opposite of pure truth isn't a pure lie, but that which has the greater power to deceive: an unidentifiable mixture which has the appearance of solid reliability, but like concrete, is never pure. And since the pure cannot be impure, the nature of concrete isn't reflected by the common use of the term.

123. An unconventional person won't be seen attending any conventions.

124. All man-hating women, since all are born of men, are just another species in a long line of patricidal sadists.

125. In order to effectively track every move of seven billion people, it would require an extra 14 billion people, using a 2:1 ratio, paired teams working in rotating 8 hour shifts who would themselves not be tracked. To effectively track those extra 14 billion would require an extra 28 billion people. These aren't large numbers, so it's amazing that any of the billions of PhD holders available have yet to mention any of these facts. Education is a must, since even when we have seventy-five degrees, it's evidently insufficient.

126. If we wish to know, we must stop assuming.

127. Two or more things that are obvious may accidentally or intentionally point to something that isn't.

3. The Rorrim

1. While reading about solutions, it's reminiscent of the ones that have been tried so far, which in some cases are still being tried, but haven't worked. Put simply, we can reflect behavior for two reasons (maybe more, but we're only concerned with two here): because we like it and are imitating the initial actor, or we don't and we want the other person to stop doing whatever it is.

Sometimes this backfires. What is difficult to explain is also probably difficult to understand, but this is important. Sometimes a bad example can be set to show what *not* to do when the time comes. Like ignoring someone's existence. This is only to let people know not to continue to ignore others when they shouldn't during a critical time such as a court hearing or any other important deciding moment in life. This repeated back to the first person who sent the message means nothing when the first person isn't the one in danger of ignoring anyone and the ones repeating the behavior, also running the risk of forming a damning habit by continuing to do it, *are* the ones guilty of ignoring anyone or an entire group of people. It may take a story about this to illustrate. But, this is why much behavior reflected back might be ignored. It is when we can tell the initial message was not understood nor acted upon. Not everyone does this.

2. Generally speaking, since people are only what we say they are and not what they really are, the only harm they bring is whatever we had in mind to begin with. When this is the case, the mirror reveals our greatest threats.

3. If a problem is not in front of us, we won't solve it.

4. When the left side of a rape victim's brain is shut down using doctor administered hypnosis, and rather than help the person, we decide to judge them, spread lies, promote false accusations, or condone it with silence and apathy, we can't expect a positive future regardless of our beliefs. What we did is what we get.

5. Every action has a cause. It has been attempted (however imperfectly) to show that cause to be those surrounding us on some occasions. Each cause, to be worth wasting time on an action, has to have at least three qualities that are wrong. This way, we can't become upended, since we're the one who did it, or are the direct cause. And we can't ask "why?" since all we have to do to answer that question is look very carefully into the rorrim.

6. We can always find the truth by never looking for it at all. We can always find it by closing our eyes and putting our fingers in our ears. This is both a tautology and a contradiction. It's always true of the majority and a contradiction of reality.

7. Today gynophobia is acceptable, but homophobia isn't. What if in reality, any type of phobia is unacceptable? What if a popular phobia is actually a misnomer, where a desire for accuracy is mistermed "Erratumphobia?" This would then turn into a fear of mistaken identity or "Falso Appelatusophobia." What if the actual intentions of the narrative drivers in today's world are to bring us to the circular logic and inescapable walls of the disease of Phobophobia? What if the only reason anyone would ever fully be driven to perpetual phobophobia was due to chronic Scopophobia Idem?

8. What if whatever was telling people to say "It's all in your head" was only something that was all in their head?

9. If we determine anyone can't see a glass as half full, we have decided that person is incapable of being a glass that's half full and are ourselves a person who can't see a glass as half full.

10. People who offend us while claiming to believe in a fictitious "right to not be offended" have defeated their own argument by their actions.

11. Many think voting for someone exactly like them, their sex, their race, will somehow validate their existence. But validation must

come from within, so any external aid will make absolutely no difference and self worth will still be in the same toilet it's in presently. Until we see ourselves, nothing can help us.

12. To claim we have no right to seek a balance in expressions is to say we know nothing of either chemistry or physics.

13. When it's wrong for others, but right for us, the solution to the problem is easy to find.

14. It's best to recognize our position, otherwise our position will quickly become unrecognizable.

Break the Mirror

15. Once whatever was good has been setup to be destroyed, all that could remain would be the destroyed and the destroyers. Nothing that would be worth either knowing or repeating. So, what's the point?

16. An alarming indicator is when any disagreement anywhere is assumed to be coming from a troll. It points to the advent or approach of a highly inflexible society that would rather be controlled than think for itself.

17. The decision to reflect others is a large responsibility. People will break a mirror several times before they realize the mirror isn't the actual problem, but rather what's in the mirror. Blame shifters or hypocrites typically will never see themselves until it's too late. Letting them pass unchecked won't make the world better any faster. But occasionally, that's all we can do.

4. Exploding Popular Myth

1. The path to education doesn't lie down the road of insults.

2. "Other people are just a thing that we talk 'at.' There's no reason to consider them part of reality."

3. "God is a fool's crutch." - Popular Myth

This is much said, so it's past time to discuss it.

We typically either agree with the phrase or not, but let's go a bit further for a second. According to the law of duality, God either exists or does not; we cannot have both, nor can we allow the phrase "whatever you want to believe" in terms of either logic, science, or fact. If He doesn't exist, the fool has nothing for a crutch other than a sentiment and the existence of the universe and how it is seen to repeatedly supply answers to the fool's troubles is unexplained. How the fool acquires benefit from what doesn't exist is also unexplained. But if God does exist, then consider what is happening: The person making the statement doesn't trust the one person who absolutely knows everything about everything, even before the universe was formed, and considers anyone who trusts Him to be a fool.

Moreover, the person is willing to settle for someone who knows less than everything in the vain hope their deficiency of knowledge won't prevent them from solving their problems. Besides, we have no demonstrations, other than from the willfully ignorant, of any person or group of people who call looking up information to solve problems or a public library a crutch. Turning to a greater resource for information is the typical approach to progress in any field. So the reasoning behind this claim is not only unclear, but stands without a shred of evidence in its support and may safely be termed a mindless whim. Who exactly is the fool?

4. "Memories can be unreliable."

You believe I have said 'x,' when in fact I may have said 'y' or 'z,' where 'z' is a combination of 'x,' 'm,' (being some intermediary) or 'y,' meaning you could be half right. Society has trained you to believe I have said 'x,' so you never question yourself. You sleep, wake up, remember nothing of my exact words, only what you believe I have said, which is nothing close to 'y' or 'z'. You tell this to others. We go to court. I'm forced to live with a decision based nowhere close to anything I have said since half-truths are often further from the real truth than a bald-faced lie would be. Yet, you still trust your memory while saying mine is unreliable. So are the memories at fault? Or rather is it how we immediately mistranslate direct experiences long before they ever become a memory?

5. According to the popular concept of equal, mirrors aren't an equal representation of the image.

Proof: The mirror flips left and right, but doesn't flip top with bottom, so it is therefore unequal.

6. Many mistakenly believe that what comes out of us while under heavy pressures is the bare truth. This is true of pure chemicals and metals, but not complex compositions of chemicals and metals. In fact, pressure makes some chemicals and metals unusable, which in this analogy would equate to *not* the truth. In some cases we may observe, what comes out under pressure is consistently the wrong thing, or a bare unprocessed reaction. When something isn't processed, there's no comparison check to measure if the reaction is an accurate representation of the actual character or intent, which would mean what we see is a lie. Few believe any of this, so difficulties will multiply.

7. The phrase "anecdotes aren't evidence" is itself an anecdote. And so, we've once again located a statement that cancels itself.

8. So, which one is it? If we're trying to plan for the next ten years:
The loudest squeak gets the grease? or
The largest nail gets hammered down?
The difference in cost between these two reactions is night and day.

9. Agreeing with each other isn't required nor necessary. Agreeing with the truth and reality is. Coming up with a thousand names for what we see in reality doesn't mean we know anything about it anymore than coming up with some fake name for someone we don't know tells us everything about who they are or their history; yet pseudo-scientists imagine themselves highly advanced in this regard.

10. Very few are qualified to instruct crime victims. No elaborate system of paybacks will add anything to the lesson life already taught these few who now have strong reasons to trust the universe way less than before. We can neither teach nor pass instruction to crime victims; they teach us.

5. Proverbs Book XXI

1. A nation with a strong military yet no poets is like a sledge hammer in the hands of a drunken blind man.

2. Just as one would not use a razor to drive a nail into stone, a narrow focus will not always produce a solution.

3. Before we don't remember, we should remember that we don't.

4. Program this:

string = any statement; it = any event or idea; if (string=="I don't believe it." && it==true) found = disaster;

- Wisdom Run 21

5. An excuse is like trying to wash an irremovable stain from a $12,000 diamond-encrusted suit by throwing it into a machine full of other $12,000 diamond-encrusted suits. It doesn't wash, spreads to all the others, and renders them all useless.

6. A dictionary is a word atomizer for wordsmith architects.

7. Urbanity ostensibly holds the correct take on all but avarice.

8. The ignorant can only give us what they have.

9. The fabric of almost every problem is the refusal to consider it.

10. Life is what we allow it to be, while not sitting around addicted to apathy would make it something else.

11. Delusions arrive from ideation with inadequate delimiters.

12. Specifics are a path to confusion.

13. If one piece of a puzzle is missing, we have a useless picture.

14. Sometimes the distance between intention and action is inexcusable.

15. Free will is as a lamp shining to illumine reality by revealing a vista of potential, whereas they who try to remove it with a seemingly endless number of devices are as darkness.

16. Uniformity of opinion doesn't always amount to uniform conformity with the truth.

17. Readability is 100% of writing.

- When Authors Don't

18. Good or bad depends largely upon whether or not we care about it.

19. People who refuse to look at any problem become part of it by so doing.

20. Promises are easily made when the smallest excuse relieves us of them.

- Forever Will Never See Sleep

21. The truth often doesn't have any feelings. People who hate the truth have less than that.

22. All authority is not identical. Most believe it is.

23. Living where something bad happened keeps the memory of it from becoming larger than it really is.

24. Words are intended to change how we feel. What we feel, however, is entirely our decision.

25. Worry is an illegal request for the permission or right to live.

26. They who live by fear shall die by fear.

27. If we feel we must prove our identity to or through others, we haven't yet proven it to ourselves.

28. How we saturate our mind is the dressing that coats our reality.

29. Truth is best untwisted.

30. Control the reaction to the thought, and the thought will control the action.

- The Invisible Findings

31. There is a point in each life where God reveals that we aren't the god we may think we are.

32. If we're honest and look closely - Ignorance is the primary cause for the existence of every law.

33. In general, nothing is true all of the time.

34. The most successful way to be perfect is to realize that we're not.

- The Gradient

35. Popular opinions are god, so never question them.

36. The mind that says, "I will destroy everything that attempts to educate me" is close to unreachable.

- Intractable Savants

37. Develop to improve; improve to see the process; see the process to know the value.

38. Having a relationship with what we say is difficult to achieve and impossible to find.

39. Two opposing statements cannot both be correct, but they can both be wrong.

- Binary Suicide

40. If how we say anything becomes more important than what is said, we've sacrificed truth for sentimentality. When what we say is more important than how we say it, we've sacrificed everything for the truth.

- Lost & Found

41. Better to develop our minds than our opinions. Best to destroy opinions that destroy minds.

42. The grade is a reflection of the quality of the teacher.

43. Believing very strongly that cupidity is not stupidity won't make it so.

44. Deniers of reality can never exist in it.

45. Acceptance doesn't alter existence.

46. You can lead humans to logic, but you can't make them think.

47. The fool demands evidence from the self-evident.

48. Grade regulation is not education.

49. "I don't need to be lectured" is itself a lecture.

50. Logic is anathema to the emotionally governed.

51. Denying the possible is neither scientific nor Christian.

52. Just because things are wrong, doesn't mean that chaos rules.

- Observation Theoretics: Non-Sequiturs

53. Hatred of the rich is the doctrine of thieves.

54. In today's world, trust is the most quickly abandoned currency.

55. Let him that is without oligarchy among you impeach the first criminal.

56. All hypocrisy comes with its own briefcase of excuses.

57. It should be illegal for any who are immune to logic to craft law.

58. People who won't defend the living place their own lives in question.

59. Wisdom isn't harmed when we ignore it, we are. Therefore we should ignore our surroundings.

60. Truth is the fuel of life. Wisdom finds its gradient. Understanding sharpens its precision. That few care doesn't lessen the brightness of its fire.

61. A study in regression is to find that those interested in hearing the truth can't too often due to the lies shouted by those who aren't.

62. Like birds to shiny objects, we are attracted to what is false without qualms.

63. We talk about what we don't know as if we do. This is true no matter what we say.

3. THE LANGUAGE BARRIER

ॐ

Explanation - n. a splanation that is leaving.

Persplanation - n. a splanation that by the time you're finished with it, you're dripping buckets of sweat.

Resplanation - n. a splanation that when given indicates you have been surrounded by choruses of "what?".

Undersplanation - n. a splanation that needs help. (Most splanations are of this kind.)

Equatoriasplanation - n. a splanation that circles the entire globe to splain anything which could otherwise easily be splained in 10 words or less.

a cinogen - n. One cinogen: a microscopic bacteriological insect related to the tarrofyr that dines exclusively on carbon remnants.

carcinogen - n. a group of cinogens which have collected in sufficient numbers to have built a car. Since they constructed it, this is why all cars emit carcinogens. It's a small step in a beautiful vast reproductive cycle that mother nature has created to kill people.

allegedly - a word that while absolving any innocent of guilt simultaneously allows any guilty to appear temporarily innocent. Seen in this light, is the word "allegedly" itself guilty of anything? Or is it just an allegation?

1. The opposite of disappointed is appointed.
The opposite of disturbed is turbed.
The opposite of abnormal is normal.
The opposite of abstract is stract.
2. If the opposite of moose is mice,

then the opposite of spoon is spice
the opposite of fools is vice
the opposite of loose is lice
the opposite of rules is rice
the opposite of obtuse is enticed
the opposite of flew is flies
the opposite of cruise is cries
the opposite of ewe is eyes
the opposite of use is tries
the opposite of spruce is spies
and the opposite of divorce is device.

3. We may discover that when we use the dictionary, what people say becomes way more understandable. It's even possible to understand small portions of it.

4. I went into a flower shop on 12,847th Street and Main to buy some flowers. I saw a unique rhododendron with a familiar Aspergillus fragrance and a sunburst orange plumage. I began remarking to the store attendant how highly attractive it was when the rhododendron suddenly got mad, slapped my face, told me I was a pervert and how dare I even think it would be interested enough in me to marry it. It began showing me photo albums of all its children and ancestry dating back several centuries. It then proceeded to ignore me as if I were five years old and had been very naughty. I walked out of the store buying nothing. I never went back. I only needed some flowers to put on my grandmother's grave.

- Insanity is the Face You Give It

5. It's merciful that animals don't understand what we're saying on average. The lies, hatred, and ignorance found in the majority of what people say would darken, restrict, and lower their experiences as much as they do ours. From these, they're safely caged out of reach of the caustic vitriol, housed comfortably behind the language barrier.

6. The opposite of reverse is verse.
The opposite of repetition is petition.
The opposite of inverse is obverse.
The opposite of instruct is obstruct.

The opposite of anticipate is participate.

The opposite of Antipater is participle.

7. Remember: Gossip spelled backwards is "hog piss" which in this case, has the same meaning as the word spelled forward.

8. "Thesaurus" is a dinosaur that never evolved, so no one ever reads it.

9. Some people have Cerebroclaustroscopophobia: fear of closed minds that are afraid to look at themselves.

10. Why isn't the degree to which something has been "sauced" called "sausage?" As in "The turkey was so entirely over-basted with heavy sausage that it was nearly impossible to pick up with two hands, much less a fork." Garden hoses could even be sauce instruments: "The agile gardener applied a liberal dousing of clear sausage to the lawn with a sausage-shaped hose. Upon close inspection, the sausage was deemed to be quite adequate." And why does a sausage have nothing to do with sauce?

- Word Smith Seminar, September 5, 1287

11. The word "context" means "with text" in Spanish. In a sea of texters, text in real books is becoming an unknown idea. So taking things out of context would involve no text at all.

- In Context

12. Where that is a pyopyo having spoked uncorrectationally, are they hasing a saying, or have they nothing of a said?

- Gnome Sayin?

13. We have olfactory nerves. This is an Old English spelling for "Ole Factory," which means we have an old factory in our noses. If we have trouble with breathing or allergies, we may need to have these space-hogging factories removed. Or, another option would be to renovate and rebuild the factory and become a company owner producing whatever the the factory made to begin with. We would then refer to them as "Nuefactory" nerves. This may also solve problems of rampant unemployment across the known universe. We should make sure to include this health saving tip in our radio telescope transmissions to life in other galaxies.

- Ye Ole Factory

14. Always remember: Apple & cinnamon rhymes with - [Babbly Scented Man].

15. [Dogmatic] is a robotic canine that will kill you for disagreeing with it.

16. Interactive. This is a word. If you are interactive, it means you have active innards. So, on those days when your innards don't seem very active, all you have to do is become interactive with others. Just remember not to activate your innards directly into someone's face, since this may cause some inflammatory interrogatives. Stay inneractive!

- Wernt Wordsmith

17. If we take anything anyone says the wrong way, we mistook them. If we do this again, we doubly mistook them. If we develop a lifelong habit of this, we may not accurately say that they are mistaken, since we're the ones doing the missed takes; while they're speaking in clear Antarctican and haven't spoken amiss, to a Miss, or in a missed demeanor. Even so, our language informs us that somewhere between two and a lifetime of missed takes, they are the ones who are now

- Entirely Mistooken (The Unspoken Robbery)

18. Differences in interpretation either exist in the mind or in books. They exist either in the mind of the reader or the author. There are no differences in the mind of the author. Not every interpretation will hold any earth-shattering significance. All of this is because language is dynamic. Many words now are nothing close to their original meanings. The original will never leave in spite of the cold manipulations of accuracy intolerant word smiths.

4. OUR BRAINS ARE VERY TALL

Intelligent Life In Dark Matter:

1. It's difficult to say too many things that are new and different, consequently much of life is basically a review of what we already know from some other time or place. When we run a thread forming a line that weaves between the nonsense of gibberish and useful concepts, a rare stone of truth may be seen.

2. Justice has more to do with anger prevention than sin prevention. This is why too often it fails.

3. Releasing murderers has nothing to do with forgiveness since we haven't forgiven their future victims.

4. "Could you please restate for the record...."

"Would you please relive the trauma so we can satisfy our insatiable lust for sadism?"

"Could you please restate for the record..."

"What record? Doesn't look like you're recording anything if you have to ask the same question more than once."

"Could you please restate for the record..."

"Q: What kind of record has the same thing written in it over two to three thousand times?

"A: A broken record.

"You brought a broken record into a court of law?

"What a dumbass!"

5. Though today you believe you have a reason to murder, tomorrow you may find you've murdered someone without one.

6. Agenda is a method to railroad responsibility into non-existence.

7. Since we have been discussing people who are "past feeling" or feel nothing at all, we may wish to consider the development of feelings in the evolutionary process.

I. First, the entire collection of atoms in the universe would have no feelings at all and be incapable of sensations of any type. This would be prior to the universe deciding that it needed to create an amoeba who would later be stalked by skilled hunters. In order for anything to exist, it first must not exist, then magically evolve into existence by some axiom of higher mathematics. So, here we are with a universe where feelings do not exist at all anywhere.

II. Next, the universe would have to know what a feeling was to begin with or we have no sufficient cause for this effect. Even failing this, it would have to know that it needed to have any feelings in order to generate them in the next evolutionary step. We also don't know really if amoebae have feelings or not since no one has ever interviewed one to find out if they do.

III. Arriving at this stage where we have no sufficient cause or sentience in the universe to have generated feelings at any stage of the evolutionary process, there are no feelings in the universe at all today.

IV. Since we have just proven that feelings could never have evolved, this explains why few people have any. This also explains why many produce too many feelings in a reaction to things like soap operas, weddings, and racism: they act in excess to fool everyone into believing that they have any at all when we have just proven they don't exist. It also explains why no one has any feelings whatsoever about murderers, NAMBLA, or human trafficking.

V. Either that, or evolution is a lie and there's another explanation for all of this.

8. Since on average no one hears what anyone else says, and if it's true we are all one universal consciousness expressing itself through

different mouths, we may wonder what argument we will have with ourselves when we finally realize we were right the whole time?

9. It becomes difficult, yea, well nigh impossible, to love someone and hate their beliefs while their beliefs are killing people.

10. The other reason, other than those already stated here, that our knowledge may forever remain incomplete and lacking in key elements, other than the obvious, is that we too often assume the names assigned by the various sciences are the correct ones. Often we assume it to be unnecessary to ask the element under observation what its name is or that it's impossible, and so blindly rush forward and ascribe a name that has no bearing either to the nature or purpose of the element in question. Or we assign a name that is inaccurate to the purpose of correctly defining the properties of the subject under study, such as using the word "reaction" when the word "transaction" is more accurate.

11. Pointing to what others have done that's wrong neither forgives nor excuses what we've done that's wrong, especially if comparing the severities of the respective offenses. This is the fatal and damning flaw involved with character assassination, even if performed "legally" in courts of "law." (That cannot be called law that ignores every law of logic.) It is a subclass of False Accusation by claiming one offense is excused by another when it clearly isn't or painting one offense as larger than another when they may be equal or the reverse.

False Accusations are prohibited by law. Those who commit this attempt at blame-shifting only waste time and stall real progress for science, justice, theology, communications, and humanity.

Public relations abusers have used this tactic for centuries, and to successful effect unimaginably disproportionate with the alleged level of intellect stated by the "god-makers," bastions of reason for humanity found in institutes of "Higher Learning." They use it to prevent the public from learning the facts surrounding many issues, albeit sometimes for good reasons when preventing a mob-rule mentality from its inevitable track of destroying countless lives and asking permission after the fact. But when this isn't the case, as we find today *far too often*, this creates a gap in the collective reasoning which will also, when discovered, wind everyone up on the inevitable track of destroying countless lives and asking permission after the fact.

If any find themselves doing this, please stop it before it's too late. Personal responsibility holds value outside of all religion, but eventually will lead to religion. There are true and false religions. Blame-shifting comes to us only from the false ones. This is oft forgotten.

12. We pay no attention to ourselves or others, then wonder at the effects we see around us.

13. Some efforts at solutions don't seem to have anything to do with the collection and observation of data, but rather the passing of the buck in the hopes that the subsequent reaction will be less severe than the previous. Sadly, too often, unless some data is studied and course corrections are made, the last reaction will be more severe than any of the previous combined regardless of any efforts by anyone. Better then to not wait too long to read and think about something that was written on a piece of paper in 1968, or any relevant time.

14. In courts of law, we pretend to not understand anything that doesn't make sense, while knowing that less than 1% of human behavior makes sense. In halls of congress we make sure that 0% of all laws make sense in any degree. Then, we feign surprise at the high crime rates. We make no laws to control this addiction to irresponsibility and failure to be honest with ourselves, then expect our future to not reflect the actions we're now emitting. While knowing that every action has an equal an opposite reaction.

- Sanitarium Planet

15. As often as reality makes absolutely no sense whatsoever, it's very strange that "It makes no sense" is the most frequent excuse to not believe the truth. Even stranger that this is allowed as a reason in courts of law.

16. If everyone gets laid off (as will happen as the current trend of electing people who don't care about jobs continues), then no one will be working anywhere. There will be no companies. When there are no workers or companies, there will be nothing to tax. Since no one will have money, there will be no tax from sales either. This means congress will have a $0.00 paycheck and will also be out of a job. Continuing to

support layoffs of people who put money in our pockets indicates a large sanity problem, but also a conflict of interests and confused priorities. It indicates we're conflicted about whether we should support our interests or those of others, but since we can't make up our minds about it, we support neither. If we can't be for others or even ourselves, why are we here at all? This type of person has clearly not yet answered the question of whether or not they exist.

17. What do plagiarism and ad hominems have in common? The power of deception.

18. Shamefully we may notice in almost every subject, ideas are like a doll created by a manufacturer that is dressed correctly going down an assembly line. As it goes, various hands take the doll and redress it, replace it on the line, then say due to how the doll is now dressed the idea can't either exist or be sold anywhere. But, if left alone and the doll reaches the public in its original form, the doll would be just fine and make trillions of dollars. Pure speculation is needed to determine who all these little helping hands are that think they have a right to re-clothe ideas instead of making genuine improvements to it, but here we are.

19. The "win at any cost" notion is still somehow a very popular strategy, even though it does nothing to reveal the truth, support the best choice, acquire any purity of solution whether in chemistry or problem solving, or explain anything at all about our surroundings. In fact, it does nothing at all. It's the drug of choice for "spirit of competition" addicts and probably won't be found anywhere in any universe but among the lower orders of an irreparably primitive society - those most atavistic, regressive, and even cannibalistic. Yet we gaze stupidly into the sky and expect anything up there to be impressed with our vast stores of supreme intelligence we forced into existence in some plane of reality with our violently defended beliefs that it should be.

20. There is no relationship in existence that doesn't require faith. Those that have none don't exist. Those that have the most faith are the strongest. An acquaintance can't really be called a relationship.

Amusingly, pseudo-scientists say that faith isn't scientific when there is this much evidence in front of our face to prove that it is.

Funny how pseudo-scientists believe that ignoring any quadrant of reality is scientific.

Funny how they believe selling lies is also scientific.

Sad the number who are convinced by their lies.

Funny how many are convinced they know more than Jesus Christ Himself and worship and serve *"the creature more than the creator"* [16] exactly as predicted.

Funny how many are convinced they're in full possession of the facts and that they aren't clinically insane.

Sad they are not being treated, nor is there any treatment available for them in any foreseeable future.

21. Helly slaps Adel so hard that it causes her ears to fly off. Adel slaps Belma, knowing that Helly would kill her and then remove someone else's ears. Belma slaps Carl. Carl slaps Darnel and so on down to Zetty. Zetty has a perfect opportunity to slap Helly so hard it would remove her head, but instead decides her decision is better than anyone else's and slaps Yinkle Yapper which goes all the way back to Adel. Adel wisely returns the slaps back to Zetty, who is actually the only one who could slap Helly. Zetty stubbornly refuses to end the cycle and slaps Yinkle yet again. So of them all, which one is the most guilty? This goes on for over fifty years.

22. We try to prove God wrong by creating events which can never have forgiveness then attempt to play God by assigning eternal punishments to them. Then we walk into churches and pretend God doesn't see an entire world full of these events we created from our wishes for God to be wrong about there ever being forgiveness for us while asking for forgiveness. We don't believe we can be forgiven, so we try to force our beliefs into a world that doesn't need them, then expect to be forgiven when it's all over, or worse, imagine we're on some holy mission to do so. Forcing our fears into a world that has enough of them already, attempting to kill any and every source of truth that exposes this charade. A holy mission where we try to prove God wrong, pretend He's blind, then pretend we're Him, failing to realize that if we actually could ever become Him, we would then also be, according to our own wishes, both wrong and blind. We scurry over the earth like the baby

in its crib trying to kill everything that bothers it. Then we imagine that all this is somehow scientific. Maybe those crying loudest about how "we don't see how" are the erroneous, blind gods created from and which mirror our own belief systems.

23. There would probably be a few more million people with eidetic memories, but it could be wagered and won that these same are either very often shouted down or ignored because what they know is damning to some party or other. This prevents the gift from developing itself. This should be recalled the next time we begin interrupting or ignoring anyone.

24. We apply harsh skepticism to a fictional construct while ignoring and applying nothing to real ones, then wonder why aliens are silent.

25. Urban and rural dwellers can remind us of the differences between indoor and outdoor cats. The indoor cats rarely set foot outside the door or know what to do when they do. They're scared of literally everything around them outside and don't know what it is. They concoct a strange list of dos and don'ts that isn't written down anywhere which they expect other cats to live by, all based on their fears of "whatever that is outside." They imagine that trees are full of long, pointy things that leap off the branches and randomly stab other cats in mass murdering sprees. They can't get back soon enough to the safety and comfort of their rectangular four-hundred story buildings with square rooms where everything in sight is man-made. Then they prattle on to each other on their TV shows and cell phones for thousands of hours about how much they love nature and just can't understand why anyone would ever want to destroy it.

The outdoor cats only wonder why the indoor cats are so obsessed with themselves.

26. When proving anything for further use, we spend time only on proving whether the unlikely will happen rather than the likely because this is more logical and scientific. This way if there is ever any real danger, such as when the likely holds some relevant, credible casualty in the near or distant future, we'll never know about it, maintain plausible deniability, and can continue to blame the victims instead of the real criminal which is ourselves.

27. We should all just continue to ignore correctable behavior and move on as if we're perfect and need no instructions. If anyone deigns to correct us, we have the legal right to beat them out of existence and wait for the aliens to be attracted to our genius mentalities.

28. Imagining life would be better with more psychics is an illusion. It's precisely the same as regular speech: no one listens and if they do they twist the meaning as much as possible to bring the most benefit to themselves and the most harm to the speaker.

29. Every product, act, or thought of any society at any time is unreliable, because some past or future society will determine in their infallible estimation that the former society was wrong. Are we then truly pressing toward utopia?

30. Part of the recovery process, the largest perhaps for some, is to hold the knowledge of who we really are against the lies of what everyone thinks or says we are and keep winning the argument. When this is lost, the manipulative miasma of the lies forces unnecessary guilt and actions on both sides that wouldn't be there otherwise.

People tend to say things or ask questions that only support their own falsehoods about their preconceived ideas, or what some say is "confirmation bias." Yet, these same authorities who created the term "confirmation bias" never ask questions in critical directions that may prove any of their own theories wrong. So after saying that it's wrong, they pompously perform it with metric ton force. If we see anyone laughing during one of these questioning sessions, that's why. Usually they just think scoffers are crazy since to them, the question they're asking isn't funny.

The negative reinforcement created by our own deliberate, unresearched misconceptions doesn't help any recovery process. And since there is a dearth of those recovering from hypnosis abuse and stone silence encasing any discussions about it, it's hard to find the right direction most of the time. Awarding any crime victims with either (a.) lies about who they are or (b.) suppression of any conversations about what happened to them would make any recovery process nearly impossible. However, since everyone is right all the time, we can't discuss or correct any of this. This is because we're supremely intelligent and can by force of will achieve the status of godhood.

31. If we have seen any do something in the future, they are the one who started it since theirs was the first record of the event in the time line of reality. If they forget their church lessons and do the same thing again, it constitutes a second offence. If something was done to them, it is to make sure they realize the importance of not repeating the same mistake later. It's not for them to ignore the laws of both man and God and do whatever the hell they feel like doing. This isn't surprising however, since everyone today has their ears turned off. This is how we move forward.

32. We may change ourselves by ignoring everything around us and everything anyone else says.

- Higher Education

33. Having to bribe people who don't speak our language to agree with us means only one thing: Our ideas suck *catastrophically*. *Nothing* we do or say will change this, other than creating a better idea. Changing our ideas *really* isn't that hard. Social experiments that bully people into agreeing with us is just one more in a *very* long list of ideas that *suck catastrophically*. What we give is what we get. Hopefully one day, we'll get rid of

- [Severe Reading Comprehension Disorder]

34. People usually only go so far with ideas that suck dead maggots before realizing that they do.

- Daily Self Exam

35. So the argument in the field today is whether the erasures performed by the memory holes instantiated by the agenda-driven media mind control are entirely complete and the subsequent frictional arguments arise from the Party discovering that they aren't.

Then following these discoveries are reams of ad hominems, threats, berating, calling into question whether video tape evidence actually exists, pretending that clicking a play button on a video requires 65 trillion tons of Newtonian force and so can't be done, and scores of other highly intellectual responses that we should expect from the grand halls of the heady and high-minded.

- Intelligent Life In Hell?

36. If atoms have always existed, then carbon-14 dating wouldn't be possible, since no atom would have a start date.

37. Today, we have the delicious experience of watching large flocks of adults arguing and killing each other over the color of rattle they're being entertained with.

- Technosphere

38. As a litmus test, good ideas tend to generate objects larger than an audience of one.

- Mass Cranial Suckage

39. Some think that dictionaries make people imagine they know everything. If so, they wouldn't need them.

- Nerd Shaming

40. The inflated ego would decide to fill the space between the electron and the proton, since this is just empty, wasted space, thus mutilating the function of all four.

- The Jovian Ego

41. We're only alive today because others don't believe like us that they have a right to kill us for disagreeing with them over whatever it is that we're so upset about. Don't worry, soon we will be in the majority, but that society, due to its murderous intent, will only last for maybe one week. Or maybe for seven years.

- Self Control Dropouts

42. Let us both pray and think:

What can we imagine is the exact reason why some groups focus on race this way - they complain, but never thank the ones who aren't supporting segregation and never condemn the ones who do support it? There is never one word about the abolitionists who were on their side, only 100% blame all the time with never *one word* about a solution, other than who to blame, which isn't always a solution. There is never one mention of people who aren't, or one word of thanks for not being a racist, only blame 100% of the time. They also never mention certain agencies who have enabled racism for thousands of years; yes, there's a strange silence about this behavior from all quarters today. Blame + No Solution = Extortion 100% of the time.

Because the game isn't about stopping racism at all, it's about extortion; it's about how to get away with crime, murder, theft, and rapes with no consequences. So the game is merely a deflection from the fact that the constant whining, with no thanks to any who are on their side and also hate racism, no desire to bring racism or segregation to a real end, but only *continue* and *foment* racism *forever*, points directly to

- The True Racists

43. We have mastered how to do everything fast and the competitive spirit reigns supreme in all but one area. We race to stoplights at 400 mph to slam on the brakes before any pedestrian can get there first, proving our superiority; we beat each other in sports and racing to prove who's faster. But there's one thing about which no one ever competes.

- Are You Listening?

44. Any sufficiently advanced race would be using telepathy to communicate. If so, they wouldn't need to waste gas driving over to earth to make contact. If not, then they can't be termed sufficiently advanced.

- Are the Voices You Hear Logical?

45. When we see people asking why no one told them the answers to a painful test when they've had a 66 book collection with all the answers inside for every test their entire lives, we have found a collection of dark matter.

- Yes, It Does

46. Since most of what we know was found by dead people and applies to the dead, what applies to the living is either ignored or undiscovered.

- We Wait For The Living

47. In our rabid quest for constant eye contact, we forgot about ear contact.

5. WHAT YOU DON'T KNOW

1. POV Is One-Hundred Percent of Reality

1. What you don't know is held within the halls of structures you've never seen found sitting on the shores you've never heard in lands about which you never asked.

2. If someone asks us what we're thinking, our mind immediately generates over 100 ideas, unless we're addicted to pop music. So, if we only tell one or two of the 100 ideas and leave the others unmentioned, we have lied by not telling "the whole truth and nothing but the truth."

- Every Man A Liar

3. If we never listen to what others say, always think we're right when we're not, and only have friends that agree with our narrow-minded opinions, it's very difficult to understand how we could even begin to discuss the hatred in someone else, much less understand what we're saying. If we can't defend both sides of any equation, we have no clue about the equation. If our world only involves false accusations, are we prepared to defend how we can have a right to make them? What we don't know: anyone else's point of view.

4. If the memory is as unreliable as people think it is, how do we know our memory of wherever this idea came from is reliable? If we don't, then the memory is as reliable as it needs to be.

5. I spoke with a man once. He said he needed me to relay a message.

"I'm tired of hearing people saying 'It was his time to go.' Can you explain to them what's wrong with this?" I said I would try.

After a few attempts, I was assaulted with a barrage of "what?" and "huh?", so I decided a demonstration was called for. A "what" out of place in a conversation is a strong indicator that the person is either not hearing or not listening to what is being said, usually the latter. But the demonstration was hijacked by people who worship their own fears (usually of not being accepted), so the point was lost to most. Though a bit muddied, I didn't lose track of it.

Their fears led to a man's death, so I told them, "It was his time to go." They blamed me for the death, but their fears would have killed him the same as if I had never existed. On the exact same day even and the exact same time. Fear has that kind of power and doesn't discriminate with the amount of negative energy it attracts. It hits the same targets no matter what. However, the hypocrites never stopped saying, "It was his time to go" while admitting they believed saying this was wrong when I said it. It's either wrong or right, it can't be both and it doesn't matter who says it.

The man told me, "They think it's in their hands to say this. They believe it's up to them to make this determination. But the right to say this isn't theirs - it's mine."

6. If we can't protect our self from our self, then we won't be able to protect others from our self either. The first thing to look at is the opinion set. If we notice the opinions are winding up killing other people, then eventually our opinions will kill us as well. This isn't an opinion, it is a law: *"Every action has an equal and opposite reaction."* [17] It's beyond a good idea to be very familiar not only with our opinions, but our ability to prove them beyond a reasonable doubt. Otherwise, what we don't know can kill us.

7. I was once told "what he doesn't say I think is more important that what he does." If I know that saying something is what you won't like and I choose not to say it, would you still be offended? Would you even know about it?

Fear of the unknown has long been our greatest enemy, but is it when it becomes something that almost happened to us, but didn't? Every second is a moment when something we don't want to happen can, and sometimes it does; but as some of us know, things can always be worse. It isn't worth mentioning all the times we chose to do the opposite of what people don't want, so we usually don't discuss it at all, which of course is why it attracted my attention. But how much less would worry or fear waste our time if we knew the millions of things that almost happened or were nearly mentioned, but didn't or weren't? How much relief will there be when it's finally revealed that all the things that didn't happen are what you don't know?

8. Understanding is what we are commanded to seek and very few have. If it must be sought it must be granted by someone who already has it. There is nothing we now know that wasn't given by someone else who has understanding, whoever that may be. Most of it would come from dictionaries otherwise we would understand no words, or if so, have little understanding of the words we would use. This means according to evolutionists that our understanding either evolved or came from an amoeba. But we see no amoeba now living that can read a dictionary, so we know this is false and that they have no understanding.

This only leaves the evolution possibility. But looking at the elected government, we can quickly prove understanding does not evolve at all, but rather devolves. The citizens, who are the actual government, have the understanding the congress needs to govern, but the elected government puts them on ignore, so reverse understanding, or ignorance occurs. This also results in a backward direction. So understanding is neither given by nor evolved from amoebae as was just proven.

The bible teaches to seek understanding like precious jewels. People who hate the bible are typically manipulators who are in constant promotion of ignorance to allow more facility at public manipulation. Why would anyone hate a book that promotes understanding, respect, or forgiveness while offering hate as an alternative? Saying we want to kill others because we disagree isn't love. Understanding comes only from one who has it. It's available upon request from those who have it.

9. One of the purposes of "asked and answered" is to prevent criminals from forcing victims to repeatedly relive the crime, among whatever other reasons are mentioned in schools. But it also becomes necessary from logic. We don't prove 2 + 2 = 4 by repetitiously restating the redundant rhetorical rambling of the reasonless request "What is 2 + 2?" We prove it by showing that 1 + 1 + 1 + 1 = 4 or that 1 + 1 = 2. Or in other words by doing the amazing trick never before seen of

asking a completely different question to arrive at the truth. Also, asking the same question twice is a method of coercion used by manipulators or an indicator that the listener has Alzheimer's and has immediately forgotten the answer as soon as it's stated, in which case they don't need to be practicing law. Or if they are not in law, they don't need to be asking any question other than "Where is a doctor?" It's laughable watching people who ask the same questions telling others to "Move on" when that's exactly what they're not doing.

Where does this come from? This has been seen both inside and outside courtrooms and it always has the same result - a wrong direction. Management keep repeating the same question till they get the answer they want, then smugly trot off with a puffed chest thinking they have the truth. It is the same in courts or any other private conversations where the truth is ignored and the worship of ulterior motives is preferred. Repeatedly asking the same question tells us the questioner has no interest in the truth or facts which also tells us we have no motive for reasonable interest in the questioner. If we want the truth, we have to ask questions about what we don't know.

10. We believe in Adaptation, until it applies to Imagination. We believe in Faith, until it applies to Religion. We believe anything to be true, until it's stated by someone with Understanding. We believe the world is Dark, until forced to turn our eyes inward to view the World Within.

11. For those who can truly read minds, the words appear exactly as they do in a book and can be recorded for future reference. They would measure the level of faith in the process for those who can't to see if they could even bolster enough to doubt their own existence or are saturated in mysticism to believe every tale in a vain attempt to chain down the unknown. Were this power transferable, it could be studied and developed. Fear and respect levels would be precisely calculated and monitored since they would affect all outcomes. Your future would be clearly seen and recorded, then studied to detect possible maneuvers. Then based on your level of respect, they would inform you about it. If the levels were beyond ridiculous, as they stand now for the majority, you would not be told anything about it and remain blind. The future

would forever remain an unknown while arrogance would expand beyond the largest gas giants. The blame would continue to shift to all things in creation so long as it avoided the actual source. And the houses formerly thought to shield you from the advances of the deadly others, merely trying to be themselves, would be seen for what they really are: composed entirely down to the sub-atomic particles of pure fear. And whatever that is, is on its way.

12. The most horrible ideas can't be written down. In the very real and far too often case when they aren't fiction, but provable reality, the insanity contained in the words will spread or form a blueprint for those who enjoy spreading it. Many times this is the reason books were burned or brains torn out -- trying violently, futilely, to keep the idea either from spreading or moving too far down the path of becoming a permanent memory. I'm aware of only a few of these and am still debating whether to release them. In either case, they won't be merciful. It's easy to remain skeptical hiding behind beautifully paneled doors and walls that appear to keep every danger at bay. But after the reality of the idea arrives like the worst hurricane, it will be clear these crafted items aren't nearly at all the fast, stalwart shield they now are believed to be.

13. What you didn't do wasn't lost in the shuffle of not saying what you didn't say.

14. To a greater extent than is generally accepted, one of the paths to every new discovery comes from not accepting any of the previous discoveries or ideas.

15. The reason we're advised to never discuss religion isn't as it may appear on the surface, to prevent arguments. Many enjoy intelligent discussion and this is why debate classes exist, since this is the only way progress in any field ever happens: communication, discussion, debates, corrections, etc. Education can't even happen at all without some form of discussion, written or oral. But the real reason is so that light won't fall on those involved in spreading the darkness concerning this or any other verboten, toxic subject. If we don't discuss the history of any church, we won't be able to see the schemes they are currently performing and manipulating.

This is why there is freedom of speech and also why the majority hate it. If we never discuss something, we won't know who exactly is sitting right in front of us, since we never bothered to study it or compare notes. And far too often, that person will take everything we have and more if they can. (John 10:10) Any prohibitions aren't there to protect us, they're there to protect them.

If we never discuss lies, we'll never have any clue regarding, if this is even possible to begin with, how many of them we actually believe in the deepest core of our existence and have believed since we were born. Luckily the properties of light are what they are, or there would never be any solution to this problem ever in any amount of time. *"Men loved darkness rather than light because their deeds are evil."*[18] If this weren't the case, neither would this idea be, since there would be no lies in need of sacred defense. Therefore, what you don't know can kill you.

16. The most direct way to communicate is by the careful use of beautiful words; yet this is what many ignore. They imagine words to have some innate ability to hypnotize the hearer into some unwanted action or that the words are how demons possess us and we'll no longer be ourselves. Or that a smile combined with the words means that they aren't sincere. The answer could be staring at them through the smile, but they'd hear nothing and wander around for years never knowing the critical importance contained in the answer they shut down. True, no one is perfect, but how many words are going to be ignored? And what if eternity was a careful and studious review of exactly what those words were and when they were uttered to show precisely when the problem could have been stopped and how many years it never did?

17. If someone were an agnostic chaos theorist, would they then support or not support the theory since there isn't enough proof to verify whether there's any chaos or not? How this can be: If there is any larger sentient being creating the chaos, then it's by design and can no longer fall under the definition of chaos as meaning "without design, intent, or purpose." Unless we've once again redefined the word to mean something connotatively, or outside the dictionary, which can't be a theory since connotations only address the realm of opinions and theories are always hard facts.

18. When both sides are neither listening to each other nor the center, it is not an indication of the beginning of imbalance. Imbalance has been present already long before this point was ever reached. Until one person begins listening, there is no solution possible. What we don't know: The Resolution.

19. For any who hate delusions, here's another one: Thinking that using hypnosis to ruin a person's mind, then forcing the mind to forget it even happened is preferable to letting the mind heal itself is a delusion. Yes, luckily these cases aren't many, as far as is known, but even one is too many.

20. You may see me as 'x,' but I see you as 'y.' Once you realize I have been seeing 'y' for over fifty years, I may no longer have the same value as 'x,' but something closer to 8. You may even wonder why I'm still looking at you, and then you'll realize that you'll never know. How you deal with the unknown will reveal exactly what you are.

21. *"The subsistence or substance of anything that exists is its self-identity; for the failure of self-identity would be its dissolution.'*[19]

The obvious doesn't usually need proof. So we can see here that a self-identification process can indeed fail. Imagining something is when it isn't doesn't make it so. Positively believing something is real when it isn't doesn't create anything or pull anything into existence from a formless cornucopia of matter to which we all magically have strange access. Thinking something is one thing when it's really something else only indicates a lack of real investigative precision.

Otherwise we could just positively believe very strongly that everyone automatically agrees with everything we say, which would indeed be the most positive universe imaginable (and sadly this is a very real place for way too many), and there would be no further need to discuss anything and we could finally move on to something else that's far more constructive. Having everyone finally arrive at the conclusion that 4 + 4 = 8 and taking billions of years to do so is simultaneously doing the most important thing imaginable while doing absolutely nothing at all.

22. A frog in a slow boil will kill itself by not jumping out. Reverse engineering this, we can see that placing a slow boil of circumstances

in any person's life will allow us to virtually get away with murder since the authorities never notice a slow boil. Sufficient time during the boil allows us to point to millions of other things happening at the same time as a probable cause for the harmful effects that authorities with no real education swallow wholesale or can be bribed away from or threatened to ignore. However, all of these activities don't pass unnoticed by anyone or any victim with a higher intellect than a frog. This is mentioned since it seems to not be clear at the moment.

23. If psychology were a person, it would be a massive control freak with obsessive compulsive tendencies as it passive-aggressively attempts to affix "-ive" to every word in creation while having hyper-retroactive attention deficit disorder since it doesn't realize that it already has done so. Since names will follow words, I'll preemptively get used to my name being "Jawnive."

- What You Don't Schitz

24. It will be a nice day when the criminal-enabling device of "entered into evidence" is removed by God in heaven, then the actual facts of the case can be shown and we can see real justice happen. Till then, we can't really expect much from this pack of pretenders.

- What You Don't Enter

25. To say that something is pedantic is pedantic. From this we see how things revolve into themselves, so for that reason, this isn't usually pointed out. The same thing happens when telling anyone not to discuss politics or religion: you just did. This is semi-confusing, added to which all this is said in a country with free speech. But because speech isn't two-dimensional and it actually is free, the time will arrive soon enough that will expose precisely what is wrong with its censure.

- What You Don't Say

26. If we discover that we're irrevocably convinced that Jesus told us that harassing any rape victim is acceptable, there are two things that are now beyond doubt:

We've been talking to the wrong Jesus.

We are in no way, shape, manner, or form a representative of law or justice and should retire and find something we actually want to represent.

The punishments for harassing any rape victim at any point in their lives is beyond imagining, so our future is nothing close to anything we can see or believe.

- What You Don't Provoke

27. If we plant something that's alive, more of them show up. So if we plant something that's dead, less of them should show up.

- What You Don't Get

28. Once my cat asked me, "Can't you just tell me everything I need to know?" I looked back at her and said nothing.

29. When considering cases of poetic justice, two obvious questions come to mind:

a.) Who was the poet? and

b.) Does he have a background in law?

30. Music allows us to convey our angry, forceful, and myriads of other facial expressions that are otherwise accompanied with yelling and throwing large objects; but because there is music with it, no one gets upset or threatened about it.

31. Beginnings can occur in any moment, as was said in 1985. But if we forget every particle of the past and refuse to learn from our mistakes, the future will drive backwards into the past and nothing new will have happened other than a redundancy. Sometimes forgetting the past is the precise mistake that needs to not be repeated. It was noticed that at least three people enjoyed when everyone would forget the past, because then they were free to commit the exact same crimes again as many times as people were busy forgetting the past. They thought we didn't notice or wouldn't remember.

32. If we argue with someone in a dream, to whom do we go to win when we awaken?

33. The stamping out of free speech is not just adding a dissonant chord and creating noise, nor the childish bandying of any idea chosen at whim and its opposite thrown against the same wall to form a contrast analysis. No, over and beyond this, it is the silencing of the music of thought itself.

But again, some of us have seen and heard things that, after such events and words, the mere relation of which the fear caused in the retelling would render the words incapable of reaching the end of any sentence, running to any silence is, in those rare cases, the only emollient against madness.

So from this we can clearly understand that we need a firm grasp on what is meant when we say "speech."

34. After seeing so many imagining what's in front of them is reality when it turns out to not be the case, we may wonder how do we really know, or do we ever, that what's in front of us is reality? So many imagine it's their job to tell us what we're really saying when they have no clue about what they're saying. So when can we know for sure what has been said? When we discover ourselves instructing someone else about what they're really saying, we know one thing for sure

- We're a Prize Jackass.

35. What we don't know is what we could. Where we're wrong is what we should know.

36. Since dictionaries keep changing slowly over time, unless we have a copy of the dictionary in use in that specific time for the work in hand, more meaning than we think is actually no longer being conveyed.

37. Before killing people we disagree with, remember, some of the changes we see around us are made to prevent malevolently monotonous mechanistic manipulations from driving those involved into deeper states of insanity. The changes are needed to refocus the attention and renew the perspectives of those working in highly repetitive fields, which these days is the majority of them. Unless we know why the changes have happened, it's impossible to pretend that we do. No one will see this. The ignorance of the majority will continue to dominate, suppress, and override reason and understanding.

- What You Don't Change

38. If you didn't hear anything I said when I was there, how exactly do you know that I'm not there now?

39. In general, whenever anyone says, "this group of people is x, y, and z, and this means l, m, & n," almost in every case they know absolutely nothing about either the group, the people, x, y, z, l, m, or n.

40. A good explanation takes care of itself. While there is any remainder of critical questions, the explanation hasn't been found. Any

idiot can generate endless questions like a child asking "why" every second till the time ends. Only adults know when to ask, and when the answer is sufficient. But the fool who hates knowledge also hates answering questions.

- What College Professors Don't Know Harms Companies

41. If you have quintuplets from five different men where four are fraternal twins, which one is the father? And which one will you get the alimony check from? And which one will pay child support?

42. Commonly confounded is losing an argument and losing a soul since the visible reactions may be similar.

43. We won't find any element for light on the periodic table.

44. What if we are only here to help one person? What if we had no idea about either this purpose or this person? What if God chose to move through us for this person at a time about which we were unaware, because otherwise we find ways to obstruct His purposes? What if this was all we had to do in our lives? What if God both sees and moves in secret because of His own reasons?

45. The two questions: 1. "Yea, hath God said?" and 2. "Which of these contradictions is God behind" travel in opposite directions.

46. Many times, there's a direct correlation between our lack of understanding about what's around us and our lack of understanding about God.

47. When we forget anything, then remember it, how do we know for sure that we have picked up all the pieces?

48. We may discover four things about the explanations on any subject given by others:

a.) We had misunderstood them,

b.) They were lying about it,

c.) They were telling the truth,

d.) They themselves misunderstood what they were saying.

49. Most of what we see around us isn't being seen for what it actually is at all, but rather what others or ourselves say that it is. And whether or not we believe these assessments decides its entire existence when actually very often there is none. An assessment that amounts to nothing and describes nothing = nothing.

2. Taking Advantage Of What No One Can See

Appearances are a glimpse of the unseen.[20]

1. Once we have studied, examined, exploded, and outlined how Issue A was destroyed, we not only have a method of correcting it, but also an exhaustive, detailed, and methodically planned instruction book on how to decimate Issue B, where those are similar. If caution isn't used to avoid this, occasionally it can happen without even thinking much about it. But it has been seen sometimes that people ask for the details on A only to collect, publish, and market instruction manuals for how to crush B.

2. Our concept of justice is skewed by the examples of justice in our field of view. These examples are too largely populated by crime victims receiving the punishment rightfully due to the criminals while the actual criminals are molly coddled and worshiped. This aberration is primarily fueled by power, money, and demonic possession.

3. Murder is illegal in reality, regardless of the written laws of any country and regardless of the country of the origin of the idea. This is the case not only because it is the removal, but *also* because it is the absolute removal of all freedom for the person murdered. Due to this, reality will also eventually call into question every person involved in every unreasonable suspension of justice, refusal of punishment, and all worshiping of the people guilty of murder. What anyone thinks about this is irrelevant since reality was here before we were.

- Discuss The Invisible

4. The experience of being alive is so taken for granted that we believe we have the right to remove it from others for frivolous reasons while defending it for criminals who no longer deserve or care about it.

5. Corporate war strategists are now so skillful that they can get us to argue their point without even talking to us ever, all while we imagine that we're against them. If we notice that we're not being paid by them to support their cause, taking a side either for or against them is ill advised. If we do, they thank us heartily for our attention and unasked efforts since it makes money for them and keeps them from having to pay us.

6. We may on occasion give a face to the invisible, lest any say they've never seen it.

7. If everything is a lie, as some contend, then regarding the names we use to address each other, to what does the name attach?

8. Animals don't speak because actions speak louder than words. If we say we can't understand them, we're also saying we think words speak louder than actions.

9. The purpose of misunderstandings isn't to produce or deliberately insert them into every possible situation as the majority so gleefully enjoy, and even lavish no small accolades, lengthy encomiums, and reward ceremonies for the most brilliant productions of them -- but rather to make sure that we aren't the ones taking advantage of what no one can see.

10. Something else that's almost immediately obvious from even a casual glance at Euclid is that if we don't draw the picture the right way, all the proof will either be inaccurate or make no sense at all. Even shifting one of the typically two diagrams one centimeter to the north of the page will destroy the entire explanation. Why is this a concern? The same thing happens in conversations or anywhere ideas are transferred. Liars, sadists, and manipulators typically take advantage of this possibility by shifting the picture, which in arguments or conversations no one can actually see, and begin describing an entirely different picture as if they have the right one to begin with. And using this method, the entire original idea is destroyed and heat of the argument is applied as leverage to prevent the idea from ever

resurfacing at the risk of melting the delicate snowflakes we all know we are. In reality, there is no time limit on ideas, so many of them which people have assumed are over and done with will be seen again after we die and gone over until they are understood and the correct picture is transmitted. People who aren't interested in obtaining the correct picture are easy to spot and by so doing self-identify as bald-faced liars since accuracy isn't part of their reality.

- Picture's Lines Matter

11. Speculative Philosophy should continue to exist, since all philosophy either still is or always began as mere speculation which has often been proven to be correct in the end. Seeing there are more invisible things than visible, even needless things such as

what to wear

when and where

which is written in the air

and absolutely nowhere,

there must also be some method of measuring these things, not just from necessity, but since there are such an infinite number of them. And from ancient writings we know that these measuring agents can either be sentient or inanimate and still hold reliable information. The question that remains is: who or what are they and when or where will they appear or to whom?

12. Since the Word is "the expression of an idea or the idea itself," knowing what precisely it is comes from understanding. Salvation by works is a deceptive effort intended to make us believe that something extra is needed (actions, speeches, people, objects, rituals, bat soup, alembics, forgotten texts, etc.) in order to understand what the idea is. But since we can understand any idea without even so much as opening a book, this sufficiently demonstrates and reveals salvation by works to be the lie that in reality it actually is.

Understanding is an invisible action. Deception is an invisible cloud covering the truth and prevents understanding from seeing the light of day. Many of the same tricks used in the visible world to trick the eyes, ears, and mind are also used in the invisible world.

13. To say we know everything is to say we know nothing. To behave as though we know everything does the same thing. Every false accusation has this quality as a veneer which serves as a useful, though not solitary, key for their detection.

14. Music, among other things, takes things from the invisible world and pulls them into our perceptions, even though after doing this, we still don't know what they are. This is yet another example of how we may take advantage of what no one can see.

15. We enjoy clothing all expressions of the spiritual with the grasping chains of physical description, thus producing our lack of understanding about both.

16. With the ones who have lost touch, it isn't always possible to say what was lost or what they were touching. Something is palpably missing, but since it's another invisible enemy, whatever it was can't be seen even were it yet present. They seem to know their own, while not refusing the company of any. There is an element common to most, but absent in their case, yet it isn't common sense they lack. Some even seem to have a greater abundance of it. Their understanding is missing where it would seem it should be there in some areas.

The problem is so virtually untraceable that to date there is nothing describing it either of medical diagnosis or treatment. That it is an actual problem can be seen in what among their kind is universally ignored resulting many times in many deaths of others. This occurs when what they're saying is correct, but yet lacks the socially approved form of expression. So they're misunderstood, mislabeled, the message they have becomes lost, and people are killed as a result. This happens universally, since it's never been personally observed that any scientist ever questions the accuracy of their assessments, but rather dogmatically enforces their beliefs, sometimes under threat of life, and never entertains the opposing views with so much as one second of listening. Of all the invisible problems in the universe, this is one of the most puzzling.

17. We pretend to despise the behavior of gold-diggers while turning around in our next breath and following, worshiping every one of their invisible laws written in the many volumes of their invisible books.

Times like the ones we're now in reveal what these laws actually are and precisely how much they're worth.

18. Without haze or the element of the vague, body jumping would be far more exploitable than it is already.

19. *"In Adam, all die"* [21] and so was responsible for destroying the entire human race. If the guilt and punishment is the same, is the effect the same, that of destroying an entire race? If so, what is being destroyed per sin?

20. If imagination is lacking, it's because it can be found in none of the surroundings.

- What You Don't See

21. Technology has made what was previously invisible both measurable and manageable in many fields: electricity, medicine, physics, et al. What if everything that was invisible were measurable? What if there were instruments sufficiently competent to accurately measure emotions, the future, motives, root causes, or which memories are reliable? How many more fables that we now are so convinced are true will be exploded by this new ability? How many invisible instances will be revealed to show that pretending to know these answers, as we do today, while in fact knowing nothing has caused more harm than good? How many lives have been destroyed so far by this? Probably nearly the same number or greater as those that were destroyed by the antics of 500 year old medical practices or believing lightning strikes were caused by witches. The best answer to this is nearly two thousand years old and works every time. Could it be any simpler than to just "Judge Not?"

3. What You Don't Care

1. Since we know that the justice system doesn't rule according to what's right in every case, but rather what will prevent the most violence, we can't look to the justice system as a reliable source for truth or fairness. Any who say otherwise haven't studied American Government and are also *not* a reliable source of truth or fairness.

They say this is justified by the fact that they can't be responsible for public outbreaks of violence, and this is a valid point. But at what point do we sacrifice truth or fairness to this god who actually is no god and thereby disrespect the one true God?

2. Maybe the reason why we're here is to find out the reason why we're here. Now that we know this answer, we must, unlike lawyers, ask a question to which we do *not* have the answer.

In this and other cases, it is possible to answer a question with a question. How can we see why we're here: by doubting everything or by proving everything? Where could we find the most answers to why we're here: by ignoring everything or by studying everything? Who would have the most answers: people who can see what's around them or people who can't? What tools would be the most useful: the ones we already have or the ones that haven't been invented yet? Knowing this, will repeating the same words hundreds of times give us more answers or less?

3. Whenever any beauty is created, we enjoy ignoring the fact we had nothing to do with the creation of the process that made it all possible.

4. If we are an actual officer of the law, we don't have any right to solicit a crime from any rape victim at any point in their life for any reason. If we discover we have done this, we are no officer and won't be treated as such. We may wish to keep thinking this is a lie, then Jesus Christ and several others will be discussing it with us later as we redress the grievance of harassing a rape victim. When He explains we don't have this right, the answers will be amusing. So we must make sure to have one ready.

5. Laughable how people imagine they know all about what does or doesn't prove something while as they talk they prove the exact opposite.
- Watch What You Say

6. We may now have the facade of a republic, but when anyone with sufficient intellect or money can circumvent both law and lawmakers, it's now an oligarchy since they've effectively disabled the law.

7. I can't tell you how much I agree with you when you're not listening.
- Broked Comlinks

8. There should be a psychological term to describe the growing mass of people who don't care about anything until it directly affects them, then it's a national crisis. It's doubtful that many would fall outside of this category, but there are currently no highly visible treatments being suggested for it.
- Screw Everyone But Me Syndrome

9. Man made false religion to cover up his responsibility to the true. The devil really isn't needed since fear of responsibility drives itself, but does enjoy helping everyone believe the false is real and the true fake. All that remains is the natural laziness to not give a damn about which is which to seal the contract.
- Eternal Apathy

6. PROVE ALL THINGS

1. Generally Speaking

1. Many still struggle with the question of exactly what is reality. Is reality every word we say without any proof, or is proof even necessary? Most believe it isn't.

2. When we say we know nothing, we can learn. When we say we know something, we are lying.

Proof: We only know what some other person has decided to call and define whatever it is we're looking at while still having no good idea about what it is in reality. Also, we don't know what it calls itself. We learn when any new information proves itself more valuable than that which we had already.

3. An infinite being must exist everywhere, otherwise it is not infinite.

Proof: A - B != W \/ I, where A = any object in space or space itself, B = the infinite being, W = whole, and I = infinity.

4. To demand from the infinite an adequate explanation of itself to any finite being is not proof of supreme intelligence, but infinite ignorance.

Proof: It's mathematically impossible for any finite to comprehend an infinite. Such demands for proof of this type are nowhere near the realm of true science, since they ignore this basic rule. But since a whole is the sum of its parts, the infinite can comprehend any finite. Somewhere after algebra, too many pseudo-scientists forget the idea is to simplify. However, since the infinite is what it is, on occasions it *can* render itself understandable to the finite without ever acquiring an entire comprehension since this is both impossible and unnecessary.

- Infinite Proof

5. Sometimes people are chosen or not chosen for various jobs because of their ability to connect with people. This is very easy to see in those in whom this gift shines the brightest. There is no scientific proof or way to quantify or measure this connection, but most can see it and we know what it is. Notwithstanding, we only infrequently hear any large debates about the existence or non-existence of these connections and people who can make them have a high value in many trades, mostly PR work.

It is another in the long list of frustratingly invisible actions that happen in a reality where not very much, taking all things together, is visible or measurable. Yet, in spite of this, we all generally understand this power and give it a special place free from our normal skepticism, doubt, worries, or fears regarding its existence. Who has it? Yes, this is debatable. There is no way to either prove or disprove this, nor is there as of yet any great need to do so.

What it does prove is that not everything requires proof for us to believe it. Since this is the case on issues that don't matter as much such as this one, it is most certainly the case on issues that do. And due to the existence of this facet of reality, neither is it provable that proof is more necessary or required on issues of higher import, depending on the risk.

6. The greater the understanding, the greater the chance of misunderstanding. Understanding has never arisen through apathy. Knowledge and wisdom are its companions. Rote understanding is the opposite of knowing what we believe. Being able to prove what we believe is the power to avoid deceptions. Having said as much, many things may appear to have been proven, yet remain entirely false and destructive.

7. When we consider opinions, sometimes it's possible to determine whether or not they're true; other times it isn't. The textbook chain of progression (not importance) is opinion -> hypothesis -> theory -> law. Meaning many laws, even scientific ones, only began as one person's opinion. When viewing other's opinions, we may look beyond the usual considerations of "agree/disagree" to consider both truth/falsehood and when truth isn't possible to prove, we may wish to drive further to weigh the probability.

What is the greatest likelihood of this being possible in the greatest number of cases? Or when is truth itself relevant? Most believe that in the realm of opinions truth doesn't matter at all, so they're free to believe as many lies as they choose. Even if this only hurts them, which in many cases it does, it would be invalid for that reason among others more weighty.

But lies frequently hurt far more than just the believers of them. Just as the human eye has blind spots, human reasoning, which is the eye turned inward viewing the invisible realms of thought, can also have blind spots, of which deceivers take full advantage. This, then, is why the command is critically important when it says to "prove all things."

8. Regardless of what the actual law is, any lawyer who says their client is not guilty when they are or vice versa has perjured themselves.

Proof: Perjury is lying under oath. Lawyers should be taking an oath to uphold the law, or they don't need to be practicing law. If they know their client is the opposite of what they say, they are guilty of lying to an officer of the court. They childishly imagine that none of this will be revealed one day, even though it will.

9. No government employee is capable of supplying the economy with any *new* tax revenue.

Proof: All government employees are paid with *already existing* tax money from the general pool of revenue collected by the IRS, which is *old*. If they pay taxes (which would be short-sighted and time-wasting to give anyone a dollar only thereafter to immediately snatch it back), they're only recycling the same *old* dollar. Therefore, any who are for bigger government are promoting a future where eventually every government employee gets paid $0.00. Since when every American is working for the government, there are no *new* tax dollars coming in, resulting in a net pay of $0.00 for everyone.

10. We don't need to feel more, we need to *do* more.

Proof: Doing or not doing something can cause bad feelings, or it can prevent them. Having feelings does nothing, or nothing close to the feelings generated when someone deserts their family. Having feelings doesn't change the situation much, doing something does, like returning. Having feelings about doing the right thing does far less

223

than actually *doing* the right thing. Having feelings for suffering people doesn't do anything to them, doing something for them does.

11. The statement "everything is subjective" is false.

Proof: If true, then there could never be any such thing as an objective and no company would now be in existence. There would be no such thing as a subjective objective, but everything would be a subjective subjective.

12. This belief is far too flippantly brandished. It will now be dismantled: "Eyewitnesses are notoriously unreliable."

This is false.

Proof: If this were true and any video tape is secured of the crime, then anyone watching it becomes an eyewitness and is forever after unreliable. E.g., When Dr. Garrist recorded children having sex, anyone watching it was then guilty of watching child porn and was then also an eyewitness to the crime. If everyone seeing any crime is actually unreliable, then there can never be any way to prove any crime ever happened anywhere in time. "But isn't physical evidence superior to any eyewitness accounts?" If we ever see physical evidence, then we're an eyewitness to physical evidence and are forever unreliable. Why are we even discussing this? Since we are now all eyewitnesses to the statement, our repetition of it anywhere is unreliable according to its own definition.

13. Some, who seem to hold more power than their facelessness should be allowed to grant them, keep insisting that in order to prove anything, the proof must be at least 457 miles in length, small print on thin paper, and require several thousand years of explanation by top experts before it can even begin to rise to the level of a proof. But anyone even remotely familiar with Euclid can see this isn't the case.

Proof: 1. Take a ruler.

2. Measure the length of Euclid's proof for Proposition I, Book I.

3. Notice that it is far shorter than 457 miles by approximately 457 miles.

4. Realize that whoever believes all proofs must be 457 miles long has believed several lies and is also spreading them.

5. Notice also that reading the proposition doesn't take years or hours to finish.

6. Realize that whoever believes all proofs must take several degrees and years to understand is also spreading lies.

7. Realize that whoever said this is lacking the 457 miles of proof in support of their own statement.

8. Put whoever believes proofs must be 457 miles long, take years and degrees to understand on permanent ignore since the following is the case:

- Point Proven

14. It's Not Right To Be Mother Nature

"Natural" doesn't always equal "right."

1st Proof: Aside from the obvious illegality of any of us prancing around "au naturel," when we're faced with a destructive force that tells us they will annihilate us and everyone in our families if we call the police or try to jail them, we don't do what's right and call the police, we do what is natural - fear and run or comply. Right may not even occur later if even the judges and lawyers are also similarly afraid. But this fear is not only natural, it is reasonable.

2nd Proof: If we're not alive, we can't do what is right on earth.

Why is this a concern? There's a popular myth that natural behavior is superior to modified, controlled behavior which has just been disproven.

15. The actions of others neither prove nor disprove any statement. Using actions to disprove any belief, belief system, or statement is a "passing the buck" maneuver that will fail since we aren't judged by the actions of anyone but ourselves. But, because of this, it does very well in revealing the irresponsible, since taking two minutes to consider anything requires little effort. It actually takes more energy to ignore a persistent issue than to study it and form a decision.

- Cursed Be The Deceiver[22]

16. People who only believe what they can see won't be usable in any science, whether theology, physics, chemistry, astronomy, or psychology.

Proof: We can't see gravity, we can't see holes left by electrons, we can't see space, we can't see anyone's thoughts, and we can't see spirits.

All must be accepted on faith and we must be satisfied knowing they're there from the effects they produce.

17. If we don't try to have justice make sense, it excuses every single time that it doesn't.

18. A book of lies would never have the following words inside it: Prove All Things.

19. If we know a true dollar bill, it's possible to look at several counterfeits. But after seeing so many scores of counterfeits we have to ask ourselves, "Why am I wasting my time looking at literally nothing?" It's the same with truth, facts, and opinions.

20. In this command is found most of the things people say haven't been proven or need to be proved. It's no one's responsibility to prove anything to us about anything. It's our responsibility to prove all things to ourselves. No teacher is required to prove what they say. We're required to make sure what they teach is correct.

21. Not infrequently were met those who after telling them the truth replied: I don't care. One thing is for certain: these can't be counted on for solving any problems. Some of these think they're members of some group of authorities or another. We may know that in fact they are not and must wait for the real authorities to show up.

Proof: They won't care if they find the answer, they won't care if the answer is right if they do find one, they won't care if they're looking in the right area for the answer, and they won't care if they're even actually looking for an answer or not.

They won't care if they've identified the real problem, they won't care if the solution they use actually addresses the problem long term, short term, or any term. And most importantly, they don't care if they actually have any good reason to say - *I don't care.*

22. The main difficulty with ad hominems isn't just that they're a logical fallacy that immediately concedes defeat of the argument on the part of the user, or that it accurately announces the self-declaration of the user to be a bully with a potential of possessing deeper psychiatric aberration. But it even more loudly declares the user to be apparently ignorant of the fact that no human is perfect, which is also why it's a

logical fallacy. In any argument, formal or informal, pretending to be ignorant of known facts is an immediate fail.

Proof: If there is no atom in existence that is a perfect circle since a perfect circle doesn't exist, nothing composed of atoms will ever be perfect regardless of any Utopian fantasies or struggles for perfection.

- Like It Or Not

23. Binary thinking is a lie.

Proof: There is either the earth or the sun. There is either a hammer or a nail. There is either my news source which is correct 100% of the time, or your source which is fake news, which is false 100% of the time. There is either a wheel or a wagon. There is either a horse or its oats. There is either a pen or a paper. There is either a fire or a candle. There is either a bird or the air. You can't have it both ways. (Sounds convincing, doesn't it?)

24. Man may never hear anything we say, but God does. Man may never do anything about anything we say, but God probably already has. If God were a mere construct from the mind of some or several men, there would be no way to prove either thing. But since we have the following command, we can know there is. Prove all things.

25. Granulated sugar and opinions have common factors: they both contain something empty, whether calories or sanity.

26. Everyone cannot be treated equally.

Proof: Since criminals are treated with prisons, so should everyone else be.

27. If we feel the obsessive need to restrict free speech because we are scared of confronting new ideas, we won't be in any part of the future.

Proof: Regardless of post-modernism, the future will have ideas that we've never seen before. Eventually the number of these ideas will overcome our tolerance level for them and we will die of fright. The future will also not have any of the current overstock of nannies, God's little helpers, that feel it's their sole purpose in life to regulate and control the speech of everyone around them. So even if we don't die, we will be lonely since there won't be any job for us to perform that is even remotely close to our imaginary purpose. The best news for everyone else is: we won't be there.

28. When we see any con glommer ignoring necessary cons, those needed to solve problems, we know their agenda is nothing constructive, but rather has the character of devolution.

Proof: If con glommers were on their game, more points would be accrued from the pinpointing of necessary cons over unnecessary ones. (Pros aren't counted when scoring points since there can be no logical reason for the existence of any real problem if there is a solution to be found. If any pro exists for any problem, it has at least one solution.) Since they ignore these and often are seen attacking people who do locate the con needed to solve problems (by first locating the problem itself, which in this case is them), their behavior is self-defeating. Any self-defeating efforts can never be a solution for any problem. An identifying trait is that they imagine their rectum is a mouth which they use to try to talk to others. Keep a sharp eye out for

- The Con Glommers

29. Dismissive people who try to minimize the efforts of everyone around them to gain a fleeting emotion that makes them feel as though they're elevated above the world for three or four seconds are only limiting their own reality.

Proof: Maybe someone else knows something they themselves don't know.

30. "No one may ever defend themselves ever." = False.

Proof: Aside from being written nowhere, this is a passive aggressive attack medium that's illegal in reality. We always have the right to defend ourselves. If any allege that we have no right to defend ourselves, then they are bound to prove it or be laughed at and safely ignored. Pedophiles always tell their victims they cannot defend themselves, so this makes things easier for them. If we believe we have no right to defend ourselves, we should look at the company we're in and rethink it.

31. When we disagree with anyone and have time to ourselves, consider which side has more evidence to support what they're saying. Whichever side has the least evidence also has the least reasons for disagreeing.

32. It will be rewarding to watch karma slap the dog mess out of the billions who believe it's up to them to decide where and when karma

should strike, then move karma out of the way, jump ahead of it, and do it's job for it.

How can we know this will happen?

Proof: How many times does life need to prove that sometimes everything we think is wrong? We may think karma needs to happen, but if we're wrong and move ahead to pass any sentence, karma will hit us in the face instead of whoever we're jealous, envious, spiteful, or hateful against. This all assumes karma even exists to begin with.

33. In a fictional context, we recognize and understand things not recognized or acted upon openly, thus proving that it is possible.

Proof: If it is the case that we can understand anything in a fictional setting, then it is also possible in a non-fictional, otherwise the words "we can understand" could never appear.

- How To Openly Hide From Ourselves

34. Police wannabes are greater criminals than the actual criminals.

Proof: They imagine crimes exist where there aren't any and their punishment for the imaginary crimes (which they imagine they alone have the right to enforce) instantiates an initial real crime, which renders themselves the only ones who are truly guilty. They also began a crime whereas before there wasn't one.

35. A. Proving a friend wrong is pointless.

B. Statement A is false.

Proof: C. I am my own friend.

36. Balance is necessary, but equality isn't.

Proof: The earth is neither inside the sun nor billions of miles away from it. A balanced position is necessary. No particle on earth is equal to the particles either on the sun or to those in deep space. If it were equal, it would be on the sun, or in deep space. Therefore, equality is not required.

37. Knowing nationality is a more diverse approach than thinking we all came from a box of crayons.

Proof: $5 < 194$

Notice it didn't take 1,200 pages to prove this or more than two minutes of either writing or reading. Any questions?

38. Sometimes people who worship money think that by spending money on anything that they are sacrificing to their god. But there is an obvious logic fail here: We may not offer our god to itself as a sacrifice.

Proof: It already has itself and doesn't need more of it, unless it's an arrogant, egotistical megalomaniac interested only in controlling others while doing nothing about itself, like the majority of humans do. And since money is an inanimate object, none of this applies. So, it doesn't need more of itself, therefore giving more of itself to itself is a repetitive unnecessary redundant redundancy. This obviously doesn't apply to any who don't serve mammon, the perpetually dissatisfied god of avarice.

39. Ignoring any part of reality can't be called justice.

Proof: If justice has nothing to hide, then it can't cherry pick evidence, which is the definition of discrimination, and call it justice. To avoid this, it must perform non-discriminatory discrimination when considering any case. Any habitual exclusion of evidence, sometimes excluding the precise contents of a book they swear on when taking any oath (Rom. 2:28-29), can't be considered a full purview of reality. Any less than an entire examination of reality will necessarily limit key elements that would otherwise allow justice to occur. People entering into this business only to play games with the outcome will necessarily limit this idea to where it has no effect on the dispensary of justice anywhere.

40. If bias is actually a valid basis for rejecting either an argument or anything else, then no justice can ever be performed.

Proof: 1. Those in the practice of law are biased against criminals since putting criminals in jail is their job.

2. Criminals are biased towards themselves since they not only constantly excuse their own crimes, but have been repeatedly known to pretend to practice law while releasing known criminals to harass their victims, sometimes for a period of over forty years.

3. Since both parties are biased, who then is able to exercise justice? It has been repeatedly seen in thousands of cases that neither party is in reality actually concerned with justice at all and that other concerns are far more important.

41. When we only see the positive, something negative happens.

Proof: "We all make mistakes" is commonly said, but if we're only looking at the positive, the mistakes are being ignored, since those are negative. If we never see our mistakes, which a large mass of such practitioners of this has already formed and metastasized, then we aren't correcting any of them. If we aren't correcting any of them, we're repeatedly repeating them. Therefore, by only viewing the positive, and never correcting any of our mistakes, we're forcing others to only see the negative. Since there are more of others than there are of us as individuals, this is an exponential problem that expands geometrically. This is extremely and geometrically negative.

42. Organizing anything is an act of disorganization.

Proof: We're taking something that we know precisely where it is and placing it precisely somewhere that we don't. Unless the definition of "organized" is "something we can never remember where it is." The definition more closely fits "disorganized." We don't know where it is because we can't remember it. If we could remember where it was, we could find it and it would be organized. How it looks is 100% irrelevant if we can't remember where it is. Till we do, it's only one in an infinite pile of useless items in the universe.

- What You Don't Remember

43. The ocean is in dire need of a psychotherapist.

Proof: It has been salty and angry for over 5,000 years.

44. On the molecular level, nothing is equal. If we have inequality at the microscopic level, we won't have equality at any other level. So, why are there egalitarians?

Proof: An electron is not equal to a proton, in fact they are opposite, and not equal. Proving also, things don't need to be equal to work just fine.

45. No one cares about anything until it directly affects them.

Proof: Two murderers are still alive only because the people keeping them alive didn't have their family members murdered or raped. Otherwise, they would have been executed in 1473.

- Skin for Skin[23]

46. There is a theory that by applying pressure to any object, this enables us to see its true nature. By this theory, shining light on an

electron shouldn't cause any deviation in its orbit, otherwise it's not an electron. This is how we know this theory is false.

- Electrons Are Fake

47. In heaven, actions will be immediately followed by reactions and consequences. This is one of the main things we're here to develop - a preparedness to live under these conditions.

Proof: In heaven, time doesn't exist, therefore, there can be no time between any action and its consequence. How consecutive moments can occur outside of time is a different question.

48. Remembering that life is a complex resonant structure, whining that life isn't giving us what we want because of what we are (female, wrong color, no education, <insert whine here>) isn't as useful as being what we actually are, allowing people to be who they are by removing all the intricate manipulative control mechanisms, and seeing what life actually brings us.

Proof: Calculate the energy cost of doing both. Follow the path of least resistance.

49. God is already in the places we haven't realized yet.

Proof: An unrealized location is a place, or it couldn't be called a location. God is either everywhere or nowhere. If He were nowhere, no language would be possible since, as has already been shown, the obvious is not common. If there were no language, it would be obvious there would need to be, but since the obvious is not common, no one would ever see this to invent one. If God is everywhere, He would therefore also be in every unrealized location.

50. Any who are scared to fight won't be a reliable resource for solving problems.

Proof: They will never overcome their fear of fighting their own reluctance to solve problems in order to achieve any working solution.

51. We can tell electronics were made by humans.

Proof: pushing a button on any electronic device and talking to most people has the exact same result —

- No Response

52. Proof regarding those who have lost touch:

Produce to the precise atomic count the number of atoms involved in either what they were touching or what was lost.

53. Old age is a proximate, but not fatal, argument against the concept of Free Will.

Proof: Most of our time is spent doing something we never decided to do and never even thought we would be spending so much of the last years doing at all.

Example: Forgetting everything that just happened three seconds ago isn't a conscious decision on our part.

- Find Wisdom So You Can Forget You Ever Had Any

54. We are admonished to trust our instincts. Yet none of this seems to be taken into account when we observe each other. The amount of pathetic judgments would be scaled back considerably from what they are currently if this were not the case.

Proof: If anyone is following their instincts, what they do may appear outwardly to not make sense all the time. When others imitate this behavior and throw it back in their face, as many have been noted to enjoy doing, they never asked when or where the person was following their instincts, so they can not possibly or reasonably have any clue about where or when the instincts were being trusted. And, sometimes an instinct is to follow a command that no one else is even remotely concerned about. But in order to have known anything, or even show that they remotely even cared, all they had to do was ask. From observation, no one ever did.

55. *"Seest thou a man wise in his own conceit? there is more hope of a fool than of him."* [24]

This is similar: A fool is wiser in his own eyes than all who came before and all who will come after.

Proof: We pretend we can't understand any of the great writings of antiquity because it was just for that time and no one can fully understand what they're saying today. And any advice from our children is laughed off and ignored.

56. It is impossible to prejudice an impartial jury.

Proof: If they're truly impartial, they will pass every temptation to prejudge, rendering prejudice an impossibility. Either that or they're not actually impartial. Every fear of prejudicing the jury only indicates

a.) we're trying to prevent evidence that would prove a crime, b.) we don't know what these words mean and/or

c.) we don't understand yet that

- You Can't Have It Both Ways

57. 1 is equal to 5.

Proof: When it's 5 after 1, both hands are on top of each other and therefore equal.

58. All anecdotes can never be evidence: False.

Proof: To say $(\forall x)(Ax \to Ex)$ isn't the same at all as saying $(\exists x)$ $(Ax \to Ex)$ where A is "anecdotes" and E is "evidence," and conversely. Since we know $(\exists x)(Ax \to Ex)$, then anyone saying $(\forall x)(Ax \to {\sim}Ex)$ is provably false, which was done this time using a different method than the last.

To prove $(\exists x)(Ax \to Ex)$ we only need one example, which is this: Every word in our brains is hearsay unless we invented the word ourselves. We put full faith and credit into whoever told us every idea we have and even our own. This also proves that our own ideas are hearsay in that we heard it from ourselves. Since most of us have no idea who we even are since we never bother to examine ourselves, this is equal in effect to hearing it from another person. But we also know words are used in court to prove cases and they're called either written or oral testimony. So words *can* be used to prove anything that can be proven with them. Now we can clearly see there are over 600,000 examples that one is true and the other is false.

On the other hand, by similar methods we can prove that $(\forall x)$ $(Ax \to Ex)$ is always false. If anecdotes can never be evidence, how is it that ad hominems and character assassination can be?

59. Of all things people say it's impossible to prove from a film, this is possible: delusions.

Proof: People in stories on film or in books or TV actually listen. So we spend great amounts of time seeing examples that no one ever follows (proving further that setting good examples does absolutely nothing) of people listening and responding logically to evidence, both verbal and physical.

This creates a delusion that there are actually any of these people walking around on earth when the facts prove otherwise. We may prove this to ourselves: go try to find one. Today, finding anyone who listens or responds logically to verbal or physical evidence has lower odds than winning the lottery, which is less than 1%.

- PWL (People Who Listen)

60. Imagining paper stacks prove anything (other than the dendrocidals) can occur with people who confound proof with popinjay scratchings.

61. Expecting results from liars is a type of insanity.

Proof: All Men Are Liars.

62. It is insignificant who agrees or disagrees, but rather that each person ensures they can prove what they believe to themselves first, others second. Even though both agreements and disagreements are valuable in themselves for their respective reasons, it's preferred that everyone we've ever known in our lives would find the truth and fall in love with its beauty and ability to deliver from every known snare that foul and foolish men could ever fabricate. But that's not an external decision, it's the decision of every person to do this for themselves.

If this occurs, then one thousand years from now, we will see them and things beyond our imagining. Otherwise, we will neither remember them nor anything they said or did, and neither will anyone else. To infer that anyone who isn't an overt sadist is desirous of this outcome is either a lie or based on a gross misunderstanding.

63. You can prove to yourself if I've heard what you've said by hearing what I've said; howbeit, this step is prodigious and typically shunned.

64. Too much of reality is illusion.

Proof: Silent letters in any word is an audio-visual illusion.

65. Unlike deception, what's in the bible isn't proven with the right kind of light, but with a sufficient amount of light.

66. If the justice system can be wrong, vigilantes can be more wrong.

Proof: If a group of individuals can be wrong, then one individual can be wronger. It was just proven that an individual can be wronger. No further proof is needed.

67. Responsibility is a yes or no question. Apathy (I don't care) is an invalid response to a yes or no question, and as such is a non-answer.

Proof: Do you have the ability to formulate a response?

68. The sun is unscientific, and as such, when we can figure out how to kill it for disagreeing with the scientific community, we will.

Proof: The center of the 365 day year is 182.5, which is July first at noon. But the sun argues this point by making the 21st of June the longest day of the year, which is the precise center of the earth's orbit. How the earth can be at the center of it's orbit while still riding along the perimeter is another argument altogether.

Since we know the scientific community have been ordained by their infallible god, Time, to be the unchangeable bastions of perfection, we know their answers are always correct and have never changed since time began. Any who disagree with them are summarily shot on sight to prevent offending the Time god.

As soon as the sun submits to our idea of equality, it will become the same size as we are so we can shoot it with a fire hose. Till then, it has the advantage provided by its earth-swallowing size which is the only thing keeping it alive. Help us convince the sun about our concept of equality so we can shoot it for its flagrant offense of disagreeing with a known god.

- The Solar Dilemma

69. We may not prove things to other people.

Proof: Deciding when something does or doesn't amount to proof is a decision on the part of every individual. We may only make decisions for ourselves. Therefore, it's beyond easy to say that even hard evidence such as large blood stains on a blue carpet, oral testimony, and missing people aren't evidence and thwart justice for over fifty years. We may only prove things to ourselves, and expecting others to do it for us is pure sloth.

70. The point of 2 is for 3.

Proof: Eyes, ears, and noses are paired to triangulate surroundings. Two-dimensional paper is needed to make three-dimensional drawings.

- Two-thirds

71. Some aren't interested in the work involved, but "Prove all things" is a command where the punishment for disobedience is exacted by life and experience itself only on the one who doesn't. Taking what we know from before, that "nothing is true all of the time," this means, which is obvious anyway, that not all things can be proven. Nor is proof required for all things. This is clear once any work to prove anything has begun.

Some have misconstrued "not all things can be proven" to mean "prove nothing at all ever." For most, this is a life they enjoy existing in, even though curiosity will eventually argue the point. Others, in courts of law and elsewhere, believe that shouting "that proves nothing" and issuing a choreographed dance of death threats and menacing gestures is all we need to do to disable the supplied proof. This is obviously false. Either admit the proof amounts to evidence and move on, or admit the entire sixteen years of education was insufficient to recognize when this is the case and redo the entire sixteen years until the understanding and maturity takes hold. But either way, once the evidence was supplied, those who recognize it have already moved on, with or without any dissenters.

2. The Majority Is Highly Excited To Be Wrong

1. Better to have the truth on our side than the majority.

2. The majority spend their time brainstorming complex methods to bend the will of others, sometimes only for its own sake, with no other purpose, but usually to some end. Guilt is, here again, the primary tool used to accomplish this.

A better way is to do the opposite: Using no guilt, spend several years simplifying methods to bend our own will. Doing this is the only place where real changes are made. The rest are temporary when we realize someone deceived us, then we go back to what we were going to do in the first place. Why waste time? Just realize from the outset that the majority are always wrong.

3. Telling the rich man he needs to give us his money since he has it is not only stealing, but a form of slavery. So, a majority now in the world who claim to hate slavery are actually slave owners.

4. A belief of one "football team" - By a holy decree of eternal infallibility, we maintain the sacred ensconcement of the ability to determine who is or isn't guilty of anything while creating victimhood status for ourselves against those who have asserted whether we are or aren't guilty of anything. Due to our position of eternal infallibility, all truth is irrelevant. All self-aggrandizing appointments of guilt made by our team are permanent and never require review or reevaluation. Once one member has made any appointment, all other members shall assiduously enforce the punishments required by the guilty status without any reflection, consideration of reality, or any critical thinking

whatsoever. All of this must be the case because our team is always right. Any breaking of rank or disagreement with the above stated eternal decrees shall result in permanent excommunication.

5. It isn't surprising that even after repeating the same ideas sometimes for over forty-five years that people still don't understand what's being said. Even though there may be millions of books written on any subject, which does sharpen the focus somewhat, there still may be no actual understanding. A very strong, but not absolute, proof that something is worth understanding or has been understood is when two people who don't know each other have said in two different times and places the exact same thing before either knew about the existence or statements of the other.

In reality, there may never be any absolute or conclusive proof about anything, not the kind most think of when expecting absolute proof anyway. Especially when the majority keep mouthing off about "no absolutes." When it comes to proofs, we may have discovered an exception to the rule about absolutes maintained by the majority. When this occurs, the proof is closer to being absolute than when it doesn't. Proof of these claims:

> *"But in natural language, words are vague and ambiguous. Words are often not defined very precisely and are therefore subject to the interpretation of the disputants in an argument. And since words in an argument may be interpreted in different ways or according to different standards of precision, they can be used in a fashion that is friendly to the case of the arguer and unfriendly to the case of the person to whom the argument is directed. Words can be used as weapons in an argument."*[25]

I had never seen these words before yesterday, but seeing them in the behavior of others has been too obvious to overlook. Nearly the exact same thing has been said here before, not so well stated at all, but still here. There have been numerous arguments that after hours of discussion wound up only being one word for which each party had a separate definition and use. At a guess, over fifty in as many years in discussions between both friends and people barely known. How critical then, before discounting any writing, to make sure an accurate understanding is obtained? How many people on the face of the earth now make sure to do this before opening their mouth to cast hatred on any book, most especially one they've never read before in their entire lives in any language, much less the original?

- The Majority Is Always Confused

6. The right to never be offended, if allowed, grants exclusive rights not covered by the freedom of speech.

Proof: a. It grants to anyone an exclusive right to falsely accuse anyone else for offending them.

b. It grants the exclusive right to provoke others to anger, violence, or both by continuous streams of false accusations.

However, the freedom of speech grants no one anywhere such rights and whoever chooses to be offended lives with their own decision. The majority believe the opposite of this.

7. Using the ideas of debate, cooking, and chemistry, many today feel that adding twelve metric tons of nitroglycerin to every pan of eggs is a "good, healthy" meal.

8. If someone does something to us it's not the same as God doing something to us. Relieving the pressure on the responsible party will only ensure we'll be seeing the same thing happen again later. We ought to blame the guilty when they are and stop sloughing the responsibility off onto God or the devil when only humans were involved. Things change faster when we attack the source of the problem and not some random party completely outside of it.

Proof: Free will.

9. If the majority subscribes to and promotes a bad philosophy, any pharmaceutical products will necessarily reflect this bad philosophy. This may explain why there are so many deadly and debilitating side effects to most of their products. If so, this only proves that teaching and believing poisonous ideas will only produce more poison.

10. The people who say, live, and believe that words don't mean anything, it applies both to most of what they believe and when they make the statement: "Words don't mean anything."

- The Majority Are Always Deaf

11. We don't need a brain to vote because thinking is a right.

12. A primary (not the only primary) tool of manipulators is the ad hominem. The ad hominem itself is a manipulator. It attempts to manipulate the mind into ignoring the actual veracity of any statements whatsoever made by anyone and replace them with a verdict of "lie," when often the opposite is the truth. We may know the degree of the delusion suffered by the manipulators by the degree of their love for ad hominems. It provides a false sense of security by causing humor at the expense of the person whose character is being assassinated. They are illegal in both formal and informal debate and signal both the end and the loser. The loser is the person who uses them. The manipulator is the person who is addicted to them.

An ad hominem means the person using them lost sight of the point under discussion and has no further ideas about it. It is a sign the brain has reached the end of any useful ideas about the matter. It is a sign of a pressing need for further education in order to have the hint of a clue. It is an unspoken request to the opponent in the debate to provide this education in order to continue towards any solution, which request is usually denied, but may be offered in direct proportion to the attitude that comes with the question, if any use could be found by so doing.

All of this is in direct opposition to the popular behavior which indicates the user of ad hominems has won based solely on the quality of the slam. Here again is further proof that the majority is always wrong.

13. The most effective or devastating deceiver won't be overt. Their best tools are nuance both in expression and movement, holding good form; manners are their motto. The wrong in their wake is scarcely perceptible, at least for that day. They give the audience what they want. They aren't always interested in death, but when they are, it isn't always traceable to them. Coincidence and accident are their currency for bail. They surf waves of others' trust and belief better than any Californian wave hawk. Their power to cause mass worship of Hypnos

rivals Houdini. The best of them require no lawyer. The majority believe the opposite of all this.

14. If the majority is wrong, a large group of people will find out after a very long time that everything they just did was incorrect. This is either true or it's not. We may vote for not, but unfortunately, too often, the majority look like they don't know how to read.

15. Faith begins exactly at the point where we abandon concern for any incipient cause. An assumed cause is taken on faith as to its existence, evolution, and governing rules. Yet the majority imagine themselves to not be persons of faith.

16. Since we all have hidden qualities, the brightest gems among us aren't always the ones that are visible. Sometimes, the brightest are merely a reflection of someone they know who is brought to the rest of the world through their medium. Few act on this knowledge and only pile accolades on what they can see. This is why the majority is often wrong.

- Premanonic Gem

17. We don't like the bible because it shows a God who deals with each person only for their own actions: "*So then every one of us shall give account of himself to God.*"₍₂₆₎ This would be the inverse of an account of five trillion other people while never including ourselves. This runs directly opposite of every human behavior, that holds every person accountable, punishable, and executable for every single real or fabricated action, belief, thought, or farts of people existing approximately 17.5 billion years ago.

18. When the majority are only interested in creating excuses to relieve themselves of responsibility, it makes little difference what we say.

19. The majority believe that concentration camps are what makes murder acceptable or not by whether or not these are used to do so.

20. Lobbyists: How the minority rules the majority.

21. "*I know everything I need to know by ignoring everything you say,*" said the majority.

22. Leading the witness = *bad*!
Leading the masses = *Fantastic*!

- Majority Logic Fails

23. Not only is it far easier to destroy than create to the extent that no demonstration is needed, but neither is one needed to see the frighteningly prodigious amount of excuses applied in the direction of each. We fail to give because that would be creating and it requires effort and we're taught to be lazy yet claiming that we're all "hard workers" while no one gives substantially in all areas where giving is possible. We don't give, and destroy many other things besides, making similar excuses that "this is the way things are" or "they deserved it," since it's the lazy way out, involving little to no effort whatsoever to accomplish and no creative energy at all.

When he said, "Give," he didn't mean give destruction, but that's how the majority interprets that statement, since that's all they do.

Money isn't the only thing that can be given. Time, ideas, inventions, presence, forgiveness, probably a thousand other things.

- Interpretation's Lives Matter

24. Since we know that when people are excited about something they do it repeatedly, and we have repeatedly proven that the majority is always wrong, from this we can conclude the majority is highly excited to be wrong.

3. Sometimes Everything You Think Is Wrong

1. Prove where it's written that karma gave anyone any permission to do it's job for it at any point in time in any universe for any reason. Proof must be submitted in writing in at least three languages. If we can't do this, then we know that karma will strike the assailant instead.

- Sometimes Everything You Karma Is Your Own

2. It's amusing to watch people who never saw the crime pretend they know everything about it. Lawyers do this as well as judges or juries. So why are people who never saw the crime more reliable than the ones who were there? As we can clearly now see, if we weren't at the crime watching it, *we* are the ones who are unreliable. And this all now helps prove that sometimes everything you think is wrong.

3. Our relationship with everything around us isn't what we think it is.

Proof: Most things around us, including people, have no idea who or what we are. If there isn't an understanding in both directions, the relationship is only one way, which experience proves doesn't work well or doesn't last long.

Further Proof: Ask it if it knows who or what we are. When it doesn't respond, we have our answer.

4. Absolute self-sufficiency is a lie.

Proof: It imagines the entire universe was created by the self and nothing other than self is needed for anything. The opposite of self-sufficiency is not dependency, but rather respect for one's surroundings. We use language without depending on it, otherwise there would never be any silence. Language was not created by any one person and amoebas don't have one. If we cannot possibly have a circumspect perspective, then we also cannot be self-sufficient since the part we miss is what we don't have, generating a self-insufficiency. One day, we discover that what we have is entirely insufficient for whatever is in front of us. This happens daily to everyone, so therefore, no one ever is entirely self-sufficient.

5. Since we have seen that no one is perfect, and that nothing is true all the time, then this applies to all beliefs. Since this means that every belief is wrong at some point, and we know this applies to everything in our heads, then this becomes one of those moments when sometimes everything you think is wrong.

6. If we were actually as smart as we think we are, it wouldn't matter who lies and no one would act on any lie ever. There would be no need to curb delusional behavior since no one would have any.

"But groups of deceivers would still pay others to act on their lies even as they do today."

Yes, but since no one would believe them, no one other than that small group would be acting on it and the larger group would be laughing at them for being slaves to money and ignorance, even as smaller groups do today at the larger groups. These are now expanding alarmingly while being paid to spread lies and highly visible rewrites of history easily deflated by logic taught in kindergarten math, studying the actual history for more than three seconds, or getting past the first chapter of any book on any subject we could name.

"How can we actually be as smart as we think we are, or really be more advanced than previous societies throughout history, instead of hypnotizing ourselves with endlessly repeated lies to the contrary which place former ages beneath us, inflate our egos, and feebly attempt to stem the downward rush of our vacuous self-worth?"

By realizing that we're not and that sometimes everything you think is wrong.

7. a. It is impossible to prove anything to people who require proof for everything. "Prove all things" doesn't mean to prove everything in existence, otherwise we should be wasting time proving the proof or

245

proving the need for ignorance or every unwise decision to be a vital necessity.

Reason: Proof for everything is a requirement of idiots.

Proof: Proof for anything from which there is no substantial gain is not a requirement.

b. Unfortunately for infants and whiners, when a message is interrupted, whether we hear it or not afterwards, we are responsible for the entire message.

- The Disruptive, Ill-mannered Lawyer

8. Even though every article or book about either memory or the brain wastes no time stating that no scientist in existence really knows how the brain works or what makes it function, the educational system appears to hold the opposite view.

Proof: They only use a handful of techniques to build memories, if not just one or two. If they truly thought they had no clue about how the brain works, they would try *hundreds* of techniques.

9. In math, if we get one part of the process wrong, the answer is wrong. Imagine if we have misdefined a word (which some dictionaries do) and used that to make an assessment about ourselves or others. Or could makeup make us more attractive if we used the incorrectly defined, sometimes conversely defined words as taught in some college classes to arrive at any conclusion about anything? Furthermore, we may consider why we would think we know the entirety of an event, but have no idea what happened in the mock trial, or that the mock trial and the real were reversed in meaning and sentencing. If we don't ponder these things, we will soon be pondering why sometimes everything you think is wrong.

10. Since most don't make it in the end, which regardless of belief, the amount of supporting evidence is overwhelming, this only means one thing: That most of the things that happen to us and around us have no meaning, not as addressing the ultimate sense which usually does, but only as found in the original intent and/or what we may think it means. It means that due to this one thing, everything that happens may mean something entirely different, widely separated, and even opposite of what we may have supposed it to mean. Because this one

thing, which is also one of the main causes for it's nearly 99% failure rate, is the fact that in most cases, we have been

- Judged By Dead People

11. Soon, [Piss & Moan] will be offered as a degree at the highest universities, to go along with [Point Missing], [Gainsaying], and [Lie Swallowing] already offered.

12. When baffled by large ideas. Pull out just one sentence, then meditate on it for about five minutes. Often the "big idea" impression will be discovered to only be an illusion. Many times, the block is seen to be just one or two words, which after looking up, the entire picture becomes clear. No decades of study required. Unless it's written in Latin, then even Spanish speakers have no clue what it is.

- Boiled Noodles

13. On occasion, we may admit to gross stupidity. We could live for over four billion years trying very hard and never be as stupid as we are now.

- Huh?

14. Sometimes, when people say, "I don't agree," it means they don't understand. Having said this, I don't entirely agree with this perspective.

- Disagreeable Denouement

15. The term "conspiracy theory" implies there are no conspiracies ever anywhere on the planet at any time in history. This is itself not only one of the largest conspiracy theories, but it's also unprovable. Are we still so sure we don't support any known conspiracy theories?

16. Say it with me: My ideas are beautiful!

My ideas are wonderful!

My ideas are fantastic!

- Unless They Suck

17. Before we didn't see how lynch mobs could form,

Now we do.

Before we couldn't see which party would form them,

Now we can.

Facts become expendable if they don't conform to our confirmation bias.

When ideologues become greater than human life, we know once again we're at that point when sometimes everything you think is wrong.

18. For those who feel that a copy is somehow a diminishment from the original, I have some seriously bad news.

Proof of the bad news: Every book is only a copy of the printing press that made it. So everything you ever read in your entire life was only a copy. Same goes for handwriting: It's a copy of the idea from the head of the one who penned it.

- Drown In Your Sorrow

19. Know ourselves so that we may know more for ourselves.

If we are part of the growing number who believe that absolutely nothing amounts to proof, not knowing this about ourselves will be why nearly everything we think will be wrong and why we arrive absolutely nowhere most of the time.

"Nothing could be more beneficial for even the most zealous searcher for knowledge than his being in fact most learned in that very ignorance which is peculiarly his own; and the better a man will have known his own ignorance, the greater his learning will be."[27]

7. BELIEVE THE LIE

Beloved, believe not every spirit, but try the spirits whether they are of God: because many false prophets are gone out into the world.[28]

1. Generalized Lying

1. An effect with no cause is neither provable nor scientific. Yet all such objections that there can be stem from the question of whether we or someone else will make our decisions for us. Proving what's around us is our job, not someone else's.

2. Believing everything we hear is the first step toward insanity. We might not disagree about the fundaments, but the qualifiers. Sometimes the qualifiers are themselves fundaments.

- Instructions for Brain Warping

3. The art of fiction is an accepted deception. The actors are pliable, only capable of a flat iron press by use of clumsy and false opinions. We only think we know what we see in them, because they appear in boxes of plastic, metal, and glass as solids; humans moving through time and space. But in reality, we don't know what we are seeing in them. Who do we really see or hear? We can't say, because the best actors are of greater malleability than a pool of fresh silver; and the images they create have no greater substance than the initial idea.

- What We See Isn't

4. If we apply the standard 3% margin of error across the board, that means 3% of all the lies are true and vice versa.

5. Believing something and doing something based on that belief are not at all the same thing.

6. Truth is cruel. Facts are harsh. Reality is unforgiving. Chance doesn't care whether we exist or not. So we lie to ourselves and avoid the truth at all costs so we may have a life free from harsh cruelty. Most do this.

7. When enough people believe strongly about something that isn't true, a large section of reality is created that isn't true.

8. We don't need to prove to ourselves whatever we saw that has happened. When we don't care what others think, we don't need to prove what we saw to them either. We can't prove that something didn't happen when in fact it did, since such "proof" would only be a lie in reality. What needs to be done in most cases is to prove that the event or words *didn't* happen. Anyone who wasn't at the event has no ability to prove anything about it - *ever*.

Most admit there is no value in caring about what others think. There is no proof to the contrary. Therefore, we may always say, and always should say: "I don't need to prove a damn thing to anyone." If we believe otherwise, then we believe the lie.

9. Both the thief and the tax collector attempt to get us to believe that giving them money is in our best interest and that we should give as much as possible. This is why there is often little to no difference between the two and history lumps them amongst the undesirables. Unlike the publican, the thief doesn't return later to render a future service other than to steal something else.

10. collude - *to act together through secret understanding.*[29] This describes the actions of every lawyer with their client. Both sides strategize about how to successfully prosecute the case. The degree of evil implied by the word depends on the facts surrounding which side performed the most, or greater degree of crimes. Too often, judges reward the wrong side for colluding. This happens since there are more laws protecting criminals than there are to protect their victims. By exercising fear of harming people who too often aren't innocent, we punish the victims of crimes who actually are by providing them with little to absolutely no protection. This is advanced and scientific.

11. Some like to talk face to face instead of reading what is on someone else's mind so they can interrupt and ignore everything that comes out of the face and pretend they have "communicated."

12. We call other people liars for absolutely no reason whatsoever not to reduce our responsibilities, since this is a static value, but to reduce our personal awareness of our responsibilities in a typically successful

act of self-delusion. For that of which we are blissfully unaware, can we have any responsibility whatsoever?

13. Lies are a common tool used to polarize. Polarizing is needed to gather people for our cause. This only works on a group with low or no education. Education only happens when we refuse to believe the lie.

14. If understanding is light, then confusion is darkness. Lies are a source through which darkness spreads. Those who willingly believe lies have blinded themselves; too often this is permanent.

15. Far too many fully believe in imaginary unforgivable sins which they place in the debt records of others, meanwhile imagining that God will fully relieve them of their own which are quite real. Among the greater is this very thing itself: playing God by assigning guilt and debt to others while excusing themselves when God had no part, nor was ever even asked to be, in either verdict.

16. There is one statement above others that nearly everyone believes as soon as they hear it. It is never questioned. No proof of its truth is ever demanded by anyone - no officer, no journalist, no lawyer, no judge, no faction. The existence of this is a large problem and has caused cases to fail in the past. It's surprising that so much trouble comes from only three words - "I was lying."

Not one person ever thinks the obvious question: If they were lying before, how do we know that this statement isn't also a lie? Yet so many imagine themselves to have supreme intelligence and that every particle of their belief system is 100% truth - never questioning themselves.

- Believe the Lie (Now You Know You Did)

17. In reality, there are three kinds of things:

1. Things that are true.

2. Things that are lies.

3. Things that make no difference.

Proof: 1. To say this is correct would be true.

2. To say this is incorrect would be a lie.

3. Whether you agree or disagree makes absolutely no difference.

18. In truth, nothing outside of yourself is provable, but must be taken 100% on faith in the written or spoken word of whoever. So,

events we haven't personally seen take a back seat to the ones that we have. It doesn't mean we don't care about whatever it is, it's just that we can't do anything about something we can't prove, should we even want to.

People are so obsessed with lying to themselves and everyone around them there's no way to tell to what degree they're operating under any deception. Too often this deception is intentional - they know exactly what they're doing. There are few who care or fight this. We've advanced to the point, it's unclear how long ago, to where many deceptions are both reasonable and believable. That criminals should have more rights than the victims doesn't fall in this category, yet millions believe this. The time has never been greater to judge ourselves (check every belief in our system), but most would rather believe the lie.

19. Reasonable Doubt Dilemma: In the absolute sense, reasonable doubt cannot always be generated, since it either exists or it doesn't. But, a sufficiently high intelligence can cause a sufficiently low intelligence to experience reasonable doubt when in fact there is none. Any sufficiently high intellect will see whether the doubt is true or contrived in each case. Where we begin to experience false reasonable doubt is the precise point that we decide to believe the lie.

20. If what takes longer than five words to explain is a lie or can't be true, then all college professors lie and every college textbook is unreliable. Every course split into more than one semester is then an even a larger lie, and should be rejected. If people getting interrupted five words into their explanation is behavior A and college courses are behavior B, and the interruption is C, this goes a long way to explain why most people hate math. Since adding AC + BnotC = a contradiction, the realization of this would require either A, B or C to change. But since C is a massive, nearly global addiction unrecognized or treated by the psychiatric community, it's far easier to continue to hate math and believe the lie.

21. What if our reaction is what we decided to have? It was.

What if our neglect to consider this prevented us from seeing we could change our reaction? It did.

What if everyone else doing the same thing made us mistakenly believe we were right? They did.

What if we, after developing a decades-long habit of choosing bad reactions, habitually blamed others for their beliefs or actions when in fact there was essentially nothing wrong with them? We did.

What if we, after blaming others for feeling nothing for so many decades, have now subconsciously done the same thing, following their actions which we claim to hate, and now feel nothing about any of this ourselves? We did and we don't.

22. Any time a sentence begins with "Are you trying to say....?", we know one thing for certain: the person asking this question has no attention span, hasn't been paying attention to the theme or topic of the conversation, isn't interested in the truth and is trying to confuse the issue. Usually this is for no reason whatsoever, but sometimes there are ulterior motives of hiding some type of corruption.

23. To not correctly interpret the words of habitual liars is the path to suicide.

24. A blind person, a lawyer, or a corrupt judge would tell Euclid he hasn't proven anything.

25. Most deceptions have this quality: a concealment of the mean and the extreme.

26. If life appears from nowhere, and nowhere exists on every planet in our solar system, and if life sustaining planets can appear out of nowhere, and billions of years are required for life to appear out of nowhere, and each planet has allegedly (with no supporting video tape evidence) been here for billions of years, it's not at all believable that only one out of twelve or more original planets (Vulcan, asteroid belt, and planet X either were or are still planets, and there are planets beyond X, and recent studies have revealed even more than this) appeared with both life sustaining ability and life on the exact same planet.

Neither is it believable that no other planet would have life sustaining ability since all have survived billions of years of existence. It is neither probable, nor believable. Believing any of this requires a larger degree of faith than most other belief systems. "It just is" is not a scientific explanation. And since all of this contradicts the law of cause and effect, teaching that any of this is factual is a bald-faced lie.

27. One of the first things, among many, people do after they die is, as we might expect, that they're surprised they're still aware of anything since most of their lives they were taught that death is final. This then turns to anger at those who lied to them about it, but it quickly fades and is replaced with a greater concern.

28. We enjoy forcing others to be flexible so they'll flexibly accept our inflexibility.

29. The difficulty with training any followers that the truth only comes from one source, a flaw of not just a small number of organizations, is that:

1. they won't look for truth anywhere else,
2. they won't think truth can exist outside that particular building,
3. they won't learn they can discover the truth by themselves,
4. they will never believe the truth can find them.

This is both known by and the purpose of the deceiver.

30. The scornful think unbelief is a super-power while applying full faith and credit to everything they think.

31. We believe whatever we want. If we care about caution, safety, or our future, we don't.

32. Since everything only depends on how things are interpreted, this means that all science is based only on the scientist who had the most money and was able to secure the best lawyers to correctly "interpret" their theories and distribute the "correct" results to the scientific community and educators. They spent long hours debating over the most "accurate" interpretation of whatever was in front of them and laboriously defending it against their opponents for decades. Which means that possibly all science is based on lies and rhetoric, not reality. We can say this only because you can believe whatever you want.

33. The more intelligent the liar, the more believable the lie. Trust will be the first thing they try to establish, so we may not presume the normal "judge of character" tests will see through this. They work long hours and are paid well to lie as much as they do. Their backers only pay for the best, so doing no research at all is a good way to have them

eventually take everything we have and kill us one day. Don't believe this? Do nothing, take a chance, and find out.

34. What if others weren't what they appear to be, but are only so because that's what we think they are? What if psychics knew what we expect from others and decided to give us what we wanted? We should expect this would produce greater control over thoughts and engender more responsibility. But in a few brief, personal experiments, what was generated wasn't more control or responsibility, only hundreds of more excuses. This is why in the absolute sense we aren't obligated to follow the common understanding of

- Giving The Audience What They Want

35. Facts will never obtain any interest to liars. That's how we may tell who they are. So, we can remain positive when people ignore facts in front of our faces. We now know exactly who we're talking to. Also, one piece of information that's true taken out of the context of the entire series *does not* equal a fact.

36. Many today believe that without any kind of physical evidence, nothing is provable. Something was written around 300 B.C. that disproves this. All thirteen books of Euclid have no physical evidence whatsoever. Unless oral or written testimony is physical evidence (and it is, but it isn't considered to be such by many today), then Euclid provides no physical evidence for any of his hundreds of propositions. There is no dead body, no smoking gun, no bloody knife full of spider's fingerprints, no suicide note, nothing. Yet every proposition is entirely proven with perfect finesse and clarity. So, if we think nothing can be proven without physical evidence, we're not only obvious, but are among the majority today who believe the lie.

37. I first learned about victim-blaming in a court of law. I also learned when they say "tell the whole truth" that this is the reverse of what they actually mean.

Proof: 1. By refusing to arrive at the correct question, the truth is necessarily avoided. The usual approach to this problem is pure apathy and being oblivious to any existence of the concern for truth, whether by feint or pure ignorance.

257

2. By mischaracterizing the answer the truth is purposefully avoided. Attempting to define the question so the answer is accurate isn't philosophy, which was one of the many false accusations at the time, it's accuracy in truth. This shouldn't be any obstacle, since it is what was stated to be the purpose from the outset.

3. Interruptions. Enough has been said about this already. So I will intentionally interrupt this proof. What hasn't been said is that this is a highly effectual, intensely offensive method of obstructing the truth and is in many cases a form of mind control.

Proof: The aggressiveness of the interruption is intended to make the person who knows the truth fly into a flight mode where the entire subject and even the surroundings are entirely forgotten in an attempt to avoid any further conflict. In too many cases, the fear for their lives is very real and not at all imaginary. So effectual is it, that it's used almost exclusively above any other tactic by the majority.

So, when one of these three methods, apathy applied to arriving at the correct question, mischaracterizing the answer, interruptions, or any other methods of avoiding the truth is granted sanction by the judge, the victim is blamed and sentenced. This occurs by the victim being forced to live the rest of their lives with no justice performed whatsoever and supposedly only themselves to blame for it.

Luckily this isn't the case of the matter at all as it stands in reality and only exists in the minds of those who worship and love nothing more than to believe the lie.

38. What is the grand attracting force which makes ignorance so irresistibly appealing that nearly everyone today is mawkishly addicted to it to the extent that they become violent and kill people if they are forced to face the idea that they can no longer have the same amount of lies they had yesterday? They may not now have the same lies that were believed by all, so lower popularity or fame for believing them, nor the same amount they can force down their own throats. What is one, among many, of the key elements?

"It puts the ignorance on its skin
Or it will find it's wrong again."

39. A form of mysticism is to deny that any crimes are happening anywhere in hopes that this will stave them away from our particular existence. It's neither true, nor provable that this works. Law of attraction is real, but doesn't extend to delusions, wishes, or fantasies when applied to imagining away reality that's already happened. But in this we are free, since it only hurts most the ones who do it, to believe the lie.

40. Since we can interpret things any way we please, when considering a relationship between any two things, is this a quality or a quantity? If only a quality, how many connections are required to establish a basis? If only a quantity, how do we improve the quality of it?

41. Today, people religiously believe more lies in one second than billions of people living five thousand years ago did over the course of one thousand years cumulatively. Since they are their own demonstration, no proof is needed here.

42. Prior to Christmas Eve, there is Christmas Eve's Eve. Around twelve thousand years ago, no one knew there would ever be a Christmas Eve's Eve, so they did nothing. In the future, the psychics from that era will be separated and severely slapped for not warning anyone about what they all knew needed to be done today. If we had only prepared yesterday for what we knew we had to do today, no one would ever need to be psychic or slapped.

43. The popular concept of "deserve" or "karma" doesn't work the way most believe because of free will. Others can give us what we either do or don't deserve regardless of the facts in any situation. This is why some people hate the idea of free will, because very often what is deserved is ignored and the opposite happens whether the result is good or bad. If they can't get us to be like them and believe that their concept of just deserts is reality, they try to attack free will by saying we have no choice but to accept the karmic desserts. This is done so that after we find out (if we accede to their argument) that karma does exist, at least some of their hyper-inflated, hate-powered, intended misery will spread to us.

Consequences are not deserts, but are rather a natural reaction. Rape victims don't deserve to be harassed for over fifty years by anyone, regardless of any excuses to the contrary, but this happens far too often.

Border patrol agents don't deserve to be murdered for doing their job. They don't deserve to be called liars by people insisting that their murder never happened simply because the news of the event of their death isn't adequately covered by media sources that are paid by drug cartels to not report it. Drug cartels don't deserve to have as many people working for them for free as they do today by pretending they don't exist, that the entire problem isn't there at all, and it's only a politically motivated creation with no basis in reality.

But consequences are different. We may believe our car is made of ice and try to drive into a volcano, and we will still be dead when it's all over. What we think or believe doesn't change reality, but quite the opposite over the course of five hundred years:

- Reality Will Change What You Believe

44. Constantly leaning in one direction is a bias. Constantly hating the opposing team is a game. Doing both while counting the truth irrelevant is suicide. The way to enforce all of this is to believe the lie.

45. When we entertain any opinion, knee-jerk or otherwise, we bend all the powers of our senses to destroy the quality of whatever we're observing to such an extent that we may continue to disapprove with guilt-free abandon and even conscript others to the cause. Here a study of causal chains would be a valuable docent.

46. Whenever the mob is convinced of x, y, or z, its perception is so skewed, even if only slightly, imperceptibly, that whatever it imagines it sees in front of it has absolutely nothing to do with reality. This is even more the case when, for over several scores of years, lies have been repeated to reinforce any jaundiced viewpoint. Their eyes will see, their ears will hear only the products of confirmation bias that have slowly bubbled to the surface from their putrid, festering, unattended belief system.

47. It may be the case that since many problems have been here for over two thousand years that we won't solve them, or maybe not. But it is *not* the case that by taking sides with whatever most definitely cannot solve, but rather does intentional harm, to any issue that we can't possibly make things any worse. It is possible from this to assess sadistic intent and proceed accordingly.

48. In myths and fables we pretend to fully understand concepts that no one has ever fully understood or even remotely collected enough interest to begin thinking about for even one second.

49. People who think controlling free speech means they're not control freaks and forcing their views down others' throats are self-deceivers.

- Art of Deception

50. Fake news on both sides is either intended to confuse the real psychics or raise the bar to produce a higher breed.

- A+ Lie Exam Certification

51. If we believe that biased opinions are always evil, then people with no education in law know more about it than those who have one, since the educated have been biased by their teachers and are therefore unreliable eyewitnesses to the inner machinations of legality. Even though this is facetious, sadly, it's also true sometimes.

Proof: Every case where the victims are punished more severely than the criminals. No person without a law degree would sanction this reverse justice, unless they too are criminals. Here, the bias of law is apparently blinding the ones familiar with it to the results of their own actions producing an effect that can't be called justice. We may not imagine that crying "we try" will save us. It's not feasible to imagine that God could be satisfied with wishes and whims since He's a "results oriented" type of person.

52. If we meet someone who knows the future, make sure to ignore everything they say. This is how we show that we love them.

- Drink Ignorance

53. If any person says or does anything wrong, nothing they say should ever be believed. This idea is almost universally accepted. Since no one is perfect, everyone either has said or done, or will say and do something wrong. When someone who has said or done something wrong says that anyone who says or does something wrong should not be believed, we may therefore immediately disbelieve it.

54. Dreams are amazing liars - our entire environment changes on a dime, yet we still think we're awake. We notice nothing out of place or cause for alarm, until we wake up.

55. Some people can call you a liar with their eyes. It's the most wonderful feeling in the world.

- Psychic Fire

56. If we believe anything to be true about anyone that is in fact a lie, we're more of a threat to that person than a friend.

- For The Record

57. If we discover our political wins and losses have become equivalent to our sense of our right to exist, we may need to examine things in more detail. When this happens, there's about a 99.9% chance that we Believe The Lie.

58. It's wonderful to be in a society that's now selling [The Straw Man] as the newest, best kid's action figure.

59. When lies are brandished to spread a corporate war of choice, eventually warriors of truth will be a barrier.

- Bruit Force

60. Swallowing too many lies has been scientifically proven to alter speech patterns. And if it hasn't, this is yet further proof that the public education system is a waste of tax dollars.

Proof: With as many people today as believe lies wholesale, the research time for this study would take mere seconds, and the benefits provided by spreading the truth about this disease would remold society. This is so because due to decomposition, standing still is moving backwards which is the same as not moving forward.

61. *"Thus saith the Lord; Cursed be the man that trusteth in man, and maketh flesh his arm, and whose heart departeth from the Lord."* [30]

So today they're angry that we no longer trust them, or they're just realizing that we never did to begin with? At least the light is beginning to dawn on them. Waiting over twenty-five hundred years to pick up a book and read it doesn't look very good for any who claim to be supremely intelligent.

62. "You can't believe everything you read" is something that you just read.

63. It is a rare sight to observe either party talking about human trafficking. So, any party suddenly pretending to care about children points directly to ulterior motives and as such isn't believable. The same

is true for those endlessly discussing global warming, but never once mentioning the great pacific trash heap: a pointer vectoring directly at ulterior motives. When our stock and trade is ulterior motives, why feign surprise when everyone ignores us?

What can we evidentially infer from these things? In the case of sex trafficking, it becomes alarming. Not discussing an obvious problem can indicate:

1. The people refusing to speak of it have family members either kidnapped or under threat of death if they do mention it, and/or

2. They're being paid by the sex traffickers to keep silent about it.

This is bad enough when it's a regular civilian, but far worse when it's *every single* public official, of whom we hear only a handful even barely mention the subject today. Only one is now mentioning it repeatedly.

But we may feel free to keep opposing those speaking out against this, then think that anyone is going to support or believe us about anything. Our disappointment will be sad, prodigiously large, and richly deserved.

64. After removing a sufficient amount of insight, whatever was said wasn't.

- Ignore Reality

65. Why are so many upset? Because compulsive liars and control freaks lose their minds when no one is believing their lies anymore. In today's society, these are not classified as mentally insane, even though they are, and societies of the future *will* classify them and treat them as such after sufficient research mounts to prove their deleterious societal impact. Their earmark is the non-stop insistence about the low education of their opponents and no actual argument strategies at all to sell their shams, but rather a consistent stream of mendacious, slanderous ad hominems.

All real argument strategies are shelved since they have no truth in their rotund pouch of products sold to the gullible. The gullible, starving for any available confirmation bias to shore up their illusory view of reality, are quick to purchase the lies sold by these dime-store hucksters, many of whom know precisely what they're doing, how to do it, and how to get the most money from it, which is more the actual reason than shoring up Utopian fantasy worlds. Ask them to solve any real crimes, and none can be located for the task anywhere on the surface of the earth, Moon, or Mars.

66. If we wish death on anyone, our future isn't what we imagine, no matter how many churches we were baptized in.

67. We see things in fictional movies and we believe them since the movie proved that they actually happened. This adequately prepares us for real life, so that when we see anything, we can say we don't believe it since life didn't prove that it actually happened.

68. If it is true that everything is subjective, i.e., that it can only be seen from the inside, then tanks of toxic gas, dryers, and rocket engines can only be seen or understood from the inside. So we have to climb in and turn them on to really understand them. Similarly for Jupiter and the sun, we must stand directly in the center of each one these to fully understand them, otherwise we can know nothing about them with certainty. From this we can see that it isn't the case that "everything is subjective," but rather, it is the case that

- [Every Man Is Deceptive]

2. The Unbribable Truth

1. When we say we have seen something, yet another person says they don't believe it, if what we have said is true, they have falsely accused us of lying. The onus probandi is always on the accuser to prove the accusation to be true, never the reverse. False Accusation Syndrome is a fatal disease that claims billions of lives as they spin webs of lies into a universe of illusions far from reality to the point where their minds are unrecoverable. This remains so until they wake up and realize they've been dead the entire time they thought they were alive. Those addicted to false accusations rarely recover and should always be considered to be the danger that they are in reality, since their lies are believable and spread rapidly, killing billions every 500 years or so. Since few ever really know what is right in front of their faces, it's difficult to tell when this is happening. The best way is to choose carefully who we decide to call a liar with our unbelief. Calling any victim a liar has never been found to have no consequences whatsoever. Some of these consequences will land approximately 16.5 trillion years from now.

2. Too often, when people clamor and yell for proof or evidence of anything, they already have the proof and it has been in front of their face the entire time.

3. Since both sides can be bought, the center is the safest position with regards to the great assize.

4. Only worry about the truth, since logically, everything else is irrelevant.

5. Choosing a side involves the least responsibility. More is carried by locating the truth that always lies somewhere between.

3. Chunk Drenched Skeptic Retch

1. People who say there's no God because we can't see Him sound like people who say there's no wind because we can't see oxygen or nitrogen.

2. Lessons in any story are now lost in the overwhelmingly greater number of criticisms against it.

3. Why is it important to take people's word without evidence that what they say is true? Why should we train our minds to this level of discernment? Or should skepticism become the universal religion that it appears to be forming today?

Because when we don't, if everything we've said up to this point is true, if like attracts like and what we fear shall be visited soon upon us as we entertain the fears, if we truly receive what we give, then sending out a signal that we don't take anyone's word for what they have said is the truth will not have a return that we will want when it arrives. It is saying that no one's word should be taken ever, even when what they've said is both true and provable. This is stated on the deepest levels of consciousness and in the highest courts of existence. Our wish will be granted.

Then, no one will take our word for anything ever, and the universe will fill with people like this who only lie to get what they want. Even if we never lie, since our word won't be trusted ever, no one will ever act on anything we say. It were better to stop this before it starts, begin to take people's word when they tell us what they have seen and heard, and drop the skepticism before it kills more people than it already has. So, should we believe everything, or doubt everything? There are far more than two ways to go.

- Taken At Their Word

4. Skeptics never doubt the one thing that would make any real difference in the world - themselves.

5. Projecting a negative image onto others in order to devalue them is like painting a Lamborghini to look like a Ford Pinto then trying to sell it. It is to be wondered why they never realize the Lamborghini would make much more money for them, but this rarely happens.

6. Since we know *"God is not the author of confusion"*[31] from both logic and written testimony, whenever we see doubt, aspersions, false accusations, hasty conclusions, slander, hypocrisy, and a host of other things, or in short, any questioning of everything but ourselves, we know we're looking squarely into the face of

- [Operation: Slewfoot]

7. Being believed isn't required, but being heard means something. Being ignored means something else.

8. I will become the doubt, so we can see whether we really want to buy it or not. Usually not, but still most never throw it away.

9. There will never be physical evidence for a belief. The fact that we're demanding it explains why we don't have it.

- Don't Ask

10. Giggling and tittering at reality ≠ facing it.

- Time To Grow

11. When we were younger, we didn't know we should doubt God, so we were taught to do so. Now, when we have at our disposal so many reasons to doubt provided by a wondrous, loving society filled with supreme intellect and brick bats, and yet say, "No, I'll keep my milk and meat provided by the Word," it does much more to destroy the pinions of the world than before. Fears unknown can't be overcome since they don't exist. Even though God requires no faith to exist, the pinions and structure of the world do, and doubt destroys those when applied to them as much as it does faith.

- Forcing Doubt To Destroy Itself

12. There is one thing to which skeptics always apply full faith and credit: Every single doubt they construct.

4. What You Believe
Can Kill People

1. *"Beloved, believe not every spirit"* [32]
From this we may see how that any person or group who recommends not to read these words, even for several centuries, which was just done not that long ago, is a deceiver. This same group never admitting their deception was precisely what it was, is still in a state of ongoing deception. Whoever says the bible is a lie, by recommending that we should believe every spirit and ignore these words, is also a liar and deceiver. Whoever recommends to follow a false prophet *is* a false prophet. Whoever says that everything but this is true has added subtlety to deception. Whoever is dismissive about deception has probably already been deceived. Whoever is apathetic about this or the many thousands of other ideas in the bible has already been impregnated by the spirit of apathy.

2. Insults are only actionable when the lies contained in them can bring certain physical harm. They are not actionable for the more popular reason, that being when the insulted doesn't know who they are. This is more so the case when the insult doesn't accurately define the insulted, which is over 70% of the time. The other 30% is when it does and the insulted has yet to come to terms with it. The most popular error in this is when someone is murdered for calling someone else a name. This won't be justified either here or in the hereafter, like it or not.

3. Many have a false concept of religion in that they imagine that since God is in everything, that even inanimate objects are in love with them. But the reality is that they don't care. The stories explaining an

uncaring universe show this. They imagine their belief systems will be accepted wherever they go due to this error. Unfortunately, not only every inanimate object could care less about them or their belief systems, but also probably a few million other sentient objects as well, perhaps more. If this were understood on a larger scale, more would be more careful about the thousands of daily things they automatically accept without question as well as attempt to "prove all things" throughout every facet of their far too often dilapidated belief systems. Taking someone else's word for whatever we believe about anything, which the majority do as a sad, ubiquitous habit, is the absolute worst thing we could possible do to ourselves.

4. Fear supplies its worshipers with pseudo-intellectual reasons for its goals enough to make arguments against it appear invalid or at least questionable in order to perpetuate its existence. While appearing to have a consciousness of its own, and it almost does, it doesn't. It is only given this facade by its slavishly devout worshiping shills that sell its wares at every opportunity and kill the non-believers if they can get away with it. If not, perpetual ostracization also works for this end.

This is the phase we're now in. If what comes next is worse, yet it could indeed be much better, our survivability will be less tolerable and will also be questionable. Very little, if any of it, in either case, is acceptable in reality.

5. Any belief that kills people should be abandoned.

8. PHRIXIONAL ASSENTION

To ascend requires friction, to descend doesn't.

1. General Assent

1. What is here written is what was expected to be seen somewhere in other books, but hasn't been yet. This doesn't mean the ideas don't exist somewhere. Instead of waiting for the right time, which often never happens, we may live as if maybe there really is no tomorrow, since it's not promised to anyone. We can't say what will or won't help someone trying to find a solution. Some of the trainers even make sure that we think outside of convention, which we should agree to do, since convention is too often a source of problems.

Our minds are limitless - we can skillfully see ourselves both as part of this society and outside of it, looking back to see what we can improve. If we're trying to keep things simple, the easiest things to change will be the obvious. This requires no explanation or proof, hence will offer no friction from the resulting idea itself. The only friction remaining will come from habits, preconceived ideas, imbalanced minds, or egos. But since these conditions are mercifully not universal, it remains a possibility that someone, somewhere will be able to use the solutions.

2. Friction is used to gain traction to provide any object or idea with the ability to travel from point A to point B. Since change is necessary in many occasions, so also is friction, disproving those who say, "friction never accomplishes anything." Some of the time, the changes are irrelevant and fall under the category of "free will." (Flossing your toes, putting ketchup on ice cream, whether to eat spam or bacon, etc.) But other times, it is necessary to prove that a shift from A to B is necessary. When this can't be proven, the applied friction should be dropped until such proof arrives. Often in these cases, people think they don't have to

prove anything when in fact they do, especially when it matters. Aside from the known command to "prove all things."

3. Since lies aren't critical, it doesn't matter when we tell the truth. If lies were as critical as some believe them to be, we would be able to hear a lie as soon as we read or hear it. Since we can't, it's obvious that lies aren't really a major concern. (T/F)

The quick answer to any issue, though convenient, only offers short term solutions, if even that. The long answer requires several processes and large doses of time, but provides long term solutions. Today's society only knows the quick answer, so the problems exponentiate.

4. Upon review, the books which many have trouble understanding were written by dead people. The dead don't write as well for some reason. They may be educated in something, but they're not aware of (or don't care) what communicates a message and what doesn't.

5. Equality and Uniqueness (speciality) are two opposing qualities. We cannot have both. If we would be equal, we are not unique. If we would be unique, we are unequal to anything else in the world.

6. All joking aside, today we should attend to a severe disease that has afflicted every human since time began. The name of the disease is NLBYDFLI.

This all-too-common affliction has been responsible for reducing the forward movement of mankind with backward-progressions and devolutionary trends such as bureaucracy and witch hunts. But it is treatable. Unfortunately most who receive treatment (which is surprisingly cost-free and self-applied) lapse back into an even worse condition of NLBYDFLI than they had previously. The notable characteristic of NLBYDFLI is standing stock still and not moving even when they're on fire, almost resembling the behavior of a large rock. Help raise awareness and stamp out this often fatal, catastrophic disease: NLBYDFLI (Not Listening Because You Don't Feel Like It).

7. When people always do the opposite of what they say they will, we can't speak to them normally, but must speak to them in opposites. Otherwise they will hear what we're saying.

8. The dissenters are majority blind and deaf. The acceptors are their victims. Ignorance and irresponsibility say there is nothing to dissent or accept.

9. Don't be mad at the partner who isn't perfect. Be mad at the mindless who told you they should be.

10. Everyone wants me to see things from their perspective. Wait till you see it from mine.

11. In some cases, the current abuser is merely a continuing extension of the original. Far too often the former is being paid by the latter using some type of currency.

12. What many truly want doesn't exist in one person. It exists in a society that isn't here yet.

13. The few people in charge imagine themselves incapable of miscalculation. If true, this is their first miscalculation.

14. It is possible that when the innocent stop feeling guilty, the guilty will stop feeling innocent. But this is a decision.

15. Not only will something change once the mind is able to *"correlate all its parts"*$_{33}$ (if that ever happens), but once anyone begins to correlate all the subjects in existence something else will change. Mostly shock at the number of wrong assumptions. There is a relation between what changes, the lack of correlation, what doesn't change, and the false assumptions.

16. Since many things both in life and the sciences travel in circles, we've probably already seen the solution to every problem we'll ever face. We just haven't recognized it for what it is.

17. Fire only touches things that can burn. To not allow others to touch us, we must become something that can't burn. We must become something that doesn't react - something that doesn't fume - that doesn't ignite into a blaze of fury. Something that waits patiently for the fire to pass overhead and is aware of what it is in itself, what it must become.

18. What's fun about changing our own behavior is we get to see someone actually doing what we asked them to do. This rare sight may happen only a few moments in a lifetime, but it's still an amazing view of global latent potential.

19. Lies make euphemisms into an oxymoron. Euphemisms maintain a silent purpose of protecting the delicate ego from either bruising or the mind-shattering pain of recognizing itself, and as such appear as a friend while the lies prove that they aren't. It is impossible for genuine concern to exist in the heart of a deceiver. Some are self-contained oxymorons since many euphemisms are themselves lies.

20. If we have no clear idea about what it is, we may not freely speculate about what it isn't. When this becomes important:

a. We may not speculate that it is not our responsibility.

b. We may not speculate that it is not in our future.

c. We may not speculate that we had nothing to do with its existence.

21. Hypersensitivity can be a sign of boredom.

22. Universal forgiveness is imaginary. Unlike math, the term *imaginary* can't be used in any spiritual setting or doctrine in the same way as math uses it. Any attempt to force things to have a meaning when they don't in reality will have only succeeded in creating a false religion. Only pure religion deals with reality. False religions are imaginary, not in that they don't exist, but create billions of people who believe billions of things that don't exist.

23. One of the biggest obstacles to progression, be it relationships, education, company expansion, or the spin of the earth, is this: Saying it is when it isn't.

24. When someone doesn't explain something, neither will they.

25. Arguments are not invalidated, but red herrings are validated and pursued through the eons, by spelling or grammatical errors.

- Give Ignorance the Time of Day

26. Defending, understanding, or believing any position can be three separate things altogether. But, if we never try to understand positions we don't believe, we probably have no real concept of the ones we think we do. The only way to really understand positions we don't believe is to defend them against an opponent. If we can't find willing participants, make use of all the free ones that aren't. The ones who aren't our friends won't care what we believe anyway. If they're really our friend and really want to know, they'll ask us what we really believe if they're not sure.

27. A word that describes what we are has no power to stop us from moving on to become something different, unless we say so. In that case, it still isn't the word that is stopping us.

- Euphemisms Are a Backdoor to Insanity

28. There was once a person who had a concert in the back forty. The person was a child who could actually read minds, not like the fake psychics who serve mammon. The child saw that the greatest change would happen by showing the audience their deepest fear so they could move past it to an idea that would actually be worth having. So, he told them what their greatest fear was. Being confronted with such an accurate representation of themselves, they were given an unique opportunity to remove something from their lives that they didn't need. They then made the only possible choice in the universe when it presents a fork in the road - They killed him.

Delusions arrive from ideation with inadequate delimiters.

- For Those Who Cower In The Vagaries

29. People are seen to say words with the letter "o" in them. But their mouth is crooked and it crimps and screams, it chorzles and crabbles the "O" to the point where it shouldn't sound like an "O" anymore by all the laws of physics. However, the tone doesn't waver, warble, or susurr into another alphabetical element in any degree. Yet, no matter the misshapen prancings of the piehole, the "O" launches into the air perfectly unchanged by the warped, melted tool that created it. So here we see that a perfect circle actually *can* be generated by a rugose, scrimpled cave. Some contend every product of man must forever be imperfect.

- Garbled Gambridge

30. Confusion Litmus Test: If we find ourselves over-explaining the unnecessary, understating the under-explained, or barely mentioning the "sine qua non," congratulations! We're confusing the crap out of whoever we're talking or writing to!

- Public School Textbook Authors, Before Publishing Your Nonsense...

31. When someone steals good from another (we may create our own situation, there are millions), it's because they don't have any of

their own. But even after they steal good from another, they still have none, since they don't have any of their own. This is why they must steal again. And the joy they have from burning through the good of others lasts only until they inevitably face the depressing fact that they have none of their own. So they seek another victim and create thousands of excuses about why they have a right to steal from them. Again, there never is nor was any such excuse.

- None of Their Own

32. (Due to recent free speech assaults), if our mind is so composed as to be overthrown by a word, as is evidenced by our denial of free speech, then who exactly are we going to protect when words defeat us? If we can be defeated by words, then words are what will be used to remove us. We are protecting no one in reality.

33. Open-mindedness is believing we're right and they're wrong over ninety percent of the time and habitually refusing to discuss why we're wrong. The world is very open-minded. Rather, if we can't defend what we believe, then we have no clue about what it is that we believe.

34. Any information we have, taken as a set, usually trends in the direction of certain vectors. While the information can be true, the vector can be false.

35. Whenever there is a human death, a meeting of three worlds convenes to arbitrate custody of the deceased. The representatives are already in place. Eyewitnesses are also there.

36. Not all blades of grass in any yard are the same color. Finding one brown blade doesn't mean we poison the entire yard, discarding the entirety as unusable. Yet some do just this by exclusive usage of the [Brown Grass Blade Theory].

37. If we're going to have One World Order, who is the waitress and what are we all ordering?

38. Ignoring the point or blame-shifting doesn't prove that an argument is based in science. It does prove that it is based on ignoring things, which by definition is based in ignorance.

39. In order to center our minds on peace, we have to ignore the rest of the world, which creates friction rather than peace.

40. When taken for what it is and applied to what it does, we have more tools than we need to do anything we want.

41. When we treat a friend as an enemy when they are acting as a friend, we create a destructive, unnecessary friction. When we treat a friend as an enemy when they are acting as an enemy, we create a corrective, ameliorative friction. When we treat them not at all, we create nothing save possibly abandonment. But since desertion creates a vacuum, it qualifies as nothing.

42. For every statement, there are implied at least ten others. The implied statements aren't always true. Some implications are obvious, some aren't. On occasion, the combination of three obvious implications will grant one that isn't. This is how we find what was lost.

43. Often, after all the mysteries have been revealed, we are left with the realization that the best things are what we already had in our hands to begin with. The firm grasp that *"There is nothing better for a man, than that he should eat and drink, and that he should make his soul enjoy good in his labour,"*[34] "the grass is always greener," etc.

Even if ever there is something better,

It's moments are fleeting and sometimes unseating.

44. God hands us rope and scissors and watches to see if we will hang ourselves or help keep others from hanging themselves. Some throw down the rope God hands them and make their own. Others kick the scissors all over creation instead of taking the two or three days it takes to figure out how to use them. Some try to chain the ropes together to drag down many at once. A few figure out how to tie the rope to an anchor.

45. Irresponsibility and blame-shifting are an insanity no one wants to touch, since almost everyone would have to be treated.

46. People who ignore problems create them with the condoning seal of omission. Any who solve problems must be prepared to face every aspect of the problem in order to see the best possible solution. Since *"the way of a fool is right in his own eyes,"*[35] it's best to solve problems as a group. Finding people willing to sacrifice their time and energy in a world of selfish distractions is nearly impossible. In spite of this, we must continue to solve problems, despite the outcry.

47. Some have mentioned "stream of consciousness" without really saying whether this is good or bad. It could be good given today's linguistic caliber. In any speech, we should be able to track a "stream of logic" for determining the value. With this once applied, "stream of consciousness" might be preferable to today's typical dosage of the "stream of ignorance" now extant.

48. While researching something unrelated, we may see something that does. While studying something that isn't interesting, we develop something that is. By changing our opinion, this can be inverted.

49. Misery is a definite case of where like attracts like. If after collecting data for things that fall under the categories of "like attracts like" and "opposites attract" in an effort to determine what forms the dividing line between them, would it then be apparent as to which group could explain the existence of the other? In some of these results, would there be any explanation of why we all know these two opposing statements are both true, yet this point is never even popularly discussed?

50. Sometimes, when people say "work," they actually mean "not work" in the normal sense of the word. A clear mind is more capable of ideas than a mind filled with working on worrying, working on being anxious, working on frustrations, working on being manipulated by others.

Work is effort towards something. The only effort needed to clear a mind for focusing is the effort of relaxation, which isn't work in the normal sense. From one of the religions we learn an empty glass has a thousand uses; a full glass only has one. Therefore, sometimes all we need to do to work and become productive is nothing whatsoever at all.

51. When any dignitary produces a mein of respect on any given occasion, it is typically intended to prevent dishonoring the wrong spirit after a bait and switch was coaxed into reality. But if the dignitary would not have used bait and switch, they would have a larger possibility for gaining respect. Here again it is clear how we can too often be our own problem.

52. The entire universe implies an eternity of contemplation as seen from the vast complexity of its design. Whatever seems unnecessary only appears that way or isn't part of the original design.

53. People who say something intelligent don't think they know everything, nor do they care if we follow their advice or not. Because if we don't, it only hurts us, not them.

54. The mind reveals to itself only as much as it can handle via the subconscious, which has several avenues with which to communicate both to us and everyone around us. In trying to get nightmares over with more quickly, it hasn't been seen that pushing these revelations too far awards any positive affect. The subconscious is fairly accurate about the limits it chooses. Instinct speaks rarely, making getting in tune with it more difficult. But imagine the day when the messages from our instinct are clear and distinct. Instinct, or some say insight, or the art of anticipation, is a condensed message from our subconscious.

But, because the subconscious is somewhat dependent upon what it is fed by the conscious mind, in the beginning our instinct is often wrong. Marking and enjoying the moments when it's right can make it more accurate and powerful in the future. This is indeed the case in theory.

55. Things are the way they should be. If this were true in the absolute sense, change wouldn't exist. Change occurs when things *aren't* the way they should be, *and* when they are. The degree of mental aberration determines which things get changed. Control freaks make change for the sake of change which causes devolution, destruction, and senseless, reasonless frictions. Creativity and imagination change things only where the most positive effects may be garnished, where solutions to problems may be most effective. They avoid change for the sake of change, only move with careful precision, and cause evolution. There is one who governs all chance and all change.

56. Some wounds won't be healed by crossing the barrier of death. They will form a permanent reminder both of our character and our interaction with others. Past the death barrier, both mental and emotional wounds will probably also be visible. This is due to our greater power of awareness in that realm as well as the fact that in that place there will be nothing hidden. So, whether it's visible or not, the truth is here.

57. When we understand how to extrapolate, we have. Extrapolation doesn't merely apply to math, but it does. Through extrapolation, a perception may be formed which seems to carry forward in a direction, but by altering the course just out of the field of view, a deception, rather than a perception is formed. Occasionally, light will do this. However unlikely, if studied, we could avoid further clashes with any

- Field Fractured Perception Generator.

58. What we learn is heard and understood. Then what we learn is forgotten without our permission or knowledge. What we learn is remembered, but only sometimes. If we read what we have learned again, we may remember it, sometimes clearly, sometimes as a dim, fog-encrusted memory, an invisible finger on our shoulder sending a dark chill through our ribs. Sometimes we see what we have learned once again, but it has been so completely forgotten that it seems like an entirely new experience.

What is the use of a computer that has nothing on it every time we turn it on no matter how much we put on it or how many times we repeat the process? Sometimes we expect people to remember what they have learned since they should. Sometimes people expect me to remember what they do, but I don't and I smile; because I know that what we learn is never really learned.

- The Permanent Reminder

59. "Why don't you agree 100% with anyone?" asked Compy Lacent.

"There's no reason to. A better question is, Why don't I agree 100% with myself?" replied Eilyenn Ward.

"Well, yes, why then?" Dr. Lacent acceded.

"Because if I did agree 100% with myself, that would mean there's nothing left to correct, which would mean I think I'm perfect, which thought would immediately prove that I'm not," concluded patient Ward.

- Inductive Deduction

60. Each life and each person is so complex, they are an entire universe. So, when anyone asks us, "Do you believe in other universes?" we may say, "Yes." Then smile as they walk off thinking we're crazy.

61. Sometimes, instinct is an angel that we're too blind to see standing right in front of our faces.

62. Ofttimes taken for granted are the people we see alive that were prevented from death. Given how greatly our decisions, even the small ones, affect the entire world, how much worse would things be without the ones who were kept alive? From this, we see that using only our eyes and not our minds to practice clear discernment is a form of blindness, shielding our thoughts and prayers from the ones still here who would otherwise have a tombstone over their heads. And with close attention, even the ones who have passed on still speak.

- The Reality of the Situation

63. Our mistakes remind us of who we are and give us a way to break habits. Those who hate us for our mistakes reveal that they never learn from theirs and are in a refusal state of mental development. We may term these: The Mistaken.

64. Jealousy often desires the death of its object.

Jealousy is an admission of complaining about the present conditions while refusing to look for or make a better one, rather than simply accepting the conditions as they are.

Jealousy is a form of idolatry, elevating the object to a higher status than it probably deserves while threatening violence in order to obtain it. Most content themselves to a complicated system of paybacks once it has been perceived that the object is most likely entirely out of reach. From this can be seen that jealousy is one of the higher forms of ignorance, or a refusal to see the reality that no object is worth whining over, paying back anyone for, worshiping, or killing over. But consideration of this is far too complicated to worry about. If ignorance smelled as bad as it really is, everyone would now be dead.

- The Gas of Ignorance

65. Too often, the people who have done something wrong try to make the people who haven't feel guilty. We may consider this next time when deciding whether to feel bad about anything.

66. It is better to love things that provide a view to endless possibilities, which doesn't include being told to shut up or face death because we've expressed an opinion, fact, or corrective remonstrance.

67. Linear thinking is the cause of many errors, mistakes, and misunderstandings. It indicates we expect logic and reason in a universe where there's little to be had. And what is there must be sought as for hidden treasures, and remains as little likely to be found.

68. When presented with both truth and lies about the same event, object, or situation, it is up to us to find the truth about it. Dismissing the responsibility to anyone else isn't usually a healthy option, even though sometimes it's unavoidable. Refusing to arrive at a decision about it is both telling and irresponsible. It tells the most about the irresponsible.

Telling ourselves it is up to someone else to reveal the truth is the same as saying we would love to be deceived about everything in life forever and ever. Since this has been written down for over 3,473 years (8,549 if we believe in the theory of evolution), we have no excuse for doing nothing when presented with both truth and lies.

"See, I have set before thee this day life and good, and death and evil," [36]

69. Even though courts are constructed to avoid punishing the innocent as a result of taking one person's word over another, in the end, since the jury or judge takes one lawyer's word over another, that's all they wind up doing.

- Punish the Innocent

70. Spiritual blindness is difficult to detect or diagnose since:

a. We mistake physical sight for spiritual.

b. We mistake understanding things of small or no moment for larger.

c. It is only provable to the individual from the inside by recognition and admission after receiving the truth of sufficient external evidence.

- Come, Let Us Reason [37]

71. Amazing what we will do to avoid three small words. They aren't college level words, they're first grade level. We will steal, fight, lie, falsely accuse others, and kill to avoid them. We waste decades doing nothing to prove them true or false, only to find out too late they were true. The words, which have more healing than harm in them are:

- I Was Wrong.

72. It's questionable whether studying anything really helps anyone discover more about reality, since it narrows the focus to a few sets of multiply redefined words and precludes any other possible explanations or reasonings from any superior method. This creates centennial habits which future generations only laugh at, thus *reducing* the number of things we know about reality by force of direction.

73. Argument is the friction of change which applies a force to ordinarily immovable ideologies. This is why people hate it, or at least bristle at its approach. Change is one of the largest delivery systems of the unknown known to man.

74. We have long heard that "familiarity breeds contempt." This, having been proven in more than one field, then indicates that only people whom we *don't* know have the best picture of who we are. But this is wrong also, since it doesn't have any of our history which our friends or family know and have seen. So, in reality, only we know who we are since we have both pictures. But even this is blurred by that with which we're most familiar, being less blurry than with others, since few tire of themselves as quickly as do others.

This is why we ought to avoid hearing about someone through another person, since the only thing we will get is a fat lie. If the person is dead, we may read what they wrote and never read what someone else wrote about them if accuracy is a goal. Avoiding this is fine, however, for those who are in love with lies. Even better for those who love spreading lies about others. Even if people don't like lies, we may meet few, if any, who cross-reference what they hear with other people. But even this back-checking can be colored by leading questions, which most don't avoid since they aren't in a court of law where this isn't allowed. We don't ask for lies. If any volunteer them, we may cross-reference as many as we can remember. Then, put absolutely no faith whatsoever in anything we hear, unless the person is psychic. But too often, even these are wrong for extremely superficial reasons. Other methods work better.

75. At some point in the future, regardless of the outcome of any case here and now, the victims will decide the punishment of the criminals. These may entail the retracing of any events, or their inversions, or any combination thereof. They may also be repeatable. In the cases of false

accusations, both the accusers and the system which failed to notice the accusations were false will be in receipt of the punishment.

76. No two people will ever have precisely the same form of ideas or formation for each idea. This is why retributive strikes will typically fail - the second strike will not be fired from the same trajectory or motive as the first. If any element in the first is missing in the second, the entire strike is meaningless and actually counts as a first strike in a new series, which is usually an ignorant, purposeless one.

77. Being able to identify, define, or describe something is *not* equivalent to solving the problem posed by the identified object.

- Psychological Failure

78. When millions of wrong things continue to gain status as acceptable courses of action, the focus will necessarily narrow.

- Why Is Your Focus So Narrow?

79. We're in an extremely complex system. A candle destroys as it gives light, becoming involved in an exchange of matter that no instrument can adequately track, measure, document, or explain. Some of the transactions can be observed, but not every one simultaneously. Any who imagine a simple solution which barely addresses one angle of any issue could have a long-term effect are deceiving themselves. Irresponsibility uses laziness to spend next to no time to avoid solving problems which have eternal consequences, while pretending to have solved everything. Therefore:

- The Simplest Answer Is Often A Liar

80. Half-truths, euphemisms, and shifted definitions are tools of the deceiver. They enable it to both fool their audience and remove themselves from the guilt of being responsible for deception. We may say "it" since deceivers aren't human.

81. Words are the distillation of concept, idea, and/or experience. A declining number understand very much about either of the five.

82. Many are counting on failing memories to take advantage of the people who have them. This is done nearly automatically while not considering that if there was no initial offense, they will be setting themselves up for a future they will neither want nor be able to handle. They also have failed to consider that after death,

- The Memory Returns.

83. Many enjoy feeling every possible way imaginable - guilt, tears, smiles - except the way that leads to change.

84. We are all blinded by the limitation of being restricted only to what we can see. When this stops, we will wish our behavior in most cases was one-hundred and eighty degrees from what it now is. Imagination, creativity, and understanding are the only ways to fight this blindness.

85. You are yourself. You see this. You see other selves that aren't yours. You see other selves standing in your way in every direction you are trying to go. You see yourself. You also see that you are standing in your way in every direction you are trying to go. You are yourself.

- Scopophobia

86. Considering the end, we may reasonably expect there to be some type of end when either few or no one is trying or even pretending to attempt to determine the message that comes with every series of words. As time passes, more are acquiring degrees in Missing the Point and Ignoring the Subject. This is considered by most to be appropriate. When no one cares what anyone else is saying, we can expect something to end. One of the first things that can end is our relationship with those people.

- The Finish Shall Beginning

87. Showing mercy to a criminal is showing hatred to their victims. We can't have it both ways.

88. Given how frequently reverse psychology works, it's possible that truth shares some of the properties of magnetism, where poles must be aligned in opposite directions in order for any connection to be established. If only there were a class called: The Magnetic Properties of Truth, we could discover the answer to this pivotal question.

89. Blaming the wrong thing involves no responsibility - blaming the right thing does. Blaming the wrong thing requires no thought, research, or conscience. Having an attitude of insouciance afterward gives the appearance of being correct. Unfortunately for the unbelievers of any of this, both have consequences - only one of them will be what is wanted or enjoyable. Time is irrelevant.

90. What if there was another dimension where the truth is visible? It could either be where a police officer takes out a pen to write down what we're saying, but he's actually taking out a rope to later hang us with in complete disregard for any truth or facts of the case, and this is acted out in the alternate dimension. Or another instance would be where it appears someone is gandering at what we have, when actually they're stealing it for themselves and this is broadcast on the nightly news in the other dimension. Or a case where someone is saying they're glad we're their friend, when actually in the other dimension, we can seem them digging a hole in their backyard to bury, forget, and ignore us. Or a scene where a politician saying they mean what they say, but in the other dimension they're laughing in our faces, telling us they hate us and don't really care if they lie to our faces or not, nor do they care if we like what they're doing with our money, nor do they respect the fact that we're writing every check they take home. Since truth is quite visible to an Almighty God, we may believe there is in fact an

- Alternate Dimension

91. Hatred comes from a type of pain. An expression of hatred isn't always exactly as described by the expresser. However, the expression is pointing to a kind of hatred. Pain comes from lack of recognition. Not all of this kind of pain stems from self-pity, though some does. Being recognized by others is unnecessary, except in an emergency, so is otherwise useless. Therefore, hatred comes from the pain of not being recognized by ourselves.

92. Through over-sanitization of any culture, society, or world, a vacuum will form. Through the haste and friction of things rushing in to fill this void, more and larger mistakes will occur than would be present by leaving the area unsanitized. This answers the questions: Why are some things here we don't want? And: Why can I never find anything after I clean up?

93. We can choose to see any idea not subjectively as our own, but as something external found through arrangement. It was always there, waiting to be seen, but can be possessed by no one. Agreement, belief, faith - these make us become part of the idea, but never make the idea

ours exclusively since others can arrive at the same terrace of reality. Only when the idea itself is sentient can it decide to become ours.

94. A mistake would be allowing the people who ignore us to prevent us from what we need to be creating.

95. Blaming others for our own guilt is an admission of a deliberate continuance of failures. But even doing this, people who aren't blind won't hate us, they only wish us to see our guilt is removable. After removing the guilt, the failures vanish.

96. The willfully blind will always ignore the real value of both words and concepts. They typically also ignore and hate both dictionaries and analogies.

97. If we're truly all equal, then we don't need a word from some authority figure before we can admit whether something is true. If we can all be whoever we are and say whatever we want, we don't need some certification to be accurate. Most of the time, these same authorities deny the one true Authority while they blind their own masses. All that is needed for either accuracy in truth, or truth in accuracy is for what we say to be correct. Anything more isn't necessary. This is mostly, but not only, because we are all equal in this aspect: If it comes down to a yes or no question, everyone is equally capable of making a mistake.

- Problems With Authority

98. Any unaddressed problem will necessarily *not* get smaller, nor will it remain the same size.

99. It is more enriching for things to be the way they are, where not everyone agrees, rather than to have a universal following of any one person or group. Non-violent disagreements are preferred. This only regards opinions or realms of the unknown, not rights violations, freedom infringements, and so forth. This way, whether we agree or not, we can say it's good. Why is this good?

Two lines starting at the same point traveling in two directions must increase in separation the further outward they travel. This represents one viewpoint, bound by it's limits on either side forming a perspective or point of view. If everyone had the same view, only what is between those two lines could ever be understood. After traveling a sufficient distance out from the center (that being when we were born), the answer to this question would eventually be

- Infinity: What Was Left Out?

100. We wonder if people suffer before they die if they're sick or about to be executed, but have no concerns for whether healthy people might possibly suffer when we say we wish to kill them or have them severely beaten simply because they don't agree with our highly enlightened, limited point of view. All points of view are limited, as just explained. Those that are about to die are actually luckier since they soon will no longer have to be sadistically assaulted by and driven to points of wondering whether to commit suicide because of our - [Limited Point of View].

101. Not considering the writings, views, studies, or opinions of others is merely another high-powered tool to limit our reality, keeping us from seeing what it really is. Interruption, evasion, euphemism, and many other forms of hatred are used to accomplish this. We think by doing this we are manipulating the world, but all we're really doing, due to the effects of prolonged refusal to see reality for what it is, is hardcore

- Living In Fantasy

102. Between this lies everything else. Between this, most minds usually rest very far from the ending, thinking they have considered everything necessary. Occasionally, there is something that comes before this. Often, there is something which follows this. There is no normal limit to the number of things to which this may be applied. This exists with or without belief. This is possibly provable. This is a large measuring spoon. This creates a photograph of unlimited detail, found when observing

- From Zero To Infinity

103. Our competitive society has indelibly trained us to believe that zero has no value. Though it may have no quantitative value, we overlook the fact that it's still a number. So, no number (zero) can still be a number. The number that has zeros in it is actually larger than the same number without them. We're trained to throw zeros away, but if we did this we would stupidly turn one million dollars into one dollar. So next time we see a person that we judge to be a zero, remember they

may just be an indicator of something larger that we haven't met yet. This something could be an idea, a person, or both.

- Brother Zero

104. We may evaluate words or music not by how it makes us feel, but by any other standard, or if possible, see it for what it is. This removes the expectation that others have to make us feel a certain way before we will consider whatever the piece is to be good, bad, or indifferent. Or we may go further and try to imagine ourselves playing or writing the same thing - could we even?

105. Many arguments stem from a blind refusal to accept things for what they are or the way they are; yet everyone says they do.

106. Words have atmospheres. Sifting through or rearranging the atmosphere can disclose the original intent or motive of the words. A qualifier for some atmospheres is power. Teachers are sometimes more familiar with the appropriate atmosphere.

107. When we're old, we try to recreate younger days. What is different? At a pure guess, does the strength provided by our growth hormones engender the free certainty that we will live forever? Through those days, we were growing so fast that time is meaningless and freedom is rather felt than a debated fancy. But hormones are just another of hundreds of chemicals driving through our bodies. So, is what we wish real, or yet another chemically based delusion?

108. From experience, life is a slow, sensitive, complicated, and delicate process. Most people don't treat it in this fashion. Expecting to have no consequences to any action isn't the best way to study or learn from this process. Understanding furthers, yet seems to be one of the slowest parts of the process. This explains much about why most put little to no effort into trying it. A several-angled approach works often, even if occasionally time consuming.

109. Not studying what we believe, not proving all things, or not examining at any length any other view than our own is a form of suicide. Being forced to watch others commit suicide is necessarily offensive. So long as these remain heedless of whom they offend, so may we. Offending for the sake of offending (a popular practice) is the same as refusing to examine beliefs.

110. If it is the case (and it is) that on some occasions "God works in mysterious ways," then the following must also be the case:

a. God is under no obligation to explain His methods to us for any reason.

b. When He does, the ways may neither make sense nor be logical.

c. Whatever methods He does employ always bring about the result He desires, or it couldn't be termed "The work of God."

d. This is not only because He is an individual, but because He is an omniscient and infinite individual.

e. The ways of God are rarely acceptable to the majority since the majority believe the exact opposite of 1-4.

f. These are some (but not the only) reasons faith is required to accept the works of God for what they are.

g. Whenever anything makes no sense, this is no proof that it isn't the work of God.

h. The doctrine that "The work of God is indestructible" is a lie. The final work of God may be, but that is a far larger issue.

111. On occasion, why crimes remain unsolved, ignoring semantics, is due to the mind's built-in protection where it erases whatever causes instability, when this function or ability exists within it. If we have no clear picture of events, there's no way to determine an appropriate solution. Forcing victims to relive the events in any way sometimes causes confabulation for the same reasons, the mind sparing itself from more unnecessary pain. Most cling to what they would like to see rather than what actually did happen regardless of the actual memories they have. Add opinions to this, to which the majority are permanently married, and you have entire groups of people traveling in the wrong direction unconcerned about the outcome hundreds of years later.

In the near future, however, each deviation from the truth will be examined and the motives for the changes which were enforced will be exposed. Many think darkness can cover them, not realizing there is something far more accurate than night-vision goggles.

112. Change is antithetical to stability. Stasis is antithetical to progress. Change must occur in any progression even when the goal could be the acquisition of stability. So, a degree of instability is required

in order for any change to occur. This is why those who promote change are labeled as pessimists, because the labelers over-inflate the instability and ignore the necessity of the progress.

113. Ofttimes, the original emotion does not fade with time. And if the circumstance is rare or a one-shot, it may move the feeling into the realm of the invaluable - or even a dream.

114. What if the number of demons released is proportional to the number of people who don't care about the crimes the demons commit?

What if our enemies aren't merely physical?

What if we're actually this responsible for our own actions?

What if the universe is actually that balanced as it is in every other field of science?

What if reversing this prevents the more powerful demons from entering?

Could we then invert the six-thousand-year-old attitude of not giving a damn unless it's something that affects us directly?

- Errors Over Balance

115. As we watch the world slowly handed over to the jealous damned who care absolutely nothing about it, all we can do is hope to remove ourselves from them long enough to be saved from the destruction they bring about by themselves. We need only one unshattered hope to stay far from the poison of mantra chanters babbling their long disproven theories like so many priests of Moloch. We hope to be far from the time when the "*elements shall melt with fervent heat.*"[38]

- Love Not The World[39]

116. Since I started studying communication when I was three, I see it fail for numerous reasons, mostly due to selfishness. That's only the *why* of the failure; more interesting is the *when*.

Some things aren't worth consideration, but this doesn't mean they can't be evaluated. Fails were seen where people shut down conversations when someone says "If this or that happens" as if they were planning on doing those things. The word "if" doesn't mean nor indicate something will be done; many times it explains why something *won't* be done. But refusing to hear the end of the sentence prevents this important fact from reaching anyone's observation. So, what is critical to look for isn't *why* someone says *if* something will occur, but *when* they say it will occur.

117. If we set as a mandate that others have to have something in common with us before we'll deign to feign any relationship with them, we've revealed that we have no capacity or willingness to accept others as they are.

- Parity of Reason

118. Page 294 won't look like any of the other pages. It has what you need to move to the pages after 294. And it's there because of what was written prior to page 294. Expecting every page to be the same is to both enforce and expect ignorance since we're all equal.

119. Sometimes when we think nothing matters anymore, we may remember something that does. When looking at some processes from the beginning to where they are now, we have to remember what people said who are no longer here, since many processes often don't make sense. Sometimes the memory of what a few important people have said will be all we have to get us through whatever is around us.

- Memory of the Few

120. The list of things we haven't done will always be worse than what we have done.

121. A part of math is that i = sq. rt. -1, which means that $i^2 = -1$. Seems to make no sense, but it is possible in math, electronics, and very likely other things. Meaning that without this equation, some things can't be explained or accurately calculated. This points (as do other arguments) to the fact that reality often makes no sense with our current level of understanding, but if humility is kept we can try to understand it anyway, and many succeed in this.

This refutes many arguments which claim that "x, y, or z" can't be the case because it doesn't make sense. Unless sufficient proof is supplied to show that it isn't, the claim remains invalid.

122. Some will have accuracy or nothing. In spite of this, it doesn't seem to depend on the accuracy, but whatever secures our highest interest, even if somewhat inaccurate, is that from which we learn the most. So, to learn faster, we may find some way to become interested in what we're doing or studying, and we'll learn more from it. Or we'll

learn the most from studying whatever we're most interested in. Many times what we're most interested in lies behind the things we never look at.

123. In physics, we discussed imagining a frictionless surface. There's no need to imagine at all. Realize that we are owed absolutely nothing and we have removed the friction through which the rest of our life will slide. Taking advantage of people who use and believe this way will do the opposite: it will create one of the most frictional surfaces imaginable.

124. Everything we see is a chemical except light. Everything we hear is caused by chemicals vibrating. Reality is there whether we study it or not. Gradients are there whether we find them or not. When we do, it helps us, not them, since their existence is immutable in many cases. We may follow their path to help ourselves. Some gradients can be shared. Other views are too complicated to be comprehended by anything other than direct experience. Any complicated involvement of stages can't be reduced to a simple sound bite for the quick digestion of the lazy. Claiming any experience doesn't exist doesn't change the availability of the experience when it does exist. It only changes us by making us less than what we could have been. Being able to prove the experience doesn't exist may change others.

125. A note found in an abandoned garden:

If you take the time to find out who I am and what I believe, you will discover that I'm nothing close to what you told yourself that I am or believe. Then you'll realize the enemy you thought I was is only yourself - your perception of me and not who I am. However, if I'm still talking to you, I'm here with you and I knew this the whole time. I was just waiting for you to wake up.

- A Friend

126. His servants have killed thousands with their apathy. Their concern for truth or any fact is effactually 0% as is their commitment to their own words. Fear is the motivator for more to follow him. No proof is possible against him since proof doesn't exist. The tears of the dead and dying aren't traceable to him. The cries of his enemies aren't heard since anything taking longer than three seconds to say isn't

comprehended. Yet each day, more followers are added to the trillions who serve, worship, pander, kiss, and marry

- The God of Convenience

127. If it's true that we can ignore our children because we always know more than they do, then since we're children of whoever wrote any book over two hundred years ago, they can ignore any complaint we have about what they wrote.

This is true for better reasons, but also because of the one under consideration. We also can't use any complaint to debate validity of, argue application of, or refuse to even bother to read what they wrote since that never works on parents. If parents are the example to follow, then we should follow it when it's a good one. If our excuses generally don't work on them, then the excuses of the entire living world won't work on anything written over two hundred years ago.

If we don't like this, then we should change what we believe or prepare to face the obvious results. There is no tie between what parents ignore and to what degree we ignore them since bad examples shouldn't be followed. The only good thing about bad examples is that they can be used to run the other way. Advice not followed never harms the one familiar with its application. So, is anyone truly respecting the elders?

128. Feelings of responsibility too often hit those the hardest that had the least to do with the problem.

129. A misunderstanding between friends is not much different from a high explosive. The end result is the same: you never see them again for the rest of your life.

- Hostile Environment

130. The Future is your Jailer. Both it, and Death catch their prey. Both place an impenetrable limit on what would otherwise be infinite. Both Dreams and Belief have long been used by many as an ineffectual method of escape. Preparation is the only way to survive

- The Prison Sentence

131. Two children, having been rewarded with a granted request after they suffered more than should have been allowed, knew fairly soon what they wanted after taking counsel on the best question to ask. So they asked to see a psychic to find out precisely when it was a

certain man's "time to go." After the request was granted and the time drew near for the man to go, the children staged the scene to appear as if he had been murdered by stress, which wasn't the case. As expected, all but those who knew the psychic spread rumors of racism and hatred as to the reasons why the man was now dead. The majority believed the lies and proceeded to harass the children till they were both over fifty years old.

This was far from good, however both knew that when it was revealed they had nothing to do with the death, but rather that it was the man's "time to go," the full weight of bringing harm, judging, and harassing the innocent would fall reflected on everyone who did so all at one time on a sudden. The full weight of each act and word would be measured and sent back to those who gave them since they were only inaccurate assessments and evil surmising from the outset.

Added to this also would be a different punishment for each second of unnecessary suffering over the last fifty years. This was all done at the request of a certain Lord to prove that it isn't up to humans to decide whether or not

 - It Was His Time To Go

132. Logos is *"the expression of an idea."*[40] Once enough words are combined to form several sentences, these words become a larger idea, but still the idea is only one. Once the ideas are applied, they can become an action or even a reaction. So then the opposite of a word would be the suppression of an idea.

Suppression is done most commonly by those who, while hearing everything quite clearly pretend to hear nothing, yet expect to be both respected, heard, and treated as adults. With an idea the size of the entire known universe (which also includes the unknown since we know there are limits beyond which we can't see), it would be rewarding to discover what exactly is the intent and content of the communication.

 - The Word

133. If anything is possible, then being wrong is also possible. Since this is the idea that is least frequented in the aggregate sum of all currently available thought processes, it is then the

 - Least Common Factor

134. The silence and/or transitions in music and other places can be thought of as a cracked mirror. In the cracks is where a problem can exist. If the crack is barely noticeable, not glaringly offensive, or painfully disjointed, the mirror is still useful.

135. There are a few things to keep in mind during the vicarious, identity-validating search. This search can happen in more cases than just once every four years:

a. There is no such thing as a perfect person.

b. Searching for a perfect person while we know there isn't one only proves the point, makes us less perfect than we could otherwise be since we have no real idea of what we're searching for, and demonstrates that perfection isn't actually our goal.

c. Those running around pointing out every flaw in sight to prove that someone isn't perfect are preaching to the choir while beating a dead horse.

d. Running around fault-finding in an attempt to look busier at finding the perfect person will have no effect on the final outcome - they won't be found.

e. Many have no clue that this is what they're doing. After reading this, we now no longer have this cloak hiding us from our self-deceiving prophecy.

f. Finding a fault in our enemy doesn't make anyone on our team perfect, only proves the point even further, and is fooling no one, except perhaps ourselves (see (e)).

g. Faults and crimes are two widely different things since there is no necessary connection between the two.

h. Perfection is a goal that usually is never reached. It can be when the proper conditions are understood, but can never be reached based on the common concept of the term even given an infinite number of eternities to do so.

i. When our carefully selected perfect person (or our self-appointed enemy's) winds up making a mistake, we may not pretend we're surprised at their imperfection - no one will believe it.

j. Bottom-feeding is not optional.

136. Most know that habits take a while to change. Those who don't may see this if they look carefully at themselves or others. Anything (organization, book, church, stray moonbeam, etc.) or anyone which expects any habit to change instantly is not only being unreasonable, but also precisely embodies why the habit won't change faster than it otherwise could. Many of these kinds of barriers have been applied to those trying to change their habits both in life and fictional stories and we may well wonder why they would rather be part of the problem than part of the solution.

Often the right things happen, granted, but too often they don't. Instant changes not only require the highest degree of work applied, but also create the most friction, which may create more problems through mishandling than there were to begin with. Allowing things to change at their own pace requires patience: a habit which too many have either not developed sufficiently due to ignorance, apathy, or the aforementioned barrier, or not even begun to build.

137. When calculating the maximum survivable sacrifice, the most difficult calculation isn't the sacrifice, but the survivability.

138. This is a butt.

It needs constant attention and is responsible for producing a wide range of natural disasters including flooding and ear-shattering sonic anomalies that are capable of startling animals and forcing people to suddenly drop their plate of grilled liver and onions. The noxious toxic fumes produced by it also rival any of the spectrum of fragrances found in either Pasadena or Baytown combined.

Yet for all this trouble and high maintenance, all it gives back are a collection of various states of matter that no one can use. It makes a noise like it has something to sell that everyone needs, but then provides a product that no one will pay for unless it's for the removal of it.

Don't be like a butt.

139. If everything were one color, we could neither see ourselves nor anyone else. The air would be grey, our skin would be grey, the water would be grey, the football would be grey, the grass would be grey, the television would be grey, our tamales would be grey, and our brain stems would be grey. Luckily atmospheres come in way more than seven colors.

140. We can claim to have an open mind and be tolerant of others, but it's much better if we can prove it using any of the following methods:

a. Let anyone who disagrees with us do so without us threatening to kill them.

b. Let people who hate abortion be who they are.

c. Let gun owners be who they are.

d. Let Christians be who they are.

e. Let people who seek justice from the execution of people they saw with their own eyes commit a murder then molest children be what they are by allowing the execution to take place without standing in the way of it and obstructing justice.

f. Let people who wish we would speak English so they could understand what in frog piss we're saying be who they are.

g. Let people who can prove a belief is wrong be who they are.

h. Let people who disagree with our "right to gynophobia" be who they are.

i. Let people who oppose our active aggressive struggle to revert to a system of pure democracy be who they are.

j. Let people who don't invent reasons to kill every person in sight be who they are.

k. Let people who disagree with our obvious rewrites of history be who they are and understand that nothing historical can ever be proven in a court of law.

l. Let people who either hate or love the invisible world be who they are.

m. Let the statement, "Sometimes everything you think is wrong," be what it is.

- Phrixional Assention

141. Generally speaking, implication and extrapolation are the two most common major vacuous regions in the reports of modern investigators. Arriving at conclusions with accurate, sufficient evidence isn't far behind.

142. If certain violently disposed homophobes or gynophobes will, the both of them, attack or rape anyone, is the problem really gynophobia or homophobia?

143. Problem solving is about preventing undesirable outcomes. Then, conversely, it's also about creating desirable ones. Too often, in an uncountable number of cases, what we believe is not only a contributing factor, but alarmingly a major direct cause of an undesirable outcome. If we discover this is the case, then removing ourselves from the entire situation may be all that is necessary to produce the maximum desirable outcome. Or, what would have the same effect, change what we believe from being something that kills or harms others into something that doesn't.

The majority believe that this is impossible, that what we believe at age two never changes after that. It is unadvisable to subscribe to this lie, since many have changed what they believe several times since age two. Many believe we're all equal, so if true, then anyone else can also do this. One of the largest obstacles to all of this, among many, is apathy.

144. Does naming things, sometimes with billions of seventy-five syllable names for every square nanometer of material, mean that we understand them, their nature, function, or existence?

145. We will never find perfection in anyone else, except one person whom most people hate with a passion. We may only search for it within ourselves, and with some understanding it may actually be found. And no, this doesn't mean we're always right, even though many think they are already.

146. This has been dealt with in other works by minds better than this author will ever have, but it's good to remember that, as said previously, "Nothing is true all of the time." While bearing in mind all that was previously said here and moving forward, we may see this has a double meaning. And moreover that one almost proves the other and maintains a balance between the two interpretations.

The obvious meaning is that there is at least one situation where any given collection of words either doesn't quite fit right, or is just flat out false. Much of the time this is due to some misinterpretation.

"But then the statement is still true," one may object.

This may be in the absolute sense, but in a subjective sense it certainly won't seem or feel that way to the people involved in it and to argue about it then would only construct a devolutionary, forgettable memory. A few examples may help illustrate this, so they won't be provided.

The second view, which isn't as obvious and is closer to being a riddle, would be that in some part of reality, there is nothing, and that this is always the case. In every place where there is matter, there must be the space (nothing) in which it sits. Also, inside every atom is mostly space with very little matter contained in its circumference.

This is a tautology, or something that is always true, which may appear to contradict the first view, but it doesn't. If nothing is true all of the time, then it also applies to this statement, which then means that occasionally, some things are true all of the time.

And the second view, by being true,

provides the balance between the two.

One caution on the first view: to constantly find when anything isn't true is easy. Remembering when it either is or could be true isn't, and is many times a journey of days, years, or lifetimes.

"Then this means that anyone who affirms anything to be true has already contradicted themselves," our assiduous objector may notice.

They have not done so intentionally, and finding the true motive is never a useless exercise, even if in the end we can never actually find any. This is also not the case if we keep the exception to the second rule in mind. It does mean it's up to us to work to "hear, understand, and remember" to what it does or does not apply.

- Nothing is Something All the Time

147. In the vein of the second view just mentioned, before something happens, nothing happens or it would have happened sooner. Up and until the point in time when something happens, nothing is happening. So in order for the one second when something actually happens to succeed, several seconds, or several thousands, even billions, of seconds of nothing must first happen. Therefore, nothing is the setting, the bed, the foundation upon which all things happen. So nothing is actually something, but it's something that doesn't happen rather than something that does.

As an ubiquitous example, on too many computers, startup requires about twenty minutes of nothing happening before something actually happens and we may then use the machine. This nothing is a critical requirement or an advanced genius would have designed something that starts much sooner. Or similarly, people saying they're going to do something sometimes seems to take fifty years of nothing happening in order for them to do it. Or people saying they're tolerant while remaining intolerant may take several decades of not seeing it (seeing absolutely nothing in the mirror) for them to actually see it. So nothing is actually very important in many operations around us. It is so much so that nothing is happening more often than things that are.

- Nothing is Happening All the Time

148. Metaphorically, allegorically, or symbolically speaking, we first consider that during December we are in our closest approach to the sun which for us causes winter and the coldest temperatures of the yearly cycle, unless we're in Australia. Through this and the surrounding months, the sun doesn't appear in the day as much as in the summer. For this reason, the deeper parts of us, which have no clue about what science is, despair of the sun ever returning again. So we get depressed in order to coax the sun back into appearance with sympathy for our tears at its departure, which after some months of pondering about it, it actually decides to do.

So what does this mean metaphorically? It means what we see is an illusion and a lie if taken at face value, since we're actually at the closest point and not the furthest. Does this mean the chaos or Creator wants to deceive us about reality? It could mean we are to refuse to trust everything we see or hear and use a better method to prove both our experiences and what we can say about them.

It's also a way to illustrate that before any of this ever happened, there was nothing, represented by the cold, dark, long winter nights. This may or may not support the "ordo ab chao" theory. A more direct way to see this is in our own heads: before we have an idea or solution for anything, there is nothing. What creates either isn't always our profound desire to do so. There may be other clues in the metaphor which could shed light on other aspects of the creation process.

-Learn to Create Nothing

149. By putting together consideration, understanding, and meditation the combined result is greater amounts and sometimes quality of all three.

150. What if there was something that is so important that needs to be done, and we're the only ones who can do it? Sometimes, for each person, there's more than just one thing, and each is the only one who can do any of them.

151. Can a crushed spirit be excited or directed?

152. What if we have a love/hate relationship with the actual concept of love/hate relationships itself? Does this prove or disprove it? Do we accept it or reject it?

153. Feelings are such unreliable indicators of reality or motive, it's amazing that anyone uses them at all, much less demands them at all times and failing this enjoys throwing the brand of "anti-social" or "sociopath" at whomever they feel deserving of it.

But when reflecting, to establish a better method of dealing with the same events in the future with less undesirable effects, it's better to turn off the feelings.

Proof: Feelings are unreliable messengers to start with, are used by hypnosis abusers as a highly destructive tool of manipulation, and after time and memory slash away at everything in the events including the feelings themselves, they're exponentially more unreliable later than during the actual event. Some psychologists claim any shutting down feelings is sociopathic behavior while prescribing drugs to calm down people who have too many, so their mixed signals aren't even clear to themselves since none of them have yet explained this standard behavior. But not turning them off when it's helpful runs the risk of having the same ill effects repeat in the future, and this could be seen as attempted suicide, given all the negative variables life inserts wherever it can. It was never observed where feelings inserted into anything ever made it better. (Love is doing, not a feeling.)

Skilled manipulators have been seen to use feelings to drag everyone by the nose into a far worse situation, then blame everyone but themselves when everything inevitably goes to hell. They use feelings about cuss words to ignore any vital information conveyed by the words surrounding the cuss words. They tout the feelings of the criminal to avoid any necessary punishment, while continuing to deliberately ignore the feelings of the victims and even allow the same criminals out of jail repeatedly to continue to punish and harass the victims. Any arbitrary tool randomly applied by manipulators to facilitate their sadism would be precisely the toy best removed from the child to keep it from harming either itself or others.

Since it's obvious no one has a clue how to evaluate which feelings are more important in not only these examples, but billions of others which there aren't enough bookshelves on Jupiter to hold, it's better to avoid them entirely when making any serious decisions. Actually, some part of navigating events over a lifetime to find the gradient is avoiding the bad feelings or attitudes while trying to find or create the good ones.

We can easily see this when it comes to money: "Don't dump your bank into the hand that tickles," like the used car salesmen, some churches, the candy clown spraying favors down the neighborhood, and so forth. But if money isn't involved, we seem to suddenly be blind to the dangers and even insist on yielding to the feelings, glaring at everyone who doesn't follow suit; even though we know from experience, if not in the moment, that they will lead to a far worse scenario.

Obviously this isn't and won't be an exact science when applied since we may number on one thumb the people who are even considering it. It's apparently taught nowhere, or it would have appeared on the news already as an available college pursuit, so we must not allow mistakes to prevent further experiments. If we succeed, we actually have moved on and left the past behind, which so many choruses around us continue to sing praises of so doing.

154. Why do we argue so often about whether we're "understanding exactly" how anyone feels when emotional feelings are entirely unprovable in any direction? No one will ever understand exactly how anyone feels, so there's no use in a hot-tempered debate about it for any reason. Rather, we should struggle to

- Feel Understanding.

155. Sometimes watching how people react to what happens to them may make us want to avoid all human contact. The amount of information in front of them seems to make no difference, they'll keep getting it wrong and continue to think they're right regardless of who it hurts or who gets killed.

Maybe what someone did to us was done to prevent us from doing the same thing later in a far more critical situation where the consequences were more devastating, so that when we got to that point, we would remember how bad of an idea it was, and then wisely choose against it. A correct interpretation of this has been seen to happen, but it's rare. Most of the time people are too obsessed with paybacks and vengeance to interpret it positively. This usually is because they're both lost and dead. If not, they still haven't sacrificed their vengeance on the altar of humility. Maybe someone can locate an accurate textbook on "Reviving the Dead."

156. We can't expect perfection in all things, but what if society does? By this we mean to include all nations, not just one. What if editing out all the mistakes and accidents in shows, movies, stories, or even historical accounts, trains our minds to expect perfect acting and no accident scenes anywhere else in our lives? And what if this expectation is negatively affecting every other relationship, including people we don't know and see in the news? We're expecting perfection and so avoid people and situations that don't provide it. This may be low impact since if we asked anyone they would quickly admit no one is perfect. But what if this behavior lies outside our radar where we can't see it, but we're doing it anyway? What if it's similar to the hapless city folk who kill the very spider that would have eaten the Culex mosquito that winds up killing them?

- Watch What You Do

157. This applies to where it does, as do most things.

If the energy we have for dealing with our surroundings isn't infinite (death proves that it isn't), the following assumption can't be true: "Throwing anything into the equation won't change the outcome." Throwing the unnecessary into any equation changes the amount of energy we have for dealing with our surroundings. Life adds its own obstacles to nearly everything without people adding their own to it. We may term these *necessity fails*, since someone thought they were necessary to add.

A few examples of *necessity fails* among the millions:

a. Universities that hire professors who can't spell or speak English,

b. Putting any commercial on any media form when no one has a job to buy any products,

c. Playing the same song four thousand times an hour instead of playing different songs because a mafia drug lord paid them to do so,

d. Any of the several groups and individuals who preach that just by believing anyone has enough money for college that this is sufficient to magically make some appear in the bank,

e. Saying that any group of people have money automatically means they do, and that since they do it's acceptable to steal any or all of it,

f. Making excuses not to take money anyone is trying to pay us instead of taking the money and helping the economy,

g. Not paying employees up to the cost of living, which is tantamount to stealing directly from the economy - the list is endless.

With these or any of the other *necessity fails,* what suffers is progress. Excuses for any of it won't make the progress show back up after being delayed by centuries of thwarted goals. If we claim to believe that everyone has the chance to live their dreams, then we should prove it by making sure not to supply excuses for any and everything that adds to any equation in existence

- The Element Of The Unnecessary

158. Among the true conspiracy theorists are the neo-Malthusians trying to violently enforce their fears of overpopulation into the world through abortion and human trafficking. Far deeper plans for enslavement have been brewing for years which may soon now rise to the surface.

159. What will happen when all the ones we've labeled as crazy turn out to be the ones who had insights that science has yet to prove? Their dilemma only arose due to the fact that there is no way to verify their observations, since we currently lack the instrumentation to do so, other than the human mind, which is currently falling out of use. This was also exacerbated by everyone in creation calling them a liar. What will happen when the future judges us the way we have the past by labeling every era other than our own "crazy," "barbaric," "unscientific?" What would have happened had the Catholic Church burned Galileo at the stake for his findings? *"Galileo was interrogated while threatened with physical torture."* [41]

307

What will happen when we get to the point where respect is due to us, but doesn't arrive since it's something we never did to any elder of our past as we label them all over a hundred different ad hominems and never bother to spend more than .5 seconds reading anything they wrote?

What will happen when we receive precisely everything we gave to others right back into our faces?

- Respecting Elders Is An Earned Behavior

160. As we go through the year, we may try to watch for signs of things that have happened due to a self-fulfilled prophecy stemming from the belief that odd numbers make odd things happen. We should realize that whatever it is isn't happening because 2017, 2019, 2021, etc., is an odd number. As we look and see ourselves being a part of whatever it is, we know that this is the only thing that's making it happen or exist in the first place.

161. Where this should be done won't be arbitrary or indiscriminate. It should rarely occur, but more often these days than the many which have come before. Only in cases where it is clear that death is the only result of certain intricate patterns both taught and formed over centuries of miscalculations and swallowing the lies from the status quo herd-tamers.

In this case, killing the head of the snake won't necessarily kill the snake, since they're all afflicted by the same spirit. Singling out a scape-goat to beat won't work either, since in many cases, more than one person is responsible. Death must be brought to the door of the affliction itself in the form of exposure both to what it is itself and the truth necessarily opposed to it. This book is actually intended to help perform such a procedure. It may be a long, but needful project in order to perform on a grand scale the requisite

- Deep Systemic Psychotomy

162. When we believe that any political system is the religion that will save us, it is clearly time for a Deep Systemic Psychotomy.

163. When deciding not to cooperate when either the result would be good or make no difference if cooperation were afforded, remember that without gaining or losing electrons, there would never be any electricity

or molecular compounds whatsoever and none of us would exist at all. Even water wouldn't exist. The oxygen in every water molecule shares two electrons with both hydrogens, one per each. What if they had a free will and all decided to afford the level of cooperation currently seen exemplified by the majority? How long would we survive without water? Would cooperation then be considered a disposable item as it is today? Would the excuses for refusal be as flimsy as choosing the wrong color of refrigerator? Would we then be able to flippantly toss hard facts into the "Opinion" box the way we now do? When we realize these things have always mattered, will it actually?

- Molecular Elemental Isolation

164. For any who are violently disturbed by and actively aggressive against all fake news, here are some mind-blowers for consideration:

a. A two-by-four is nothing close to two inches by four inches. It's not even within one-sixteenth of an inch, or one-eighth.

b. The term *specific heat* from chemistry is neither specific nor does it deal exclusively with heat.

c. Colors only appear to us as they do because of how our brains are constructed. Other brains may see them entirely differently or not at all. This is why scientists still have no idea how the world looks to a cat or many other creatures.

d. No one person, agency, or system is correct or accurate 100% of the time, except one. And that's the one everyone is either saying doesn't exist, is busy spending their lives calling him a liar, or ignoring him entirely. So, the one person who is 100% accurate always is ignored while they worry which of their smaller groups have the highest degree of accuracy between themselves. It is to be wondered where exactly their inaccuracy lies.

e. Since they have no power of self-reflection, no computer in existence is capable of objectively analyzing data.

- Who's Fake Now?

165. Sometimes things are the way they are for a bad reason, which is nearly the same as no reason. But for many of these, simply because there is a bad reason doesn't mean that at this time it's possible to change any of them. Because changing them in the direction the people who

created the situation are intending by their actions would bring about an exponentially larger set of things that would be the way they are for no reason or a bad one. To date, there is only one area where this applies more than others, and for that we may be thankful. Let's try to keep it that way.

166. The stated purpose of the baby, at least according to those with whom we may inquire, is to be able to cry as often as possible, get a pacifier throughout its entire life, and to have larger communities of people with the exact same goal. It now appears (but this is believed to be the incorrect response) that the majority fully intend to hand them everything they want on a platter.

- Hey, Baby! (The Baby Syndrome)

167. *"But that too was a position of ours which, as you will remember, has been already refuted by ourselves.*

We remember."[42]

Every process leading to motive, every art which brought these words about, every environment where they could be said without being interrupted with some off-topic point, which gave rise to these words is a lost practice. It has rarely been heard, if it even was, that these words were said by anyone anywhere till now. They used a process of error detection that is a phenomenal rarity in conversation, though computers use them sometimes, although not enough even for this case. We may remember this when listening to people speaking of a utopia claiming that they are gods on earth, yet never mention these words even once anywhere, any time, for any reason.

168. An example of another ignored 3:16 -- *"For where envying and strife is, there is confusion and every evil work."*[43]

A few movies have dealt with this issue where striking examples of it may appear, which are as soon forgotten as declared by the non-existent popularity of the films. These stories reveal crimes committed by one or more which they blame on the weaker personalities, getting away most of the time unpunished by using threats or high levels of violence to force everyone to believe them. All done while pretending to be angry at the falsely accused for doing the very thing they're in the bedroom every night doing themselves to their own daughters or sisters. People sometimes become jealous and punish others not because they think what was done is wrong, but because they're jealous that they themselves didn't get to do whatever it is, when there isn't anything good about any of it in reality. They imagine their motives are passing unnoticed, but if we can see them, so can someone who actually is a judge and will be able to deliver consequences about them soon.

Why would it be confusing? This question is worth exploring. Because by appearing to do the right thing, they're still wrong because eventually they'll realize punishing anyone for what they themselves want to do won't get rid of the initial desire, which will emerge in some other form one day. It's important to make sure when we say, which should be said rarely, if ever, that we want to kill someone that we're not just jealous of what they've done and trying to cover it with a false cloak of anger. It is visible to the right people. Especially if we're not for executing anyone who actually did commit murder, then our motives may as well be spelled out in large letters on a mountain side. It's fooling no one.

169. *"And philosophy is the acquisition of knowledge?*
Yes, he said." [44]

This puts the issue into a far larger arena than some might expect, becoming literally everything we see or hear, and also makes the art of measurement, referred to in the same work, that much more important.

170. If we can arrange things so when anyone doesn't keep their word it results in their own destruction, we've illustrated reality.

171. Today, we will study Outbursts. By this is meant any sudden, unexpected, or startling blast of noise from a person due to insanity or emotional depressurization. Insanity is here meant to include silliness.

Some jobs indicate universal displeasure at any type of outburst or blurting out of any kind. After watching a few of these for many years, we may wonder that with any successive runs of major or minor outbursts whether this could lead to any larger sudden explosion. Or, that is to say, why don't people who are given over to daily, successive outbursts just suddenly explode and disappear? Realizing that we typically attempt to monitor or control outbursts for the sanity of others, we may further wish to consider if this disappearance is even possible. Then we should also be on guard for securing these uncontrolled, widely scattered, successive sonic eruptions to prevent a possible spontaneous combustion. Or another thing to look at is: To what degree is logic and reason scared out of the room or out of the brain by outburst propellant?

Or yet again, on which occasions would stifling the outburst from the inside, using composure beyond that of any control freak, only lead to a larger, more devastating outburst in the future?

- The Torrential Damage of the Outburst

172. What if what we can remember of our life *is* actually our do-over? What if we've had thirty or forty do-overs already? And here we are screwing the hell out of it again.

173. A firefly was spotted wandering around in the yard alone. I'm glad they're still here. Based on where it led and where it settled, we could suppose it to be a symbol. It flew through the abandoned remains of a dwelling where a person of high wisdom once lived, intermittently illuminating the shadow streaked walls and cabinets. We could see it to be saying that those who are no longer with us can't forget about us anymore than we could forget about them. Because they are not alone, neither are we. They will watch us as they did in our lives when they walked amongst us, *"seeing we are surrounded by so great a cloud of witnesses"*₄₅ ensuring our feet well placed within our souls' safety.

The work that captivates their interest isn't alone the business of the angels, because the work itself demands a much larger audience. Driven by the mystery that appears not but as a reflection till after crossing the cold barrier, after which there is no other thought but the full view of the sacred notion to the point of drowning in it, they share. Wondering if perhaps we could help them get closer to what they themselves were looking for which sparked the same interest in us, they visit.

The things we pass through remember us as well as they do the ones who went before us. However they know, where they sit, they remind us that they see us for who we are and are happy to bear the messages of those we can no longer see. Believing this to be the case is no delusion when if it actually is the case, denying it would be one far greater and moreover an injustice.

- Firefly Language

174. When we have striving for perfection as a goal, there is no division.

175. Our concept of whatever we think we know may be entirely different or even opposite in reality than whatever we think we know it is. Triangulating can sometimes verify, but doesn't always reveal the entirety.

176. There is a group of people who are offended by anyone or any group who swallow as many lies as they can get their hands on as fast as they can. This is the actual group of people we should be worried about offending. Concern for any other group is like worrying if the count on the number of atoms in the universe is off by 7 or 2.18.

177. Hypocrisy is a wonderful type of insanity where we never have to admit we need treatment.

- Fake News Barrage

178. If what is around us is arranged in many ways according to our dictates, we should try to make better dictations. People have been seen to be killed because of some of them. We can see how they would not have been by merely changing only one of the dictates in far too many cases.

179. Forgiveness is something we give, so the word "give" is inside it. *"Who can forgive sins, but God alone?"* [46]

We may not forgive sins, depending on the sin itself, so what are we forgiving? Asking us to forgive sins of others is asking us to pretend we're God, who only can do so. So we reasonably both won't and can't. We may pray for their forgiveness, but this may or may not acquire it for them depending on their choice with regard to faith.

So here we see that by asking us to forgive criminals, people can appear to be just and holy while asking someone to do the exact thing that caused *"Satan as lightning [to] fall from heaven."* [47]

Therefore, we are allowed to forgive minor infractions, trespasses against each other, and are even encouraged to do so. Every injustice between us is to be resolved this way and forgotten. But sins against God, which many criminals have committed, aren't our responsibility. So don't ask anyone to forgive them. It isn't in our power and we should refuse to accept the invitation to be joining them for eternity. All else requires restitution or justice for the process of forgiveness to begin, which many are still waiting to see. As any recent events remove the edges from our best choices, remember to include these ideas in the forgiveness equation.

180. Once we have arrived at something we believe to be better than it was, we may then consider whether it actually is better, or was any part of it less restricted, free, or more breathable when we weren't concerned about whether or not it could be improved? How is it now compared to no comparisons?

181. We should be praying that the people who are about to realize what they've done after it's too late don't wait to realize what they've done till after it's too late. Pray to doubt ourselves as much as we doubt everything around us, or realize that we are now not equal with ourselves, our surroundings, or anyone else that's in them. Or better still, we should doubt whether we have any right to assault other people with our doubts. This is a more useful concept of equal rights.

182. We will never be the ones who understand infinity, but neither should this be an excuse to prevent searching for missing pieces.

183. Philosophy can travel for a long way down a wrong road by imagining the universe to be smaller than it actually is.

184. Considering the phrases "That's what I was afraid of!" and "You have to give the audience what they want!", a few ideas appear. We may not ask to see something that we don't want to see, then blame someone other than ourselves for showing it to us. If we didn't want to see it, then we would have never been afraid of it. If it's not something that we want, it's not something that anyone else wants either. Deciding what someone is afraid of isn't up to other people, but only that individual. Deciding what someone else is thinking when we're not even a psychic will also typically prove to be a grand failure, but what are friends for?

185. People who love you know why they should.

People who don't will find out later why they should have.

186. Are the noble gases "elemenalists?" They never borrow from any other element and always think they're on the right side. All other elements mimic them but can only make copies. Let's all be noble gases! (Incidentally, neither methane nor CO_2 are noble, even if this is typically all any bloviational conglomerate ever consistently pumps into the breathable atmosphere.)

- A Noble Pursuit

187. In the end, wisdom rewards her enemies with a devastation that's beyond imagination. Understanding meets its opponents with a reaction that is equal and opposite. Knowledge faces those who knew it not with a reality that's beyond comprehension. Seek them all early.

188. If property rights begin where one is born, then this land is mine. If they begin by conquering the territory, this land is mine. If they begin by experiencing a disgustingly horrible tragic event on an area which converts the ownership to the infringed party, this land is mine. So however you feel like looking at this subject...

- Ownership Rights Own You

189. A double standard indicates a false concept about God. It indicates a belief in a blind god who can't see there's a double standard. To some degree, this exists within every person. It can be seen by comparing how often we forgive others with how often we forgive ourselves. Again, to some degree, this is fine since in our own case we know all the facts and correctly assess that once everyone else does they would do the same thing.

The misstep is when we don't remember that regarding anything to do with others we will *never* know all the facts in order to forgive accordingly and typically never forgive since we don't have them and don't bother taking even two seconds to find out more of them. Nor do we spend any seconds discovering if we even have sufficient facts to perform whatever punishments we inflict on them, whether omissive, passive, or active.

Another misstep is the now nearly universal law, which only a few people hate, that everyone is always, in every case, "guilty till proven innocent." The misstep will be corrected when God informs everyone personally that He never wrote that law anywhere and never authorized its enforcement to the universal degree that it now enjoys.

- Inductive Reasoning

190. A true utilitarian wouldn't consider anyone to be useless since many of us are still searching for the correct time and place for our best use. Our utility is often mistaken and misunderstood to be its opposite when we laugh at arguments over things that don't seem to have one.

- Indifferent Advantage

191. Hating our decisions while not hating ourselves is easy once we discover every decision isn't a direct challenge to our right to exist. Any who are busy teaching to love our bad decisions aren't practicing psychology, but are in fact teaching psychoticry.

192. The reason we beat the daylights out of each other with fists and billy clubs and why we throw baseballs into the nostrils of others, necessitating the mass production of baseball helmets, is because we feel that by beating the life out of everyone around us they will feel threatened and scared enough to explain in harsh squeaks and grunts who and what they really are. This will save us the hours of homework and research to find out the same information on our own which could otherwise be done without all the bloodshed and crushed, baseball-infested nostrils.

- Faceball

193. Since hay is merely dead grass, kine and equine are vegetal necrophiles.

- Unknown Environment

194. When wants and needs are blurred, which is the job of advertisers, who wants the need?

- Pearl-Gilding the Limner

195. A reason, among many, that we fear the unknown is that from this comes the unexpected. From both, very often, arrive solutions to problems. Solutions mean our responsibility has increased. No one wants this ever, so we keep it away with fears both reasonable and not.

196. We may always enjoy a rich tapestry of symbolism because it enrichens the texturality of the storials. (Symbolism here: Broken communication, repetition, and portmanteau.)

- Lurn Two Reed

197. It's better to throw up a little in your own mouth than throw up completely into someone else's.

- Dr. Litmus

198. Since many modern college professors teach in equivocal terms, it's only fair we should be able to pay them using ambiguous currency such as monopoly money, car wash tokens, or carnival tickets.

- Modern Swill Shillers

199. Due to the high dosage of vitriol streaming from nearly every person who now believes their only God-ordained job is professional criticism, hearing anything has become more difficult. Due to this, something critical is bound to be overlooked and errors will only increase on all fronts.

200. Whoever votes based on popularity or likability explains to the universe why they also have no money. We may term these: Freudian Slip Knot Voters.

Whoever believes leaders should always be highly charismatic and sexually attractive may also indicate a prodigiously disturbing psychological makeup for what they expect a leader to be doing: singing, dancing, sexercising, and playing vs actually solving real, critical, necessary problems. Saying that people who aren't sexually attractive can't solve problems also points to a mental imbalance and these should probably avoid voting if at all possible.

People who vote for someone based solely on whether they imagine they would like having sex with them probably aren't listening to anything they say and so would cheer everything. This explains both why they never listen to anything anyone says about anything as well as why they react violently if we insult their love toy. They will threaten to kill us for this or for even disagreeing with them since sex is a god that must be served and because they have Only One Thing On Their Minds. These also will greatly contribute to the mass scale
- Sexual Devolution

201. Being called a *seasoned citizen* is a low key method of telling us the truth about their after death plans: They Will BBQ Us.

202. Many think psychic links or talking with dead relatives is like a phone with long distance charges, clear connections, and with no dropped calls. They also think it's like plugging into a computer where we have full access to all the data contained in the brain of the other person over their entire existence.

This, as can be seen by putting this into words, is both false and unreasonable. If anything is clear, the only thing we actually saw was a miracle.

To answer "why isn't it clear?", we only have to list everything that's actually being connected starting with our body and branching out from there. At the first junction of invisible objects that we encounter, which will be "what do we hear?", we will see that past this point, everything outside of it will be impossible to nail down. We can prove this easily by taking a hammer and trying to nail down anything around us that's invisible. Write down the results. Now we know why.

- Dropped Dead

203. If a psychic can tell we already know the answer to the question we're asking, they'll tell us the opposite and let us decide. This way, whatever happens is solely based on our decision. This centuries old habit of asking already known questions is probably based on lawyers who only ask questions they know the answers to while pretending not to know by using a form of self-delusion, calling the process "discovery."

- Psychic Minefield

204. We may believe we're all stepping stones onto a higher path for others as long as we remember we're all more than just merely something to step on.

205. We cry, screech, whine, yammer, mewl, and fabricate fantastic sob stories to release murderers back into the world from prisons where the majority of innocents were safe from them. They then kill more people, resulting in families hand-wringing, grieving, crying for long hours, and blaming God for allowing these things to happen to them.

How can a just God do such things on the face of the pure earth? How can a holy God allow such unholy acts? How can God just not prevent everyone from having a free will and make everyone's decisions for them like a puppet master to keep these kinds of things from happening? How can He not prevent it?

When we see this, we can't blame or think of God at all. We may only think of

- Murderous Sobs

206. We may think our opinion doesn't count or matter, but it always feels good to know there's at least one person on our side. And when this isn't possible, it's always good to know that at least one person is on our side.

- The Invisible Army

207. People avoid math because they realize that eventually, with enough things having been solidly proven, they will actually have the responsibility that they already know they have. And that by this, math will destroy them and their endless worship services to the gods of convenience, apathy, and ignorance, among thousands of others. This can clearly be seen with little to no education in math.

- Math Slaughter

208. If "as above, so below" is true, then this universe entirely fits into one proton of one atom of a larger universe.

- Formula C1C

209. Since schools can only touch a small surface of whatever it is they're teaching, the subject will always become something more and larger than even they understand it to be through further study.

210. There is a noticeably general fear of making sweeping generalizations, so many today avoid generalization altogether and regard any who even hint at them as a general pariah. But when we are deprived of speaking generally about anything for too long, the general interest involved in whatever is being discussed will rapidly become bogged down in a putrid, soupy morass of particularized minutia of mind-numbing minuscule molasses. And when this occurs, generally speaking, we will no longer have any general comprehension of any subject forever or any deep-rooted connection with any committed interest towards, as well as an entire general inability to recognize, respect, or salute

- General Understanding

211. a. Since it is believed that what we say to others occasionally applies to ourselves and

b. A common expression is "You don't know what it feels like," then from this we know

c. A large group of individuals is asking to know specifically what it feels like and is openly admitting that they don't know.

- How Does It Feel?

212. [Anyone telling us that we can't defend ourselves] = [A Form Of Attack]

Proof: The only reason to disarm anyone is to facilitate an assault, unless they're the initial aggressor.

213. Ignorance should be illegal. Then we'd actually hear people defending it on its open face to try to legalize it, realize how stupid they look, then change.

214. The cold is preferred because there are a few who can see a nearly palpable large reduction in the dissonant psychic white noise.

- Cold Psychic Ambivalence

215. Just because the weapons of our warfare are not flesh and blood$_{48}$ doesn't mean they won't use flesh and blood to try to win the war.

216. People think their decisions don't affect us; but as we wait for them to keep their word, the story doesn't have any ending. Any story that doesn't have an ending hasn't been completed, this only happens because...

- That's Because....

217. When anyone says not to discuss something, ignore them. Very few of us have any real commanding officers. They're only imposing imposters disguised as a quaternion of quidnuncs

218. We may notice many arguing with others, but actually the argument is with God and many times against God. These will one day have their wish to have an audience with the Most High and present their arguments. But the discussion won't go the way they expect.

219. When we assess the truth of what is in front of us based on how bored we are with it, we know one thing for sure: Truth is nothing close to what we have.

- Malevolent Monotony

220. A shart doesn't really care how careful we are with it, it will destroy us anyway. This also describes how most people respond when we talk to them about anything today.

221. "A spell that summons a mound of zombies to fall on your opponent? I love it!"

"Politics today is really something, isn't it?" - General Chat Conversation

- Shart-mouth Society

222. We ostracizicate and marginalcipitalize anyone who doesn't measure up to the [Sacred Standards] of society while never considering or even remotely thinking about whether these [Sacred Standards] even have any value whatsoever in any time, place, or dimension. Nor do we ever even care what the [Sacred Standards] of marginalcipitalization even are, were, or could be.

- [Sacred Standards]

223. As it applies to this precise second, to say we have no right to free speech is a violation of rights and proves we have no right to violate, since rights violators have no authority to be involved in the institution of them. Crimes prove their existence when finding their repercussions. Secondly, it further proves us guilty of sadism.

224. If we follow the Hollywood maxim of "giving the audience what they want" and apply this to a court setting, we see that we have to give the criminals what they want as well as giving the victims what they want. If not true, then why is it ever said?

This produces a remarkable dilemma. So, if the testimony of both prosecutor and defendant doesn't do this, then it fails to meet the standard set by the gods of this age. This makes sense because it should be up to the judge or jury to decide if what they hear is the truth or not. It's also up to the judge to make a correct judgment, or they have failed their own office. If they can't, then they have no business being a judge or jury and need to leave the seat open to those who can actually do the job.

If it is the case that we *don't* do this, and do one thing in one building, and yet another in another, how is it that we can believe that we're not two-faced? If we're two-faced, then we daily perjure ourselves by definition and our testimony either as a lawyer, judge, juror, or witness is entirely invalid.

- A World With Two Faces

225. The memory too often blocks out the worst moments, or if not block, ruins all the details. So, without the complete set of facts, it's impossible for anyone to always be certain or make good decisions about anything of a critical or severe nature.

226. Certain authorities, and not all within the same type or class either, expect to be treated as gods while disrespecting the real one. They disrespect the One True God when their job is to dispense justice and instead molly-coddle, kiss, and slaver over criminals like schoolgirls over musclebound jocks. These we may treat as if they have no clue what a god is and disrespect them as much as possible short of violence. Most violence is immediately disrespectful. They'll see why for both cases later. Respect is not a title-based achievement: we *all* must earn it.

227. Regardless of who's saying what, often it appears that whoever is talking is taking notes of how people react, then going ahead and doing whatever they hell they want anyway. Are they from the squad of Invisible Aggressors?

228. When studying anything, inexorably one or more objects enjoy providing a Dolby enhanced version of a distraction. Typically these will be human, but not always. Were it not for these, anamnesis would require far less scourging. Sometimes it's the muse of indolence, but on a breach, the mountain lost its category and that's how the air filters won the war. Most universities now even offer degrees in this blistering suavity.

- Point Usher

229. When reality questions you, question it back.

230. Looking back, sometimes all that can be seen is a vast sea of mistakes and broken moments. Mistakes lined up so far and deep, all armed with fierce weapons to destroy and crush into dust, that we can view no end. Or is each moment lined up for review for us to face them? And are they waiting until we give them the right answer or the right reaction? It is uncertain that, if they were people we could actually talk to, the conversation would be any easier.

231. Symbolism is a high sign. The symbol for the vast users of "hate speak love" is the minus sign.

- Ignore Your Surroundings

232. Think of others as more than one person. That way if you don't listen to one, you'll hear the other one.

- Life Hack #502

233. When we hear any saying, "you can't compare x to y," they're exposing the fact that they don't know what the words "analogy" or

"contrast" mean. So we can now say that you can't compare people who can't compare, or can that be said anymore? Can we compare people who say things with people who can't? Or is this better left unsaid? We should say what we didn't say.

- You Can't Compare!

234. Using intimidation tactics only proves that one is from the mafia. It further proves that one isn't for a democracy, since intimidation places an unreasonable price on action. It also proves that whoever does this thinks they are my parent, when they neither look, act, nor smell like them, but in fact smell far worse for worse reasons.

Since many of those who are intimidated are actually victims of crime, it proves the intimidators don't care about victims or their families, and as such, deserve no respect from them or anyone else. It proves such don't want to be in America, since America is based on freedom. It proves they won't be voting anyone into office who supports freedom, but rather supports tyranny and rule through fervent and frequent use of grand-scale intimidation tactics. It most importantly proves they would love to sit in jail with the rest of the mafia for the rest of their lives, which should be brought legally to pass.

- How To Locate Mob Ties

235. On average, people who typically talk out of their rectum also look up to it for sage advice.

- Actions Speak Louder Than Verbs

236. Any highly detailed description of machine-like perfection is automatically a description of a fantasy. Look for this reality-piquing element in arguments.

237. We should give to those in need, but thieves always need. So, do we live without and feed thieves for eternity?

238. Constantly calling attention to what we're not doing will only push us straight in the direction of what we're not doing, which is *exactly* what we don't want to do. This is sometimes why rehab doesn't work. If we *forget* what we're not doing, before long we won't remember why we ever wanted to do it.

- Forget The Past By Forgetting It

239. The phrase "we see what we want to see" means that if we want to see anything, we can. If not, there is only one place to find the culprit. If regarding the understanding, not seeing means we do or don't want to. As in, "I don't see why the drug of feelings is so worshiped in movies, music, books, and TV that all other considerations are ignored or mocked." Or the same words could be said in this way, "I don't see anyone discussing any of this anywhere." This is literal, and not the figurative use of the phrase.

- Just A Passing Phrase

240. The term "second" needs to be a different word, since it leaves open the question of where is the first? Saying "the first second" sounds like the person is majorly confused. How can it be first and second at the same time? And saying the second second sounds like the person has a non-tourettesian stutter. It should be called "moment," since that's what it is. Then we can say "the first moment" and "the second moment" and not sound entirely ignorant. And to keep alliteration, the hour should be renamed "muumuu." This was written at the 8th muumuu, 29th minute, 37th moment of the day it was written.

- Moments, Minutes, & Muumuus

241. We must never associate the worth of the soul with being wrong. They're not equivalent.

- The Wrong Diamond

242. As the world plunges headlong into an extremely extended period of isolation generated by the devout followers of rapid karma, who love nothing more than to help their imaginary deity by applying the punishment inviolably determined by their god to those who certainly must be deserving of it, and this done without more than the passing of two seconds and even less of this time involved in thinking about it, are we prepared for the long term effects of isolation?

- Karmic Warlords

243. Actors would seem to know how to act better than they're acting. Unless of course they're just acting. What if they get stuck in "acting" mode and can't stop? Who could ever tell? Or if they're blind, they couldn't see that the results of their acting are having a negative effect so they couldn't know they needed to act differently. Or if they're

manipulative control freaks, they would use their acting to change how others act and thereby imagine they're spreading knowledge of the craft to others. When they see others killing themselves based on the acts they showed them, can they feel it? Or do they use their acting skills to cover it up?

Is there any agency of police that can oversee the actions of actors to ensure the safety of others and would these police be real police or only need to be actors playing the part of administrative oversight committee members? Who in turn would oversee these acting police agents? Would they also need to be actors since they need to be judged by a committee of their peers? Would these also just be acting? If yes, which human would be able to distinguish truth from reality in all this circus of performers? Has the number of people who worship these actors grown past the numbers of followers of every known religion combined?

- Acts Book XII: Bad Actors Acting Badly

-Events Before Thoughts-

244. While working on the concept of, "Where does a thought begin?" we discover a dearth of information which isn't found where we should expect it to be. We know that mind is a spirit and has a spirit, but this doesn't explain the selection process it uses to fill the vacuum created by need and opportunity.

245. If oxygen to the brain is what enables thoughts, we may be able to say that thoughts arrive from and travel on the air.

246. So many studies and much time have gone into considering exactly what a thought is, how it occurs or what it's capable of. Yet there has not been one person who can definitively say the specifics of a thought have been fully apprehended. The evolution of a thought from non-existence to cognition may always remain clouded, but it's a nice point of focus.

Invisible always, even when written down, since the spirit of the law or word and the letter are too often unique, arriving from who knows where and back to nothing when nothing is done with them, thoughts and what give them birth are more misunderstood and vanishing than clearly defined or concrete.

Many use fear or apathy as a process of comprehension. But even those who use precise caution often wonder if there is cause for alarm from the fact that whatever the thought is, far too much of it will remain forever unknown.

Even any of this may pass unnoticed until a certain location is reached. But what we seek is to find the energy required and ability to adequately identify, irrespective of any amount of time passing in the process, since that's quite irrelevant, the complete universe surrounding all the

- Events Before Thoughts

-And Jesus Knowing Their Thoughts[49]-

247. What if one psychic read another psychic's mind, but didn't know it. The second psychic was getting information about a murder from somewhere else. The first psychic believed the second was about to commit a murder. Better not to judge, isn't it?

248. These five words alone, though there are others, prove the bible wasn't written by man. There is only one person who could verify whether these words were the case or not. That person is both entirely human and also isn't, so doesn't fit the normal definition of man as we understand the term at the same time as he does. As well as that he himself didn't physically pen the words, or he did. Either way, it's impossible for the writer whose name appears on the document to have begun to imagine that this was even a remote possibility. Even today most ignore them as if they don't exist at all and refuse to consider their meaning, significance, application, or consequence. How can we say this with any degree of certainty? Because this same man also once said this, *"How long, ye simple ones, will ye love simplicity? and the scorners delight in their scorning, and fools hate knowledge?"*[50]

-Worry Ward-

249. Worry is an energy that creates nothing or a vacuum. It is a thief that burns time and memory, leaving nothing but ignorance, fear, and regret.

250. a. If we worry about the success of worrying, we will have caused a worry to fail by attracting its failure through fear.

b. Once we have failed to worry, we need do nothing more.

c. Given (a) and (b), this is one way, among many, to take a negative and multiply it with something else (another negative), and make a positive. Math verifies this as well.

251. Worrying for another doesn't transfer if they already are. Now two people are worrying, which makes things worse. And yes, Dr. Tangential, worry and concern are not the same thing.

252. We ought to worry about what's going to happen if we don't stop worrying. By this, we force worry to kill itself.

-Evolutionary Scale Atavistic Recidivism-

253. It never used to be the case that every form of communication was hated to the degree that it enjoys today, but now for those who are over four thousand years old, even they get tired of arguments on occasion. So, instead we may think about what hasn't been discussed yet in our experience.

Prior to space being formed (everyone assumes space always existed, but pure science assumes nothing), there was no physical space. But was there spiritual space? The question is: What is necessary to form space itself? Was space formed from subatomic particles that haven't been named yet? Or was matter in its raw form cast into nothing at 0K, slowly heated to 3K, separated and expanded and the space we see is that which lies between the matter? And, what was the "nothing" into which matter was first cast?

We can't expect blind followers of evolution, who deny flatly the law of cause and effect, to answer any of these questions, since their worshiped theory is rife with twelve million assumptions. As far as is known, no one is even asking these questions. This is good since if there's no one here asking the questions, there's also no one arguing about them either. Arguments too often devolve into fallacy, repetition, or demanding proof of first truths. This question isn't a demand that matter or space be proven, but a question of is there a way to see how it came about. At the instant of the second repetition in a typical argument, the boredom immediately closes the conversation.

Again, this question may seem to ask for proof of a first truth, that being "Space is." We know that space is. The question is, "How did this come into existence and by what process?" And again, the question isn't *what*, it's *why?* We can't know what problems this may solve by never asking, hardly looking, or barely considering it, so let's keep doing just that.

254. Can atavism heal the effects of cultural extinction? This may be necessary if many directions aren't angled differently. The biggest lesson to be had if we notice we're suddenly in a hospital is

- You Only Thought You Had Time

255. At what stage in our ability to decide and make choices did we become enemies? If we are currently devolving, how did evolution ever happen to begin with? At what point did the ability to choose evolve? If we're enemies with nearly everything around us, which is infinitely larger than we are, who is going to win?

256. Meditation 487

Without preconception, allow one idea to become the next in a slow, pensive ponder. We may observe the remaining effect of the after-image when we're through.

Focus on why the monkey on seeing its reflection in a mirror, rather than appreciate the work of God it sees, instead sometimes tries to destroy it (and usually succeeds). Ignore the theology and assume this is true. When we (as humans) commit murder, we're doing the exact same thing. The rival or territorial issue doesn't change this, since genuine appreciation would override the instincts.

"But it has no powers of self-reflection to arrive at the conclusion that it's a creation."

This is all well and good. In order for this to have evolved in progression toward humanity, it would have needed to realize this defect. But the realization of what was missing would indicate that it already had it, thus giving rise to a paradoxical impasse. If it can see what it doesn't have, it already has the power of self-reflection, at which point the mirror would appear more a friend than enemy. So, why do we still try to kill our own reflection?

~The Disruptive, Ill-Mannered Lawyer~

257. Interruptions are one of the primary forms of hatred in use today. It lets the other person become acerbically aware of the kind, compassionate thought that they are a useless waste of time and space and should be somewhere else, or not exist altogether. It lets the other person know that we are more supremely intelligent than God and can't be bothered with ideas from other people. It lets the victim of a crime know that learning "the whole truth and nothing but the truth" is the last thing we will ever be interested in hearing.

The best thing to do when considering whether to interrupt someone is to interrupt the entire process of interruption. The most fitting thing for people who are addicted to interruptions is to interrupt them.

 - No More The Interruptions Streaming...

258. <u>Reductio ad absurdum.</u> Deceivers try to prevent this type of argument since it proves what something is by showing what it isn't. Justice is blind even to itself when it ignores these forms of arguments. And if the case has been proven to be absurd, then it can no longer be seen as normal behavior from those who were demonstrated to be absurd, and must be sentenced accordingly.

But while both judges and lawyers are interrupting during a reductio ad absurdum demonstration, justice is denied. Interruptions are also used widely in informal conversations. It is laughable, since the people who think they're avoiding something have only made their own future worse. They imagine they can prove the speed limit sign doesn't exist by ignoring it altogether.

 - Fraus Decreti

259. One thing refreshing about Plato, to any who are familiar with it, is the absence of interruptions. It's actually highly relaxing since there is nothing in the entire world right now even remotely similar to any

of the conversations inscribed in that book. If we're really so advanced, how have we now become so addicted to that which prevents ideas from developing? And while not allowing very many ideas into the universe, how can we then complain about not having answers? Yet, generally the people most addicted to interruptions are the ones who also claim to have all the answers.

Here is a strange entity: The one claiming to have all the answers is also the one preventing answers from entering the universe by spreading the disease of Addictive Interruption. But, somehow this same entity can't see that by spreading answers instead of interruptions there would be fewer problems that needed answers. And since creating an unnecessary problem is one of the many singular marks of an insane mind, we see immediately this entity in fact does *not* have all the answers, but should be ignored, along with its doctrine of [Addictive Interruption].

-The Centrist Reflect-

260. Let's discuss opposites: The center cannot be affected by opposites and speaks plain languages. The center can see and interpret all opposites once their positions are known. Hidden agendas don't change what was created at the outset. Petty hidden agendas are subordinate to larger, willfully neglected agendas which are on file.

- The Hole in the Center

261. To each side, the center will appear to be the opposite, only due to the fact that the opposite lies behind it. But this is only an illusion since the opposite can't be the center without making the center twice as far as it already is. When we can't see the center, then neither can we see the opposite and the circle has become wider than our comprehension.

A center won't be the opposite only because it is the center. And unless it moves, it won't. If it does, then something else is the center. The only way the opposite can be seen, in any case, is by removing the composition of the center. If we aren't in the center, we exist on some extreme and can't hold any claim to being centered in reality.

- Plain Geometry

-The Imprinting Impress-

262. When we make an impression, the lineaments of another impression in the reverse direction are also made. This is impossible to prevent. A decision of "yes" in any direction is a decision of "no" for every remaining direction in each moment of time.

263. People love to speak via hint, innuendo, clues, and subtle language because the tongue would fall out of the mouth if actual communication occurred too frequently. So, considering everything that was said since 1969, imagine all the clues, hints, and innuendos that *haven't* been said during this time. Not the negative or useless, but the useful hints that were mentioned are what is now under consideration. Compare and contrast those ideas with where we're currently sitting. A large picture should start to emerge at the end of which, we may see the bigger picture.

264. "There are no words..." How often have the moments outlined by these words critically impacted the shape of our lives as seen by turning around to gaze into the maze of the trails we left in our wake? This may seem to lend an edge into the "ordo ab chao" theorists credo, until reflecting on those times that are now so complex we have no known way to describe them. And if these times can so impact our existence as to create both memorable and undefinable memories, why isn't it rather called

- The Order Theory

265. Our religion comes out of our mouth whether we know it or not and whether we like it or not. This is because as previously stated, when an impression is made, a reverse impression is also made in the space left behind. This can be studied to reveal surprising detail.

266. When moving we leave impressions on our surroundings. Even those who say nothing are certainly thinking something. The less said or done, the less repercussions from those actions, usually. Sometimes doing nothing allows others to believe their impressions are correct. Often they are, but just as often they aren't. The way to leave impressions that don't judge is to see impressions as not being sent from a judge, as much as possible.

Any decision we make leaves its own impression on the universe. This renders us the form and the universe the symbol or mold. What are we creating? The answer won't be singular.

Interpreting something as an offence when no offense was given is itself an offense, which will necessarily call for repercussions. This is why the main function attacked by deceivers is the ability to interpret. Since dictionaries clear up most of this, most of their attacks are easily deflated. But in spite of all these constant fluctuations, we are still leaving an impression over time. Often it's illuminating to stop and reflect, even if only for a few moments, upon the large list entitled "What Did You Leave?"

-When The Day Disappeared-

267. For those we met before we were around fifteen or so, they hold a place like no other, even if we only met briefly. No one can take that place, change, or remove it. It's not "length of time known" that creates this bond either, since the length soon becomes apparent for what it is, an inaccurate standard of measure. Science can possibly explain what is happening here, but not why if we're looking for a full-circle explanation. Moving even ten degrees in either direction around the circle of knowledge, all explanations fail and become useless. Fixation can also burn reality into uselessness. I think people who are mean or evil have either forgotten these people they used to know, or they never had them to begin with.

- Landlines

2. Respect the Future Enough To Change It

1. The susceptibility to misapprehension should never be an excuse to prevent real dialogue. Using this can change the future.

2. Eventually, the Speech Police will have us to where we aren't using words at all, but will revert back to the grunts, howls, pointing, and facial expressions we allegedly used 75.9 trillion years ago. Then their campaign will be to kill anyone who uses the wrong facial expression, and that would be any of them. Given this reasonable fear, few will be looking forward to these next one hundred years.

3. When *how* something is said becomes an obsession over *what* is said in any culture or society, this is only one indicator that a necessary change has been forestalled for several decades. There is no indication of this improving to any appreciable degree.

4. The forces against good won't be contained in only one group or name.

5. Superstition has caused more unreasonable fear than any religion ever could.

6. We learn what we are by seeing where we've been. While others' opinions, even our own, show us what we're not, we leave the future open to show us who we are, knowing that even this is only part of the whole.

7. Slaves to fear first laugh at the ideas of others, then consider their worth almost never, through jealousy that the idea wasn't theirs. Swelling numbers who love doing this don't make the future attractive.

8. When anyone is shown the future, their level of arrogance (already nearly off the charts on average before being shown anything) goes so completely out of control that very few can be around them after that. Sometimes they recover themselves. Usually they don't. They develop such a restrictive habit of not listening (far more than average) and believing they're right in the face of all reason that being around them or not makes no difference. Most quickly see this and choose not to.

9. The bible is interested in letting both Jews and Gentiles know they can be forgiven and are through faith. People who hate the bible are interested in forgiving no one ever. The current level of unforgiveness now in the world is all the proof needed for this. Every news item is a litany of how many different ways people can refuse to forgive each other. Yet it is a rare encounter to meet anyone who either doesn't want to be forgiven or doesn't believe they already are.

But beyond the initial grace, forgiveness is a balanced equation -- input = output. Therefore, forgiveness is an investment in the most important future in the world: ours. Using this, we can see and even control the future.

10. As we look at whatever is in front of us, it not only is exactly that, but is also becoming something it may not be any more. The past and the future are both represented in everything we see, so we may actually see both.

11. If we become acquainted with ourselves, this can give us keys to control our future. Not every particular, but every particular really isn't that important or necessary to change. Not just the small things are capable of change. Most importantly, certainly never using only our own resources or power. We are all part of a circuit. Forget this and we may be electrocuted.

12. More explanation is needed than time to do so, but there are some who teach we can be gods. The easiest way to disprove this is to ask any of them to create a life-sustainable planet, or let us know when they can. There is another way. Many things are invisible that if we could but see them would prevent many deaths, accidents, and diseases. One of these things is the future. One of the reasons we can't see it, outside of the practical reasons of lack of skill at foresight and anticipation, is

our inability to adequately, deftly, or even to any degree, manipulate the present.

The present is a gift, as its name implies. One of the popular things for those who do inadequately manipulate the present is to kill anything or anyone who disagrees with any fact or opinion. This pattern wouldn't change for things in the future, for those who could see it. Fears would possess minds worse than any demon ever created, forming issues where none existed and people would be killed for no reason, even as they are in the present. All perceived threats would be eliminated, causing a tendency to separation, to be explained in a following section. So much so that the future itself becomes an enemy and is quickly annihilated by shutting our eyes to every window that ever exposed it.

Every known test where even the smallest piece of the future was revealed has yielded this result. It's difficult to say any of us could ever be gods while we fail to adequately control both the present and the future, both of which form the past. It's difficult to think we're greater than Jesus or God when He is currently *not* killing His enemies here on earth for disagreeing with Him, even though He can fully see every part of the future, proving that His fear neither controls His entire existence as it does most of ours, but doesn't even exist at all. It's difficult to propose that aliens could ever be in our future, when for the majority it can be said that we aren't even in our own future, since there are too many who display that they fear the future by continuing to ignore the present.

13. Notice that for any act of vengeance (God excepted) or payback, no proof is required. This is why it fails in most cases. Due to this, it then becomes its own case to be heard, judged, and sentenced in the future.

14. The seeds for being able to kill people for absolutely no reason and get away with it were visible in the 70s; but at the time, no one was doing anything about it as much as today. Now that it's not only being done on large scale, but accepted and allowed by law, it indicates something much worse is in our future.

As truth and facts are daily rewritten for absolutely no reason in the minds of football party politicians and their followers today, a few questions spring to mind:

a. Why are people so increasingly easy to control and their actions so predictable that any of the daily media manipulations are even possible?

b. Why can we equally attack either party and just as equally predict the majority reaction to either one?

c. And then, after knowing all of this, why do we have every person siting back and just watching as the manipulations continue without one person in law enforcement trying to stop any of it?

It doesn't indicate anything positive about our future. Luckily, this doesn't apply to everyone.

15. With enough attention to improvement, stopping to recognize where we are compared to where we were in communication and understanding is important to any future advances. We may further this by not allowing enough time for complacence, but seeing the amazing developments and appreciating them is necessary to know the next step into the multi-directional future.

16. Once there was an enemy so pervasive, that hurried and ill-conceived steps were needed to prevent the extinction of the entire human race. The only real protection against them was self mutilation by blinding or deafening the offending organs. Earmuffs would do effectively for many, or even blindfolds. But sometimes the creatures would insidiously wind their way into the sensory doorways and once inside, would cause massive damage and even cranial explosions. They came eventually to be known as the BSWs.

Even a few of the pets needed to aid the blind about their paths would fall prey to the deadly BSWs as the creatures made their way to the brain stem of the animals, invariably resulting in the catastrophic eruption of the skull into thousands of pieces, leaving the owners more blind without their aid and alone once more, if they were not killed immediately by the blast.

Scientists eventually found a method of preventing them from ever destroying another human by searing the part of the brain where the creatures seemed to congregate the most and were repeatedly observed making a beeline directly towards upon entry via the ill-guarded organic doorway. Soon, all but one scientist remained behind, unseared, to treat the future generations. The brain searing procedure became a global law in order to prevent humanity from ever again being negatively affected, influenced, harmed, maimed, or forever scarred and irrevocably changed from the hellish, damnable horrors posed by the

- Big Scary Words (The Fear Is Real)

17. The Future will fully balance every problem that has ever existed.

18. In our tireless efforts to insult others in order to ensure no one considers them to be a god, are we as tireless in ensuring that we're not becoming self-appointed judges with no future?

19. *"For the thing which I greatly feared is come upon me, and that which I was afraid of is come unto me."* [51]

This is one of the first things written. It's also an equation that forms an implication which is only false when T = false.

FTx ==> FLx

where F = whatever you fear, T = significant amount of time, x = any human, and L = lands directly in your lap. Various methods were tried to demonstrate this over the last fifty years. It hasn't been observed that anyone yet has either understood it or acted on it. Since fear is a decision, it's entirely up to us when it exists. How we remove our own fear is *never* another's decision. Many assume that it is, but this can never be proven, since it isn't.

- Fear The Fear

20. Hypocrisy is so addictive, it's doubtful very many will leave it for another lover.

21. Life eventually becomes the teacher on the level of which the rest of us failed to rise.

22. Look at this symbol: ∞

It is a finite representation of, not just a "large number," as some mathematicians call it erroneously, but an *unending* number. It is a series of numbers that never stops moving. It's not a typical variable either, since it's continually changing and isn't any one value. It can be assigned to several things at once: stars, sand, thoughts, errors, shopping malls, changes. It is both infinite and eternal, since it goes forward, up, out, and never stops. In the one mark is contained the idea of itself and its opposite. Coming up with a name for it grants us no power over it: we're all still finite, or the opposite of everything it stands for.

Narrow focus or narrow sampling arguments try to take this concept and put some limit on it to bring it into the world of the finite. Doing this is similar to the baby reaching out of its crib, pulling everything inside in some feeble attempt to understand what's around it. Look for this element in what people say. We may notice it's present way more often than it should be.

- The Future Is Infinite

23. People who want everything both ways, of which there are now a growing majority, can be summarized by this equation:

$$x = x + 1 \quad (1)$$

There is no solution for problem (1), just as there is no method of pacifying any who believe they can have everything both ways.

People who live in a fantasy world can be summarized by this equation:

$$2 + 2 = 7 \quad (2)$$

There is no way to help those who think problem (2) is a reality, unless they first admit they are mentally deranged. But then, since there are no more sanitariums in which to place or treat them, there is also no solution for problem (2) either.

- The Math of Reality

24. To a large degree, our future forgiveness is based on how or if we forgave in the past.

25. Now, everyone knows so much they never need to listen to anyone else at all about anything or read anything written by anyone. In the future, we'll know so much we won't need to listen to ourselves either, and the universe will finally be silent.

3. Proper Identification

1. If we don't know what we would or wouldn't do in a situation, then neither do we know that we absolutely wouldn't do it. Nor do we realize how many ways we're defending against the monster we think we might be which stems from not knowing whether we would do something that we absolutely would not do in reality. Everyone, for this reason, isn't who they think they are in general.

2. Speech is free, but when bodies start dropping as a result, it's obvious that someone, somewhere is trying to make it cost something. We're safe as long as we avoid this and follow reason. We remain above the fray as long as we remember what anyone else says does not define us or describe us. If we're still coming to terms with who we are, it is then impossible to define anyone else.

3. When we twist arms, spread rumors, believe everything we hear merely to see whatever we want to see, whatever we're looking at has nothing to do with reality.

- Optics: Who's Real?

4. People who think they can think, can't.

People who like to think they can think, can't.

People who know they can think are delusional.

People who know they can't think, can, but it's a slow crawl, largely due to the first three types.

5. Since we're all tempered by, and products of, reactions to everyone and everything around us, who we are is the result of a team effort. This slightly redefines the term "team," since very many of the actions and reactions on both sides are not voluntary at all.

6. To divert our minds from what it is trying to show us is to bring ourselves closer to a state of insanity. Not all insanity is curable. If we find that we're insane and are searching for the path back to reality, the first thing we will notice is that, on average, the pedants and psychomancers know way less than they should. As necromancers busy themselves resurrecting the dead, psychomancers resurrect bad psychology.

- The Pedestal of the Psychomancer

7. We may approach our future with the firm idea that everyone is dominated by some psychosis, whether diagnosed or not, whether they believe it or not, and whether or not the psychosis has yet to be discovered. Far too often, human behavior proves us right.

8. Our fear brings the object of our fear directly to us because like attracts like. We may strategically use this reaction to summon our fear in order to slay or overcome it. The greatest threats come from what we don't know. A dearth of understanding creates the vacuum of ignorance. Therefore, a lack of understanding creates an infinite cycle of death.

For this reason, too frequently, what we see in others isn't them, but a reflection of our fear. So we keep them at arm's length, not because we understand them, but for the sake of the convenience of not having to deal directly with our fear. This was also said in 1969, but all anyone heard was their own fear projected onto the speaker.

9. Monkeys With A Paintbrush

Most people, like the judicial system, think they can pick and choose words people say, painting (mostly via interruptive editing) whatever image they can to describe either the character or actions of a person. This is an illusion. Reality is *all* of the words *and* the motive taken together, not just what we feel like believing after farting on a Tuesday.

We can take words and paint anyone into anything we want, but we're the only ones guilty of painting that particular image. So who is more guilty, the image or the person who made it? Since most of the time motive is an apathetic blindfolded guess, generally the picture is millions of miles away from who or what the person really is.

10. If we're all the same, then we have no character, since character can mean one that's different from our own such as the ones played by actors, or one that stands out from the others who would be the bad characters. If we're all different, we may not have identified or accepted our character if we see ourselves as being different from who we are.

11. At some point in the future, possibly a close point, many will realize their set of values is shallow and many who are now viewed as unforgivable haven't really earned this title. This is because most people's definition of unforgivable is having a house painted the wrong color or becoming part of a series of events personally arranged by the very people who won't forgive them. Once this is seen, we will hate the system that made us this way and try to get away from it to sort things out. After running a given distance and realizing we are part of the system, we'll return to dealing with it once again. But after this happens our reactions will be more genuine and engaged. A range of things we previously thought proved nothing will be seen as proof and provable.

12. If what we believe is only true if and when we believe it, then what if there are parts of the body, functions, entire systems of some regulation, whether in or out of the body, that we can't see because we don't believe they exist yet?

13. We think we know how to feel, but characteristically default into knee-jerk assumptions about how others feel which widely misses the mark. Deliberately misunderstanding how someone feels then pretending to care isn't working; neither does judging others for not pretending to care precisely the way we do. If however we take time to do something better than a knee-jerk assessment, we can get close to the truth, while never really knowing if it's entirely accurate.

It hasn't been seen that one group of people do this more than another, and when we're fatigued everyone seems to default into it. The normal line of questioning laden with narrow-sampling and sound bite mentality will only lead us further away from any good understanding. It must be sought or what we have is only another problem in a large cauldron of them. Considering the source and ignoring it in this case isn't always a solution.

Therefore, Understanding Requires Work.

14. If anyone has any habit, we see them having this habit. Then our mind forms a habit of seeing these people having these habits. When they stop or change, our minds are in the habit of seeing them in these habits. This is what prevents many positive changes from becoming permanent. Our minds are in a habit that we don't want to take three seconds to change. It's easier to lie to ourselves and say the other person hasn't really changed than to change the thought patterns in our own minds. It's past time to change this. Either that, or watch more people die from lack of positive support for no other reason than pure laziness.

- Esse Est Percipi

15. For many or some things, depending on the subject, we must refuse to define them until they have defined themselves.

16. By being deathly afraid of offending anyone, which incidentally there is no commandment regarding this written anywhere, we conform ourselves to a mold which will eventually shape us into someone we are not. Those who claim to be being themselves while maintaining this philosophy are lying to themselves. We can't offend them anyway since they aren't who they are, but are instead someone else entirely.

- We Are Not Who We Are

4. Interpret This

1. It matters little what words we choose; the meaning will only fully be contained in the concept of those words in the ears of the hearers. The people we enjoy hearing the most only reinforce our concept of reality as described by those words, which may or may not be being used accurately or adequately.

Many won't bother to look up even words they do know, much less those they don't. The largest group contradicting this behavior would be teachers, but counted among the thousands of people encountered in the last fifty years, this group is still very small. This describes the denotation.

Connotatively, most can't help themselves from coloring every word with some detractive character screen or contextual element that bears no relation to the subjects discussed. E.g., Abraham Lincoln was a compassionate imbiber of thick distilleries, so nothing else he said could possibly be true, though it was never seen that anything he said isn't. So, everything we hear is viewed through this useless, mind-altering, character destroying, dictionary abusing filter (hard to call it a brain) which most palm off with the phrasing "good judge of character," while offering no credentials proving this capacity.

There are good, though not provably accurate, ways around this disability. Trying is at the top, if we can push past the palpably dense apathy of the age. Putting all this together, it's surprising any communication happens at all or that anything ever gets done in any direction. It's doubtful that without some miracle producing agency which most hate or needlessly fear, anyone ever in their lifetime, or several were that possible, ever get anywhere near experiencing the truth, reality, or depth of life where pure motives can be clearly seen, which we find could we ever achieve

- True Communication

2. Since some of what we read is a translation from another original language, we may wonder: Which language would offer the smoothest transition of the nuanced interstices? Just imagine if you were a nuanced interstice traveling along in your comfortable sentence when suddenly you're shifted into a language that's clumsier than a seven-thumbed hand or a sloth playing tennis. Many of the subtle shades of meaning which may or may not shed further reflective thoughts onto the subject are suddenly jolted out of existence. Or, conversely, which language could *add* a smoothness to nuanced interstices that was neither possible nor present in the original language? Surely this has already been done, but we still can't help but feel sorry for the hapless nuanced interstices that have to suffer through appearances and disappearances, sometimes forever lost, wandering through a broken humanity it could otherwise help - homeless, friendless, and too often lacking existence entirely. Is there currently such a language that could solve this or is one about to arrive?

- Cloying Compunction for the Nuanced Interstice

3. Yet further proof that the bible is the word of God:

Notice that for every other translation of anything into English (Dante's Inferno, Hegel's Phenomenology of Spirit, the Voynich Manuscript, etc.) we don't find fourteen trillion translations into English largely, if not solely based on the complaint that "we can't understand anything here written even though it's printed in clear words in English." Rather than asking God what it means, as the book itself tells us to do in several places,$_{52}$ we go to the printing press and expect to find better answers from man than from God.

This is as we would expect to find when seeing our reactions to other things. We imagine our peers are the only ones who can truly understand us. We believe only men can understand men, and women can only understand women. The same reaction is found to be applied to countries, nationalities, races, animals, aliens, and microbial genetic engineers. Only the same in kind are outfitted with the exclusive ability of being the sole souls in the universe capable of complete and reliable comprehension of everything about that kind. (None of this is a fact, but it's what we believe very strongly, so it has its effects.)

So, we see the same pattern: We have very little difficulty understanding English when a man or woman writes any piece which is then translated into English from the original. But we have the most difficult time, often rivaling the most faded hieroglyphics the Egyptians ever chiseled onto crumbling stones in any era, comprehending the Word of God, thus proving it actually IS the word of God. The pure words of man never find this obstacle, real or imagined. This is only a mental block since if Jesus is God, then He's also a man, and we actually *can* understand him regardless of our native language. Pride, darkness, and rebellion compose a large part of this problem as well. But so does what has just been said.

4. Not interpreting or refusing to interpret doesn't qualify as interpreting. Neither does taking something and interpreting it as nothing. Any ignoring the spirit or letter of the idea is ignoring, not interpreting.

5. From the following, we can prove several college professors from this day never studied either Luther or the lawyers of his time. They think it's a great elation to couch the course material in an elaborate, impenetrable haze of obscurity by supplying an endless stream of vague, equivocal terms, which they then quickly shift in between at least three separate definitions for each term under study. The same dense fog is likely preventing them from seeing exactly what they imagine themselves to be teaching or why teaching has suddenly become a problem for them.

> "For it is justly said among lawyers, 'The words of one speaking obscurely, when he can speak more plainly, should be interpreted against him.'" [53]

Then on the other side, there are some who by refusing to ever lift a dictionary, declare everything around them obscure.

- Say What You Didn't Say

6. We must be careful to remember that when hearing messages about God's will for our lives that this has nothing to do with what sadists do to us. It's beyond doubt that being forced to watch family members or ourselves tortured has nothing at all to do with God's will for us.

This has more to do with the freedom of the will and how we use it. And it is certain that any involved in performing or allowing gross or even covert acts of sadism will all be lined up in a room one day (whether before or after death, makes no difference) to give a careful, detailed account about why they did it.

Some blame God for these things, others blame the devil, when far too often, neither one had anything to do with it - not at all. Rather the fault lies entirely within the misshapen pates of the supremely intelligent, highly advanced race of humankind and their repeated failed efforts to make a decision.

7. For those of us who have had the punishment of having to copy out the dictionary, here is a small test - ungraded. It is unnecessary to advertise the answers.

a. Did you notice you weren't looking at an original document?

b. Did you question what language the document was originally written in?

c. Did you actually expect to reach the 'Z's?

d. Did you notice you were reading a copy?

e. Did you wonder where the copy differed from the original?

f. Did it cross your mind that since this is a copy, it could also be a copy of a copy?

g. Did you search the beginning pages to see who the author was if it wasn't contained in the name itself, such as Webster's?

h. Did you notice that "some man" wrote everything in that book?

i. Did you search the copyright page to see how many thousands of years ago the book was written?

j. Did any of these investigations lead you to question the interpretation of the letter "A" or its definition?

k. Did you notice a comma or semicolon that was out of joint and needed repair and put the rework into your own copy?

l. Did you redefine any of the words and place instead your own "better" version of how the original author "probably intended" the definition to read?

m. Did you ever get your work graded or returned with corrective marks?

n. Did you ever think as you were working that none of this really mattered anyway since it's just one man's opinion of how each word should be defined?

o. Did this encourage you to get a degree in etymology?

p. Did this prompt you to apply for a job as a proofreader of dictionaries?

q. Did you realize that it makes no difference what's written in this book when everyone has their own definitions for nearly every word that's in it?

r. Did you discover while writing that most people have no idea that this book even exists?

s. Did you form an opinion that this is a book of truth?

t. Did you finish?

8. These two statements have the same problem. See if it can be determined what it is before reading the explanation.

"It's not your job to influence others."

"It's not up to anyone to say how things should or shouldn't be."

Note the one thing they have in common: they are assumed to *not* apply to the speaker. If they did, the speaker would be guilty of performing against their own recommendations. And if it did apply to the speaker, they would be setting an example precisely the opposite of their statements, so the talk wouldn't match the walk.

This is the exact problem: If true, both these statements *do* apply to the speaker. Statement 1 is precisely and only intended to influence the behavior of another. Statement 2 is exactly saying how things should or shouldn't be while hiding behind words that say the reverse. A translation would be: "Things should not be where we have people running around saying how things should or shouldn't be." If so, then there's no need to say the statement, since it cancels itself out and we have become one of the ones under proscription by the statement.

Deceptions are often subtle and hard to see. These two statements don't fall into that class since it's too obvious to see what's wrong with them. Since the person is behaving opposite of their own words at the same time as they're saying them, we can safely ignore them for the same reason contained by the statements themselves.

The statements are also intended to set up a one way street, and as such, they're tools of manipulation. An attempt to place others beneath and oneself above. As we can, we work to make sure these efforts are wasted and come to nothing by seeing them for what they are. Failing that, we can tell them -

- You Can Stick It Up Your One Way Street

9. What we perceive is very often only our own decision. Countless times have passed where what was said sent someone into a frenzy of rage, but there wasn't anything wrong with what was said. They decided to interpret what was said using some assumed innuendo or hidden agenda that hadn't even been thought of and still isn't being, then decided to punish the speaker for their own decision. We may try to remove these quickly from being around us since they can't understand basic languages. They're infected with this "right to not be offended" disease or what's worse, the habit of deliberate misinterpretation to inflict maximum sadistic damage. Or it can just happen by accident from not knowing or considering

- What You Perceive Is Your Own Decision

10. How do we learn that the real crime starts at the beginning of the chain and not the end?

"Not that which goeth into the mouth defileth a man; but that which cometh out of the mouth, this defileth a man."

"For out of the heart proceed evil thoughts, murders, adulteries, fornications, thefts, false witness, blasphemies:" [54]

This isn't the end of the chain with bodies on the floor, blood on the ceiling, items or people missing, this is the beginning.

Therefore, true justice finds the beginning of the chain, then awards and dispenses itself accordingly. Every other action is false and has nothing to do with justice at all regardless of any man-scribbled laws to the contrary. "Who started it?" is more relevant now than it was when we were five. Whoever ignores this is a false representative of justice and doesn't deserve the post.

- Severe Reading Comprehension Disorder Is A Preventable Disease

5. Mind Slaves

1. The deceived are slaves to the liar; therefore those who spread lies aren't as opposed to slavery as they may otherwise claim. Not practicing forgiveness ever means we fully support abusive slavery.

2. Guilt peddlers aren't interested in anything but putting people into the position of a slave. The fact that they never have solutions to the problems they generate indicates they desire this position to be lifelong. Any who create or even have the desire to create lifelong slaves won't be the ones who have any permanent solution, if there is one. This is why they never mention the real slavery happening right now. They aren't interested in stopping it and could care less about any who are now suffering under it. They paint themselves as victims meanwhile ignoring those who truly are. Since they don't care about real slavery, their message is meaningless and the more quickly placed on ignore the better. When there are over seventy million human trafficking victims today, how long would we need to search to find even one person who cares?

3. When demons possess people, they force them to act in ways that are intended to challenge God's desire to have any humans in heaven.

"You would have this thing wandering around even in the same universe?" would be one paraphrase of their several arguments. People who release murderers and punish the innocent go a long way to help the devils make their argument. We may be fairly certain that the devil himself would love to thank them. Maybe one day he will. I will laugh.

4. Notice how math and science are very specific, except in certain key areas. One of those is calculating *exactly* what a person needs to be paid to keep up with the cost of living.

Note how the cost of living varies from point to point, but the minimum wage doesn't. This is the first clue.

The truth seems to be, no one really cares if companies are paying up to or above this cost, which necessarily only generates more poor, poverty, national debt, and debt slaves.

So, all the whiners about slavery can here be seen to actually not give one damn about it since they never mention this in their illustrious sermons to the universe. If any companies do care about this, they aren't spreading their lessons to the rest to ensure entire job health to the nations they live in. They also seem to be in the minority given the twenty-two trillion dollar national debt.

Debt, then, must be a supreme sign of intellectual progress and advancement which can prolong a society in perfect health and keep it safely on the map; otherwise, why waste time creating millions of debt slaves?

If this calculation is too cumbersome, close shop and allow the companies that do know how to use a calculator become the majority till the national debt, student loan debt, credit card debt, et. al., drop closer to zero, then we may bring back our debt slave creation which we believe will save the universe. If we don't really care, why pretend? It's fooling no one in reality.

- Debt Slaves

5. The reason why we don't hear about exorcisms as much as in former times is that today the demons have everyone so well trained that people spontaneously vomit every idea the devil would say if he were to possess them without so much as one demon having to lift a finger to touch anyone to do so. With sufficient time, any society or world incessantly and willingly motivated by demons will soon begin to speak and move as though they were the demons themselves without one devil even needing to get out of bed to do anything to bring it about. They would all be on demonic autopilot.

Something that has been alive for over six thousand years that hates us with an unchangeable passion will have no trouble using reality against us. Any ignorance of reality or expecting it to bend to our will only aids them. Not changing any conditions of the experiment is the topmost cause of failures. Even changing one thing can bring success. Too many barely make a feeble attempt at creating even one condition, much less ever changing it.

Satan now has so many mouthpieces that he no longer needs to rouse himself from the burning slumbers to attack anyone to spread his doctrine. Were there a sufficient number who were divorced from apathy, we would have accurate records of the number of possessed around the globe and would very likely see this number diminishing from lack of usable effect. There's no need to waste the energy when he has several billions at his disposal willingly providing him with free labor.

So we see here that there is another, more subtle and dangerous type of possession where one becomes possessed with the ideas of another without the owner of the original idea even having to locate any global pressure point, perform any spiritual transplant, or bother any priest.

Most believe that hearing the views of other people will cause this demonic transfer to take place, so they use bats, venom, lies, hatred, false accusations, backstabbing, knee-jerk reactions, scowls, and a host of other methods of Supreme Holy Compassion and Tolerance to keep the ever-so-dangerous, fatal opposing viewpoints at an inaudible level so they won't run the risk of becoming possessed.

But it's actually the opposite: *never* examining one's own beliefs and *never* hearing the views of others (which does the same thing) provides a near ninety-nine percent chance of positively being possessed.

- Exorcist Unemployment Checks

6. Law of Cause and Effect

1. We are not required to keep promises made to those who break them as a habit. With every effect there exists a causal chain. With every causal chain there exists a first or initial cause. Sometimes several causal chains are found to have a single first cause

2. By not addressing the root cause of any first instance, we become the root cause of the second. This works for both positive and negative instances. This is also why so many courts and judges are guilty of crimes whether they realize it or not.

3. If teleology is correct, then every interruption is only preventing major progress by forestalling every conclusion.

4. Everything we see around us is an effect of some cause. To believe otherwise requires more faith than most have or can produce. Since it's faith, it has nothing to do with science.

5. If we're in a stream of cause and effect chains which is too random too often, what we do is combine several causes into one to begin a new chain of effects. This is one way to view creation. Also, whatever is created is given force by its creator.

6. Proof of societal conditioning:

Say the antonym for misogynist in less than five seconds. If our society were truly equal, as most claim we are, then you wouldn't be fumbling for the word now. In fact, this word has never been heard by this author in any movie, news report, or TV show, and only in few books, if any.

Yet people who feel this way are a major group today, vying for control, recognition, and sympathy. Yet, under the rules of equality, if one is wrong, then so is the opposite, and vice versa. Or can we have it both ways like when we were five?

In a world where misogyny is not ok, but misandry is, this only proves further that we're not equal.

Should we still trust our surroundings?

- We're Not Equal

7. Whenever we question our existence, the question's cause is inherently wrong or our perception of it.

- Equal Right To Exist

8. When we accept something, we construct and project emanations conforming to some geometric pattern of concrementational divination. What this summons back in return will usually be both variable and unknown, which may allow to lie dormant for decades undesired seeds that spawn what can't be seen or addressed, that also could render untold destruction.

The usual caution arises somewhat from this. When we find those who won't accept the obvious, we can know through triangulation to exist at least some or a large possibility that they are aware that these forces are precisely what they're sending out. Their lack of accepting anything is how they imagine none of it will come back. This might be believable were it not for the Law of Equal & Opposite Reaction.

9. Q: What should be done with teachers who teach via equivocation?

A: They unequivocally should be handed all equivocal answers on "equality" paper that isn't quite wood or plastic using pencils that aren't either lead or graphite. They should equally hand them to the teacher's aids from other classes to see if they understand how to trans-literally communicate via the opprobrious channels. And/or, every answer should be "google it," while actually meaning to use "bing," since this is the stock answer for questions today.

Or, this should be done via the anti-incorrectational methodology of the hyper-ingregariological sanctions proffered under the maladictatorial systemics of ultra-linguistic obfuscatory committees now extant.

They can't complain about any of this, since they started it. We're just copying their wonderful example. If they like that, they can set a better one.

- We're All Equivocal

10. People babbling incessantly about climate change is producing a provable increase in the amount of CO_2 emissions from humans, so choosing to remain silent about it will save the universe.

Proof: One babbler vociferating non-stop about unprovable theories emits more CO_2 than 800 SUVs over a period of 300 years.

- Keep Your Faith To Yourself

11. Evolution created the greenhouse gas CO_2, and so is the direct culprit of ruining its own creation. If evolution had never created CO_2, which it would not have created if it were supremely intelligent, then there would be no destruction of the planet going on now. Evolution created this problem, so evolution can fix it. Either that or

- Evolution Is A False god

12. Equality. Do we apply the same hate to our own faults as to those of others?

13. Pseudo-intellectuals compose too much of the scientific community today. They can be used to see exactly what *not* to do. Where they typically assume nearly everything, we may freely do the opposite and assume nothing.

- Pure Science Assumes Nothing

14. Since every second is the end of a one quadrillion year cycle when counting backwards and nothing is currently exploding into existence from nowhere, this means that every second is proof that at the end of any quadrillion year cycle or less, any amount of matter popping into existence from nowhere is both impossible, not at all likely, and a ridiculous credulity.

15. In order for science to move any proposition from Theory to Law, it must follow at least three rules, perhaps more:

a. It must be demonstrable.

b. It must be repeatable.

c. It must be possible to perform by more than one person.

Causality (the *law* of Cause & Effect) is a *law* for precisely these reasons.

Creation is based on Causality and is therefore scientific.

The "Turtles All The Way Down" *theory* is nothing but a theory and always will be. It was told as a joke to children, and a joke it still is. Teaching a joke as a fact is *not* scientific. This theory will never move into the realm of law since there is no way to demonstrate that there can ever be any effects (such as an entire *universe* of matter) with absolutely no cause whatsoever. Also, one of sciences own laws (the Law of Entropy) proves that no combination of inert matter could ever come together to form life by itself without the active force of some external agency.

It's hard trying to learn anything from confused people (which explains why I and several billion others still know next to nothing), but it's possible.

- The Law of Ignorance

16. If we refuse to both trace and address a problem back to its source, we now know our position as it relates to any problem. If we only treat and punish the symptoms while blinding ourselves to the root causes, we now know what we are. We are the enabler.

- The Enablers

7. Answer the Question

1. When is an answer important? Sometimes if it's ever quiet and still, we can think into the future and hear some words. The words coalesce into the structure of a general question, occasionally it's vague. Often it's about something we already know, but haven't put into words. As we're composing the concept for a response, we realize this is a question from someone who read what we wrote or saw what we did, but didn't understand some aspect of it. This lack will stretch forever forward into eternity so long as we refuse to answer the question.

2. If any won't give us time to think or compose an intelligent response, they aren't interested in truth and won't be a solution to any of our problems.

3. *"What then is the result of what has been said? Is not this the result--that other things are indifferent, and that wisdom is the only good, and ignorance the only evil?"* 55

From here, we can see that people who answer questions accurately and effectively to the best of their ability are those who promote the only good, and those who don't promote the only evil. Any who refuse to answer any questions at all, or whose answers only cloud rather than clear the issue, are only teaching evil, regardless of how many letters may follow the name. We may try to ask questions that people won't answer to clearly illuminate the line between good and evil so everyone can see exactly where it is. Asking a question where we already know the answer is neither an evil nor a good since it changes nothing in terms of wisdom for anyone.

4. People are how they are to an extent due to parenting, which has a variety of styles. Those using the same style find each other like varieties of trees or schools of ostriches. Some styles are toxic to the environment, but don't believe they are because their children didn't die in the process.

These are like salted earth on which nothing can grow, vast wastelands of crushed concrete covered regions in nowise useful for any agriculture. These are largely recognizable by an annoying hallmark trait: they never ask nor answer questions about anything or anyone, especially themselves.

- The Unexamined Brain Is Not Worth Thinking

5. People who have no better idea than the one under proposition, or any solution whatsoever, can be safely ignored.

Proof: They have no solution.

Once one such person, after he was asked a question, carried on at some length of days with prodigious grandiloquent bombast, yet never answered the initial question. He was necessarily abandoned. Yet, this happens very often, hence this proof. However, depending on the event, only one behavior pattern of this kind isn't really enough to waste time thinking about. But if there is one, it's a safe bet it isn't unique.

8. I Am The Truth

1. The truth doesn't always arrive as a night and day contrast. It sometimes arrives by noticing all the small lies, removing them, then from that, as an epiphany on some random day by an Arby's, a complete change occurs in our understanding of what is around us.

2. For those who can see, truth found anywhere shines through its respective medium and glows with a palpable warmth and brilliance that can bring tears to the people who love it.

3. If you ever change your mind and agree with me, I won't notice. The person that is helped the most by believing the truth is the believer. If I ever turn out to be wrong, I typically won't apologize, since I'm not trying to be wrong and everyone is wrong about something nearly most of the time.

If we ever stumble across the truth, it is most definitely through no power of our own. If anyone asks us to do the impossible, we have either misunderstood the person/writer, or that person is wrong. Everything we need to do is possible. All we're asked of by the truth is to simply believe it when it reveals itself.

4. What if the argument between God and man actually was our fault? This isn't hard to accept when we expect others to believe the existing lies in any of our belief systems without question. Things repeated for hundreds of years, as if that makes them any more true, regardless of any proof to the contrary, are commands expected to garner universal obeisance.

But what if we actually were God's enemy? What if we wanted to kill people just because they don't agree with our point of view? What if we wanted to murder anyone, whether we actually do this or not is quite irrelevant, simply because of what they've said? While we believe, promote, or kill for any lie, we will remain God's enemy.

5. When we communicate and become keenly aware that nothing of what we've said has been heard, this is because we are not speaking the language of the hearer. There are a few reasons why this may happen, but one of them is blindness. Aural blindness happens for a few reasons also, but one is societal conditioning, another is spiritual awareness.

We may have heard the same series of words since we were children, and yet not have the understanding or relationship with those phrases that we will have at some point in our future. Since we have been warned that "*blindness in part is happened to Israel*,"[56] we must compose a strategy to eliminate as much of it as we can. If it can happen to God's most favored, anyone is susceptible. Since we are finite, it will most likely never entirely be removed where we now exist. Blindness has never been known to be cured by refusing to admit that we are. We aren't responsible for how society conditions us, or that they do, but we are responsible for how we fight the lies this conditioning contains.

Most of the time people don't try to listen to others, but this isn't always the case. Many times, from experience, it's because the person is currently blind to the words or concepts we're trying to convey, whether they define the words differently or some deeper conceptual shortcoming. This is why it is critical when we communicate to take the steps necessary to remove the blindness which ensures that we can

- See What I'm Saying?

6. Why we avoid the truth many times has nothing to do with being able to understand or handle it. We construct elaborate fantasies about other people we think we know to explain their behavior instead of just taking it for what it is. We believe nothing they tell us about their real motives, even when they're true, which admittedly too often they aren't.

Any truth will necessarily shatter these fantasies. There is no more dangerous person than one whose delusions have been shattered, save the best of deceivers. For passive, the lies increase, for overt, the violence will increase, for the manipulators, both increase.

Trying to hang on to even one small shred of the fantasy, such as the entire universe is obsessed with their wives or husbands and other such stupidity, they flail about like dying political structures as the truth slays their house of lies.

This is why, even though difficult, we may look for the truth as if for gold from a mine. Then after finding it, instead of manipulating others, try to manipulate and control our own reactions to it. .

7. Often the truth is in a balance of two or more concepts, viewpoints, or realities. But it's also frequently found in remote reaches far from the center of anything. This is because truth is an extremity.

8. The truth isn't always in official reports or history books, although it's possible it can be surmised. The truth isn't always spoken, but done when no one is watching so it's assumed to never be discoverable. I watch how people hide the facts, and then I hide the same facts from them in a different area and notice how they don't like it. The revelation, the exposure, the surprise, the anger - yet at no time did I see them stop hiding anything. The truth is hidden behind the stories that we all have to get straight before we're discovered by the future. How much of a shock then must it have been to them who heard Him say those words in their faces:

- I Am The Truth

9. Positively Negative

1. Since we have seen that dreams are exceptionally skilled liars, and we know they come from the subconscious, then it must be that some lies are necessary, some negatives are required to be observed. They are created into our reality and since they are typically beyond our choice, they are part of nature. Do these exist for us to see what they are or some other reason?

2. When we continue to do things the wrong way, telling ourselves it will work won't change the outcome.

3. When people pigeon hole us into a box and make us into something we're not, this is their own creation. When they thereafter imagine we're guilty of some crime based on this fabricated analysis, who's the criminal, us or them?

4. If positivity training or positive thinking existed in reality, no one would be turned down from any job since the positive mind would discover a way to use every job applicant. Any arguments against this idea will be necessarily negative and prove the both the point and that the arguer has no clue about positivity.

5. Believing very strongly or killing anyone who disagrees with us that $2 + 2 = 12$ won't change the answer in our favor. Believing that $2 + 2 = 12/x$ may work if we get the x right. We could say that everyone who says "$2 + 2 = 12$ is wrong" is just being negative and should be completely ignored; but this will only yield an exponentially negative result.

- Positivism Is Positively Negative

6. Whenever we hear about any individual being responsible for their conditions or surroundings (which admittedly is true on occasions), we ought to immediately check the obvious.

a. Is the individual the *only one* capable of making any decisions that affect the surroundings? A: *No.*

b. Are sentient creatures around the individual the only ones that can affect every decision the individual makes? A: No (an earthquake will affect their decisions.)

c. Is there a small, or large number of sentient creatures around the individual that are capable of making decisions that affect the surroundings? A: Large. (Over 10 billion, if we count all animals.)

d. Is the individual a CEO or congressman who can decide how much money they make every year? A: No, in most cases.

Given this and probably about 15 more questions we don't have time to consider, why is there such an overwhelming urge to blame an individual when they are only a small part of the overall equation?

A: It frees everyone from any responsibility of doing anything that would make the outcome go into a more positive direction and allows the greatest amount of selfishness to pass unchecked or even be mentioned. And, mostly, it prevents a unified voice speaking out that would not allow these things to happen were a large enough group of people to gather with the determination not to continue to allow it.

This is why the statement "Life is what you make it" is wrong. The correct statement is "Life is what we allow it to be, while not sitting around addicted to apathy would make it something else."

7. When we are clearly in the wrong (believing lies and trying to force others to believe them, etc.), we should feel wrong. If someone explains the truth of the matter to us, we should feel like changing the situation, not anger at the person stating the facts of the case. If we don't feel like changing, no one should feel like aiding and abetting our descent into self-delusion or molly-coddling us into a false sense of bliss and security when our future lies elsewhere. If we don't feel like making positive changes, then we feel like making negative ones, and none should feel responsible for sympathy toward us. How do you feel?

- Treacle Tyrants

8. We can never move in any forward direction as long as there are so many, nearly everyone it seems sometimes, taking something that is positive and redefining it in negative terms. This is in fact one of the largest elements that destroyed the case mentioned in this book and most likely scores of others, and its path of destruction is far from over.

9. If methods of proof are unwanted, unwarranted, and negative in every possible condition or environment outside of a courtroom, then we can't say they are successful in a courtroom. The efforts to prove this will continue until the courtroom methods are improved.

10. A mistake resulting from a failed effort fueled by good intentions, far from being the negative any self-appointed judge will pressure us into believing it is, is actually very informative. A second similar mistake can be used to triangulate the real problem.

11. Another fundamental flaw with the ad hominem or character assassination, is that it does what all positive thinking psychologists world wide encourage others to do: Assume The Negative. It maintains that there is one act this or that person did that is so wrong, they can never do another right as long as they live throughout eternity. It also breaks the normal flow of courtroom logic by not only presenting the assassin as "innocent until proven guilty", but "innocent even after proven guilty." It also breaks the normal flow of courtroom logic by presenting the victim of the assassin as "guilty both before and even after being proved innocent."

It is the equivalent of saying, "because this person wasted 1 penny, they can never make or give to others over $45 million at any point in the future," which is obviously a lie.

Or, "because this person wasted any value of money, they can never make any more money or give it to others for the rest of their lives," which again is an obvious lie. There is so much wrong with slander that it's a marvel anyone in court ever uses it at all. Then we pretend to wonder what's wrong with the justice system.

- Assume The Negative

12. The only positive thing about being forced to live an unnecessarily limited existence is that the balance of the universe points to the extremely large potential for a necessarily unlimited one

to follow. Over 99% of the other things involved in a limited existence are negative. Knowing this points to the insanity involved in wanting to force others into any limitation.

13. We look for answers. What if the answer is a problem? What if the problem is negative? What if sheltering ourselves from the negative prevents us from finding the answer? What if the problem is negative, but the solution is positive? In this case, being positive and closing our eyes to everything negative is actually negative itself, since it prevents the solution to any problem that falls into this class.

What if the answer is a question? What if the question is negative, but the solution is positive? Same result. What if what we think or call negative really isn't, only our reaction to it is negative? "I know for a fact that without fear, this case would have already been solved," was one example. So, in these cases, the only real negative problem causing wrong reactions which prevents a positive solution is the fear of problem solving.

14. Across a lateral line, we found the description of a unique problem, sans blame or conjecture. Bisecting this line in the middle, we found a separate, vertical line which was a calm, useful, accurate interpretation of the meaning and application of the first line. From this literary glyph we saw how to turn a negative into a positive.

15. If we have a degree, all we have are the ideas, wrong or right, of "some man." Occasionally these ideas are actually wrong, but we'll see this as history corrects and rewrites itself later. If we've read any book, we've just seen the words of "some man." If we've heard any music, with or without words, it was just written by "some man." Any idea, written or spoken, are just the ideas of "some man."

So every idea, both wrong and right are just from "some man." All the words of truth and deception are only written or spoken by "some man." Since we didn't invent any of the words we know, all the words we now know were only created by "some man." It is unclear who is thinking positively when they say this, but supposedly we're all capable of positive thinking.

Whoever this man is, he's very powerful, having created every idea of deception and truth and filling every person on the planet with every thing he ever wrote or said. Maybe one day we'll be lucky enough to meet whoever this is, who no one ever believes or hears, yet is responsible for every single thing they know, but of which, none of it can be true since they're only the misguided concepts, thoughts, and broken, failed ideas created by

- "Some Man"

16. We study conflict and aggression in order to avoid it. People who avoid solving problems and labeling those who do negative are merely scared of the conflict involved in solving them. Studying problems with no emotional reaction is usually best, but not always the solution. Yielding to fear will produce failure. Yielding to compassion and understanding usually won't. Applying compassion and understanding to the primary instigator and aggressor will never be a solution for anything. E.g., giving a tyrant everything she wants because she grew up in a bad neighborhood with no parents won't win the war.

People who will sacrifice everyone but themselves will only add to the problems, and never solve any of them. And so long as they aren't directly affected, they could care less if the problem never gets solved. People who don't have a zero body count as a goal won't yield the best solution. One person is the least likely to provide the best solution. People insisting they're right when life daily disproves them are one of the largest obstacles to cooperation. Another is worshiping the god of Convenience. When we apply conflict and aggression to our mistakes, we can begin to see how to avoid it with others. People who avoid finding solutions only extend the problem's duration and rate of exponential expansion. Self-defense is a part of studying conflict.

17. The Breath of Life. It appears more lovely every time anyone or anything tries to take it away for any reason. We draw it in and consider how many days we never even thought about it, appreciated it, or respected it. But this is a negative angle with a positive direction. It censures the times when it was taken for granted with the hopes of not doing so in the future. But there's only so far we can go with this and many other ideas: we appreciate it, then what? How long do we sit in this condition? Obviously not more than fifteen minutes on average, or time is measured as being wasted. Or is it?

18. In order for God to create any other thing with its own awareness, He first had to understand Himself to such an extent and with such precision that He would even be able to do so to begin with. How can anyone create an awareness while having no clue what it is? What are its physical and spiritual components? Not knowing this, nothing is what would be created.

For all of man's positive thinking and spiritual and self-awareness, we have yet to come up with anything close to or required by this level of understanding. The majority aren't even concerned for or looking in that direction, and don't even know the direction exists to look in, mostly fueled by their oft repeated pet phrase: "I don't care." Spiritualists perhaps have arrived a bit closer to a real understanding, but may be missing the physical components required. Failing a firm grasp of this understanding, not even the animation of the Frankenstein monster is within our reach, much less anything more useful than a dead vengeance on fire.

For all of man's believing that he knows everything all the time and very reluctantly and rarely, if ever, admits that he knows nothing, this direction should have long ago been understood and studied. Not the creation of life, but finding the precise components needed for its existence. It may be this will never be in our power, but never looking and proving this will never discover whether or not it is.

Believing we know everything has only produced over five millennia of failure. Maybe it's time to see what results if we ever admit that we don't.

- The Source of Life

19. Scientists have arrived at a late-breaking discovery about electrons. It appears that the reason electrons move when we look at them, preventing us from observing their normal behavior, is that they're embarrassed. Shining a light of any kind causes them to flee in sheer panic and confusion. They feel like they're not wearing any clothes, so they quickly try to run to a closet to put something on which they had recently purchased from Foley's, frantically searching the clothes racks for an Italian gaberdine suit or a mauve raglan sleeve sweater. But they realize quickly that they can't get away due to the fierce and unrelenting

gravitational pull of the nucleus. Which led scientists to conclude that all nuclei are mean, salty dictators and have issued a worldwide warning to be aware of nuclei posing as internet bullies who enjoy kidnapping and demanding ransoms for their captured electrons.

If they start with one of the smallest of things, an electron, where will it end? Eventually skyscrapers, planets, suns, and galaxies will be captured and forced into circular labor by these harsh tyrants, most of whom are invisible, hiding behind the clear door of the obvious only revealed by the most expensive, powerful microscope which only politicians can afford, since most people will never make $495k a year in their lifetimes, or even scores of lifetimes combined.

Instead, focus groups have been dispatched by the administration of the top scientific communities to help the electrons deal with their pent-up emotions while authorities work on some way to free the tortured cruxes of negative energies. But since they're negative, it's doubtful that anyone will ever really help them, since aiding negative energy will only draw more of it to us, according to karmic law.

So, since we're only going to be positive, it's probable that eventually these lost, tortured signals will be left in the dark to fend for themselves; hopeless, neglected, without food or clothing. Their only crime? They're

- Negative By Nature

20. Anytime others believe the worst about us, it only drives away the successes they claim to wish we had and attracts more negative situations to both them and us that usually prevents us from having more successes. It also keeps any real progress we make in any area invisible to them. Their rumors keep them invisible to everyone else. Somehow all of this is positive thinking, even though nothing positive has ever been seen to come from it.

If it weren't for science and observation, this might become a larger concern and we would be forced to believe them. Using science, we may record our own progress through observation and prove every one of their lies to be exactly what they are. A strong belief in recidivism can actually become a cause of it. It is also an indicator of what we actually wish to see, unwittingly exposing our motives to others who know this.

The audience will usually get what it wants and even though the massive potential to create something far better is always present, what is actually generated is a cascading dissolution from which there is no recovery, either due to their own views or the addiction to some rumor that's immediately believed on sight with no examination allowed, cross or otherwise.

It has never been seen where exactly this approach is either taught, preached, or recommended. So until we discover some book or church that promotes it, it will have to remain something that is apparently learned by proxy and imitation, or by brute force and humiliation into compliance which, in either case, is accepted by willing and unwitting shills, gleefully practiced and immediately believed on sight with no examination allowed, cross or otherwise.

21. Sometimes a positive attitude does the work of the devil by making the slam to the ground that much harder when the opposite of what we expect happens. Much harder than either expecting the worst or expecting nothing, which are the other two options always available. At the same time, never expecting the positive will similarly magnetically attract whatever else it is we're expecting. Ofttimes the wait isn't very long. This law is actually universal.

22. If people could transmute their negative belief systems into positive the way they transmute the correct statements of others into incorrect ones, imagine how much more wealth and less stress everyone would have?

- Gossipmongers

23. When we were teens, some of the largest things we hated was having believed everything we heard from our elders which turned out to be false many times. So, to correct this oversight, when we grew older we continued to believe everything we heard, ignored the lessons we hated when we were teens and repeated the same mistakes ad infinitum while preaching about positive thinking and imagining we're attractive to aliens.

24. CPAP - Continuous Positive Airway Pressure. This means that it forces positive, provable beliefs into the airways of our belief systems that will help remove that itching need to kill everyone who doesn't

believe the way we do. True, not everyone is psychotic and has this itching need, but who couldn't use a few billion more beliefs that you can actually prove?

- The Power of Positive CPAPs

25. Few will become their potential and perform the positive. It would be worse if we didn't have Eternity. ∞

10. When the Public Eye Has Become the Public Enemy

1. As the excuses for ignoring facts, shirking responsibility, or any version of the permanent staving off of reality rises, this creates a blind spot in the collective attention of any group of people.

2. An object behaves differently when under scrutiny than when no eyes fall upon it. The object then becomes ensnared by whatever the onlookers are drawing to themselves by the law of attraction. Whatever they're afraid they will see is the only thing they will see, only made possible by the power of their own fears or narrow sampling. Even if the object doesn't want to take part in the useless display, it makes no difference since the universe is stronger.

This is why learning to control our fear is crucial, since it not only affects us but others as well. There is more to this idea, so it will show up again.

- See What You Want To See

3. *"The act of observing a system inevitably alters its state."* - The Observer Effect[57]

This is seen in anything from computer programs to electron behavior under light. On a larger scale it is repeatedly seen altering the course of events, destiny, and even reality. When the light is strong enough, the choice of the electron becomes zero. When the light is either unaware of its effects, uneducated, or both, when does its responsibility begin? Effects caused by irresponsible light treatments are reversed or balanced by what agent or series of events?

8. PHRIXIONAL ASSENTION

The public eye has long been a known enemy to free will. Since memory can still enforce changes made by the public eye long after the eye is removed from any subject, when does the free will begin again after any amount of scrutiny, whether just or unjust? That it has caused murder is known by the fact that we have a republic and not a pure democracy. Is there any regulation or governance of this either known, written, or discussed that can ensure or protect the rights of free will against the destructive, arbitrary, unmerciful forces that elusively cower in plain sight behind the public eye?

4. *"90. In owning property I place my will in an external thing, and this implies that my will, just by being thus reflected in the object, may be seized in it and brought under compulsion. ... - it may be coerced."*[58]

If we consider reality to be the external thing, and the public eye as the coercing agent, we can see that by allowing our reality to be defined by the public eye we have been being coerced by it for far too long. This is not only alarming, but has resulted in the sluggish, desultory, deleterious progress that most people have long been sick of.

The question now is how do we bring the public eye into the light of justice to be punished as the criminal agent which it actually is? Any aggressive act, passive, omissive, or otherwise, is a violation of the free will. The public eye isn't one person, but rather a viewpoint which has coalesced from several into a unified whole and typically travels in the wrong direction, which future generations enjoy pointing out, while doing nothing to correct the base cause. (Yes, reality comprises several properties, but just as with a nation, we can easily conceive of several properties as being but one and weigh it accordingly, but this time legally in a positive direction instead of the typical illegal one.)

5. Politicians' jobs would be far easier if they didn't have to daily iron out the billions of misconceptions formed by the public eye. Sometimes these are formed purely out of boredom, other times formed deliberately out of malicious intent.

6. The generalized ultra-permeation of constant hyper-criticality seen in the public eye only means a few things:

a. Low self-esteem.

b. The relentless search for the mythical perfect person which doesn't exist is ongoing.

c. The irresistible urge to be a control freak won't go away any time soon.

11. The Atomic Recorder

1. Space is the recording device which stores every single impression created by matter on a timeline.

2. Time is a construct that allows the replay of events from any point (x1) to any other point (x2). This will be needed for the billions who will be standing in judgment crying in a loud voice, "That never happened." We will be able to replay anything and see precisely what did and didn't happen from any angle. Also, since time is a construct, there was a time when there was no time. Without time, atoms cannot revolve their necessary orbits. Therefore, matter and space have not always existed.

3. It will be amusing to see the face of all the people who die and wake up to find things aren't the way they were lied into believing their whole lives. The purpose of the atom is to create a permanent record of events capable of recall and playback on command. The examination of the atom on any level of its composition will only confirm the veracity of its movements, for those who doubt. Why is this so? Because today we have fools who go to court and say they didn't do things they were clearly seen doing on video tape. Death doesn't change this behavior.

4. A definite point in the future, perhaps even the near future, holds the technology to replay any moment in time in exact detail. For this reason, any object passing through time can neither be altered nor erased. This is a direct result of the fact that matter can neither be created nor destroyed once initially created. Otherwise, the real evidence, the actual moments in time, would be forever out of reach and no true justice would ever be possible.

5. We often can't see what we're looking at without proper instruments. Telescopes, microscopes, X-ray technology have all revealed proof of the invisible worlds which has expanded science beyond our ability to keep up with it. Prior to these proofs, those who believed in the existence of things without needing the proof were sometimes labeled crazy, killed, or locked in sanitariums till science later belatedly proved them right. There is no proof to establish what a belief is, but everyone has them. Through extrapolation we can see that in the future we will not only be able to identify the existence of, but also the objects of belief. Through the correct process, some can do this today.

6. About seventy-five levels below that of sub-atomic particles are recording devices, capable of accurately depicting each movement, sound and detail of every moment in time since the creation of the universe. This can be seen by tracing back the reasons for creating the physical world to begin with rather than choosing to leave everything spiritual. This is another null hypothesis which could prove worthy of further investigation since we are now nowhere near seventy-five levels below subatomic particles in our science.

12. Judge Harshly All You Survey

1. We decide whether anyone is worthy to be judged harshly by us based on what we choose to forget about them.

2. Most, if not all in some cases, of our reactions are based on how we look, what we're wearing, what's on our faces, the sharpness of our beak-like proboscis, the flattened mashing of our pallid pates, the narrowness of our beady eyes, the missing teeth in our sharpened grins, the fragile gait of our chicken legs--from all these we base our responses to each other.

What will happen in not too many years when these forms fade to the nothing whence they came? Will we then realize how much time we wasted making decisions solely based on the Outward Form of Temporary Housing?

3. Judging others prevents progress, since instead of them having the resources to work on their creations, they have to stop and redirect some of them to defend against false accusations which prove to be wrong. What many will try later, which won't work, will be to say they didn't know. But no one can say this since we were told.

4. It's very difficult to criticize people when they're trying to help us. In fact, once we can see the care involved in their efforts, we usually avoid tearing them down at all. But isn't this what happens when hearing information we could use to improve ourselves or our surroundings, and instead of taking that responsibility, find it easier to criticize and assassinate the character of the speaker with a plethora of ad hominems?

Even if this could be called normal to some degree, what isn't normal is stubbornly refusing to see the care involved in their efforts, refusing to remove and ignore the false accusations fired by the character assassins, and refusing to use the valuable information that will improve ourselves and our surroundings. In fact, it's suicidal, albeit not always instantly.

5. Many believe they understand people they both know and don't know by a comforting arrangement of letters, words, and sentences (too often amounting to nothing above a quarrel) that places them in "perspective" as they term it after performing such maneuver. These novelettes are chosen for their ability to both place others under them and to now magically fall under the category of "not my responsibility." The others may even agree to these novelettes if confronted with them directly. Most avoid this confrontation to save face.

But as can clearly be seen, this is all a delusion. Mostly because, just like two different dictionaries, we each define words differently. Any slight alteration in the condition of these novelettes, and the entire piece is wrong. One altered word, then positive is negative, yes is no, true is false. Apart from the obvious that no one is above anyone else, this can fail gloriously if we don't take care to secure accuracy with

- The Hinge Key

6. When we realize we're wrong after fifty years of believing we weren't, what will we do with all that hatred we launched at all the people we were convinced were wrong? Where do we think all that hatred will go?

- As You Slowly Become The People You Hate

7. If court cases go wrong, it is due to the fact that people are addicted to judging others, frequently have no clue about what they're judging, since they have no formal training as judges, and don't really care if they judge correctly or not, since their judgement only affects someone else - for now. Fictional works take advantage of this and weave it carefully into the story. The story is then more believable because at least this much of it is the truth.

8. As long as we think we're doing the right thing, this is actually taken into account at the judgment. But if we know we're doing the right thing, this will make the judgment pass more swiftly.

- The Accountable

9. We can't see this exactly because we're inside, but judgment of others has become so standard now that it is more than just a passing reaction, but rather a finely tuned, highly organized skill with its own invisible academy of agents.

The tools of judgment are now so precise, they no longer resemble tools. The people who judge are now so refined, they no longer resemble judges. The techniques they now use are undetectable as tests or exams; but their conclusions are final and the responses and sentences they pass are unavoidable. Their only problem is that they have no authority other than in their imaginations. The people of the past may well appear to provide their own, more productive version of

- The Unexpected Measure.

10. Once we've done with minimizing the efforts of others in a vain attempt to pigeonhole them into a more manipulable position, we can start to appreciate the tremendous refinement of skill which has always been right in front of us.

11. In the future, everything more than five millimeters beneath the skin will be scraped out and thrown in the trash. No one cares about what's there anyway. We will all be walking paper facades.

12. Let's tie a few of these smaller ideas into one. What is wrong with judging today is that we can know the obvious (where the obvious isn't always the truth), know what the truth is, yet still neither know nor care to do the right thing with any of it. We enjoy getting it completely wrong while knowing and becoming highly excited that we're completely wrong and enjoy the thrill of reckless endangerment. All to serve the modern gods of convenience, apathy, and dismissiveness.

- Mastering How To Do Wrong Properly

13. Being judged by others is like suddenly waking up to discover we're in a test that no one told us about and for which we gave no consent. We are not allowed to protest the results and are forced to live with the consequences of the final grade regardless of whether we feel we have passed.

14. People who only want the worst for others have the worst in their futures.

15. If we abuse someone, we have judged them worthy of being abused. If we desert someone, we have judged them worthy of being

deserted. If we talk to someone(s), we have judged them worthy of addressing. When anyone judges us using these or other methods, we may generally allow it, since even if they don't believe it, every action and word of their judgment (both good and bad) returns to them in full force straight back into their own faces. We may remember this to some degree of comfort during the grueling hours of the least pleasant judgments.

16. The best judges of character are the ones that don't.

17. Every inch of time we spend judging other people

Is an inch of rope that will hang us from the steeple

- Crime Retards Advancement (Building Your Rope)

18. When we use our tools to stab progress, we prevent others from helping us who, in most cases, don't have the intentions we assume they do, since we can only base our assumptions on what *we* know, *not* what *they* know.

So, we assume they are going to do what we would do given the two small pieces of information we think we know for certain about their environment and shunt their growth with our highly trained and intelligent doctors, laws, and hyper-worshiped authority figures. But by doing this, we only stab people who otherwise would have been our friends and would have helped us.

So, in the end, we limit our own progress more than having any affect on the sum of all progress, since the sum doesn't care about our flimsy, ill-informed opinions about what people will or won't do inside any arbitrary situation. So....

- What Did You Do? (Inductive Reason #7,283,485)

19. If we are all different, yet every attempt to address these differences and strengthen them is labeled "racist" or "discrimination" which retards the entire progress, what is the direction or motive with any of this? How does treating everyone the same take advantage or build the strengths or weaknesses of each person? Who is ultimately making all these decisions? Why are we allowing it?

20. We limit the world with our own expectations and punish it accordingly, using this active aggression to bend reality to our sacred will.

21. Some groups discover it to be an impossibility to avoid ad hominems and so liberally baste every sentence with several thousand gallons of them. Not only clouding the issue as a deceptive maneuver, but also clouding their own propositions to the point of absolute irrelevance. It's a treatable disease affecting over five billion people in the world today. The only cure is what the majority will never put any effort into doing, so due to this, it may well be incurable. One cure, among many, is to start using the ears and none of the mouth. A good way to do this is to remember that the followers of cult leaders and tyrants all thought they were right and didn't listen to anyone else, just like the over five billion people in the world today. The psychologists who don't exist yet (the ones we have currently don't care at all about any of this, and so can't be expected to address the issue) have labeled the disease

- Ad Hominentia

22. "What do you mean by 'judge?' I think you mean something different than my idea about it, which is the common connotation regarding it," said the Public Eye.

And in like fashion, when we see this word used by our Lord, it isn't believed that the common connotation today is anywhere close to either the connotation it had at the time, or had over the centuries that followed, or His own idea of the word as He was using it and is still using it as He speaks in the present.

To see whether we have judged anyone or anything, all we need to do is measure the degree of personal responsibility our words have assigned to the predicate of whatever we're discussing. If the responsibility is equal to zero, then we have fully judged the matter and are in danger of a mistake. The common dismissive approach to literally everything today will be seen in the future to have killed billions.

23. If we habitually rehearse the wrongs of others with any other motive than forgiveness or correction, we are wasting our time and bringing about a future we won't be able to survive. This has been seen a countless number of times.

- Evil Surmising

24. We look for imperfections in others so we can shatter the initial image of perfection we have of them, which is an open admission that

we know a perfect person doesn't exist, then start our long path of discovering other ways to hate them. Even knowing this much may or may not stop anything and the chain of error will continue.

25. Judging isn't just something someone says, it's also something they either do or don't do.

26. If B = the bootstrap theory, i.e., that we can pull up the entire surface of the earth with our own bootstraps, and J = how to judge others and x = any human, then we get

Bx ==> ~Jx,

i.e., we can work hard, tirelessly, and effortlessly every second to ensure that none of our beliefs, words, or actions are responsible for judging others.

It also means that no one needs to even bother to tell us this much, since we can lift the earth's surface with bootstraps. This is also because

Ox ==> Ux

or the most certain way to bring harm to ourselves is to bring harm to others. And since self-defense requires work, hard work must be applied since we are the largest threats to ourselves.

27. For being such a highly advanced, non-judgmental society, it seems far more like everyone thinks they're a movie critic, and everyone around them is another movie they can't wait to smear and destroy with snarky smarm. It's difficult to recall a day where this wasn't seen executed with flourish and acid wash breath signed with a double helping of condescension as they flip their pre-programmed heads and chalk another point up on the scoreboard. I won't be at the mixer for the final tally.

- Hyper-Critical World View 101 (Get It Or Get Left)

28. One of the reasons people hate the bible are these two words in it which would remove the world's favorite pastime - Judge Not.

29. We find children adorable, not from the fact having just left the presence of a gracious king, but because we enjoy having slaves that will always do what we say. When they discover they can actually make their own decisions and turn into adults, people abandon them based solely on whether or not they still do what we say. The best humans are those good boys and girls who follow orders, don't make waves, and do

what they're told. If they don't, we leave them to rot and that's their own fault. Even friends are sought out and kept based on the possession of this high-caliber quality.

People who think for themselves and make their own decisions, after realizing that they can, are evil hell-spawn and can never be as adorable as they once were when they were our slaves. Everyone else in the world is really only another child of ours that should do what we say if they know what's good for them. If not, we'll punish them by interruptions, ignoring them, then if that doesn't work, use the ever so mighty separation and abandonment tool. This has taught even the best of us what's "really" right from what's "really" wrong. If anyone doesn't believe any of this, they will soon find out exactly how wrong it is to think otherwise. This is really a matter of no concern since the majority is on our side. And even though we never or rarely do what we say, they had damn well better

- Do What I Say

30. Be yourself, then watch everyone say how you're doing it wrong.

- Do You, Then Get Slapped

31. *"For with the same measure that ye mete withal it shall be measured to you again."* - Christ[59]

The word "withal" literally means and is derived from "with alle," meaning exactly what it looks like - with everything (all).

People try to say this is karma, but we don't see karma punishing every crime or criminal either now, later, or any time at all. We see them living full happy lives after killing and removing life from others. That's not karma at all, so karma doesn't exist in visible reality.

But, since Christ is the judge, He can back up what He says. This is another reason people hate the bible, it actually delivers where karma fails.

What people want isn't the bible or karma, they want actions with no consequences. They want to rape, steal, and murder to their heart's content and have no jail time or repercussions. This is also irrespective of race.

Believing this verse or not has no effect on it. It happens either way to both believers and non-believers. This also isn't just about giving financially, which is where we commonly hear it in sermons. Since just one verse prior to this the subject is judging and forgiveness. So taken in context, it applies to more than just money.

Mercifully, the chicanery peddlers wishing free death and beatings for all wind up precisely where the idea began

- In Turd

32. When you favor certain minority groups over others, CONGRATULATIONS!

- You're A Discriminator!

33. Many believe that prior to receiving any degree, that this is the only time we may be fallible and the degree somehow magically conveys the power of infallibility. During this all too short period in our lives in striving to obtain this holy grail, we willingly receive correction, instruction, rebuke, or adjustments and bow our heads in graceful acceptance. But after the degree is won, that time is over and no more corrections are needed forever and ever, Amen.

They even imagine that having more than one degree increases the power of infallibility exponentially. This degree can take many shapes. It could be an actual degree, having 485 jobs per second (JPS), or having any number of kids. Any of these, or many other proud, hard-won achievements magically bestow this substance-altering panacea. The attitude towards others gives this away for what it is. But it's all imaginary, since there is no such thing as

- [Degrees Of Infallibility]

34. When weighing thy coin or gold at the money changer, which is it? The gold or the weight which holds value?

- True Judgment

35. Those of us who are honest enough with ourselves to consider the darkness in the soul of man will readily admit very little of what we do makes sense. This is trouble for people who spend every waking moment trying to compile reams of paper filled with ad hominems about others when simply changing their own behavior would be faster and do more.

It's lamentable that we expect others to make sense while making none of our own, with no efforts or concern about how or when to do so.

8. PHRIXIONAL ASSENTION

It's calamitous when we expect others to keep their promises and hold their feet to the fire till they do, while forgetting the most important promises we've made, and neither caring nor trying to remember them. It's deleterious that we think too often nothing can be done when changing ourselves is all we ever needed to do.

13. Permissive Law

1. Almost every problem now in the world can be attributed to the following: Ignoring the permissive law. Briefly stated, if we don't have permission for anything, we can't do it and conversely. To do otherwise, even if we're in a position of authority, brings a heavy fine assessed either now or in the future. It has never been seen that anyone really enjoys the outcome of these assessments. Whether anyone believes this or not has no effect on the outcome mostly because the Law of Cause & Effect is an involuntary action beyond the initial action.

2. Most of the arguments that take place outside of the physical realm have to do with the exact boundaries of the free will. Most (if not all) of the arguments against free will in both the physical and spiritual realms are false. So, why is it being allowed? Before answering, let's consider this for a while.

3. Whenever speech is limited, restricted, interrupted, ignored, or abandoned, something important is lost, if only in the form of potential. That's why "the right to the freedom of speech shall not be infringed."

4. While hearing words, if we decide to apply feelings to go with the words, we must remember it was our decision to apply the feelings. The words never asked us to do so. If the person we're getting the words from asked us to do so, this is irrelevant since they don't control our lives, we do. If after attaching feelings to the words, whether accurate or not, we decide to fabricate a retributive strike to hit the person that we imagine gave us these feelings, we must hit ourselves since it was our decision to attach needless feelings to words that we may or may not have interpreted correctly.

However today, most people deliberately *misinterpret* the words to give themselves the factitious advantage of this retributive strike. As we may now see, this is entirely an act of wanton sadism and is for that and other reasons completely illegal in reality and runs contrary to the permissive law.

- The Illusions of Freedom

5. Any who restrict the freedom of speech close the door on solutions to problems about which they will forever be unaware. Sometimes the words needed to expose a problem are ones people illegally say are illegal or inappropriate. Often it's likely these same people know exactly what they're doing, but think they will never face any consequences. But the multiplication of problems due to their actions cannot scientifically be said to never have a consequence. This is because many times, some problems may only become apparent through observing the solution.

6. Mental blindness occurs on several levels. We may believe we have correctly interpreted what we see in front of us while seeing nothing at all in reality. Some cases have taken several decades of active war against the blindness to reveal the damage done as well as the motives of the culprits who enjoy spreading and maintaining it. Due entirely to free will, a permanent cure may or may not ever be possible.

7. In the ongoing study of free will, what is noticeably missing so far, or may only exist in the unread portions we have at our disposal, is the consideration of multiple wills.

People consider God's will acting on theirs or vice versa, but never that maybe events have nothing to do with either our will or God's, but way too often, some other cluck face with less clues than we ourselves were afforded. Karma does this too, ignores other people making their own decisions. Maybe karma is only the vectored result of seven billion other decisions and nothing more. Maybe God's will isn't God's will at all, but the result of some other person's irresponsibility, ignorance, and deliberate blindness that's blocking our progress.

Sometimes this can be cumulative, brought about as the result of societal influence and several bad decisions built up over a period of decades. Maybe other people are actually responsible for the choices they make which affect our lives instead of the megalomaniacal concept that any individual is responsible for the decisions of seven billion other people, when this is both absurd and impossible. Maybe if more studied the free will issue they could be freed up to make better decisions.

Sometimes fate is only what we decide it is.

8. Why is free will important? Since hypnosis was used, it has become critical to know what precisely has happened. What does happen is that the free will is removed, even when the result is allegedly harmless, from the individual under hypnosis. And in some cases, it never comes back. Yes, this can unfortunately occur even when not under hypnosis as in the case of gravity or crimes, the will is removed and everyone has to live with the result. But for those who have experienced hypnosis abuse, it makes them more appreciative of the few actual choices we do have and how to make better ones become clearer.

So, what is the will? What precisely is under its control? Who else is able to move it?

9. If this is the last day of January, we are here. It won't come back later. 1/12th of the year is gone already. We will be upset when it doesn't come back. Like the girl who changed her name to get away from us, lied and said she would return, then never came back and stuck us with the dinner bill. When the day never comes back again, it will make us feel like the adopted family that we never had kicking us out the door onto the street with a shoe print all over our backside. It will make us feel like the leftover salad we let rot in the freezer. It will make us forget that we're alive and wander into the hall of some unused theater from several hundred years ago thinking that we're in a dream. It will leave us like the unexpired milk that already tasted sour five days early. But when something makes us feel that way, it's actually better if it doesn't come back again.

- Without Permission

10. For some, English may be their forty-fifth language, so they may not know that when someone says, "You have no right," this is the same as saying, "You have no permission." Sadly, most today don't know what a right is, where it begins, or how to even know whether we actually have them.

11. When trying to win in a game of "Root Causes," it isn't the person who most aggressively redresses offenses with retributive strikes to repay the original offense in a case by case basis, but rather whoever redresses the *original cause* with sufficient force to either keep it from happening again, or redirect its current effect.

All strikes which fail to hit the original cause will be returned to sender. We also can sometimes amplify the damage by ten before returning it. Some have wanted it to be over one million, but this wasn't allowed. It can also be passed on to the original cause if possible. But the return, by the known laws of physics and chemistry, will happen regardless of any other decisions, even if no decisions are made by anyone.

- Addressing Violations of Free Will

12. In reality, every incorrect discrimination, judgment, or act will have its equal and opposite reaction somewhere in time - now or the future. Many who today perform these acts randomly, imagining they have some exclusive license to commit selfishness, believe they shall clean escape any reaction to their false accusations and harsh judgments against people they not only know nothing about, but don't even care to know.

In reality, there is no license to selfishness, no freedom to retaliate against contrived or imagined offenses. There's actually no permission to retaliate against real offenses. There's only a right to true justice and freedom to forgive, or face a future where we won't be.

If we take any forty year period and count the seconds, we find there are over 1.25 billion. If in reality there is a specific and different reaction for each second of incorrect discrimination, judgment, or action against other people with permission from no one to do so, the future won't be what we have always imagined.

Knowing these things, *we*, not God or anyone else, control our future regarding this issue. It's called "free will." (We may say "not God" because most today blame God for the future they selected for themselves when no one wants it and it's easy to change.)

So, the future both is, and isn't, what we think. This varies to the degree of self-induced blindness.

Lethal Subculture (Addicted To Separation)

1. Q: "Why do you argue with people who have studied the subject longer than you have?"

A: "Because they think attaching large words to a sentence means that they're not guessing at the truth, but it doesn't and too often they are. There are at least two other reasons."

- Believe Everything

2. If one has already heard the truth, any subsequent contradictory statement is known for what it is. If one doesn't know whether one is hearing the truth, one has no business sitting in judgment over anything.

3. If we keep people skilled at killing alive, it means we want to see what they're skilled at doing happen again. We prepare cameras and audio recorders to capture the event. We wait with baited breath, lips slavering in spates, palms itching for action. We pay people to let them out of jail to repeat the previous traumas ad infinitum into a labyrinth of perfidious overkill. We observe separation after separation occur, all in the name of the "law." The law of death and insanity. Thank God Reagan got rid of all the sanitariums. Now they have nowhere to put us. Let us tell you how to think.

4. When we can't have relationships or think ours is better than everyone else's, we use the law to run all over creation separating as many relationships as possible which were perfectly fine before we decided to let our ego ruin the lives of others. We murder the future of others and feel nothing about it. We do this daily. We take people from

manageable situations and place them in overwhelming ones. We don't care if our accusations are true. We feel nothing and are never bothered by consequences since we can't see the future. We believe nothing awaits after death and don't care if it does. We feel nothing. We are addicted to separation and haven't admitted that we have a problem. We don't need to. The law is on our side.

5. We can easily imagine the lethal subcultures who are grossly addicted to separations finding something less childish to do with their time than to uselessly separate everything in sight. But so far, it's only a (probably vain) hope. They won't enjoy the other end of the spectrum, but there is a separation that leads *away* from selfishness instead of burying ourselves in it. If we bury ourselves in ourselves, where is anyone else? Or who cares?

Separation is God:

6. If we say or do anything, someone, somewhere will say that this fits a certain pattern and that we should be treated. The more sadistic and powerful among these will find a way to treat us whether we agree or not. Using rumor control and false accusations we will watch our job and life handed over to people who don't care who we are. We will see this when all we did was exercise our right to free speech in a country ostensibly built to guarantee freedom for all. We will be judged by people who claim to know everything, when any real scientist will confirm that the only people who think they know everything are the insane.

7. Separation is an action. Separation is always illegal when there's no permission. Sometimes they use the excuse that they're preventing further harm or damage to ourselves or those around us. When separations cause more pain than situational stability, what is better would be to separate those who habitually engage in illegal abusive actions from their power to separate. That people enjoy bringing harm to others more than leaving them alone needs no proof. Bullies are now a worldwide problem, if they never were previously. When this will stop is an unknown.

8. They destroy more than they create.

They implode more than they improve.

They're vacillating more than venerable.

They're immune more than they're ideal.

They divide more than they combine.

They escape more than they explore.

They disperse more than they collect.

They waste more than they weave.

They engulf more than they ensure.

Excessive hubris more than humble.

They addictively separate more than they aggressively secure.

They divide more than they unite.

They doze more than they dream.

They undercut more than they understand.

They shred more than they shield.

They take more than they treat.

They cleave more than they carve.

They pontificate more than they peruse.

They blame more than they forgive.

They coddle more than they convict.

They diffuse more than they condense.

They shift more than they sharpen.

They forget what they said more than remember what others said.

- Divided We Stand

9. We're all just human and do human mistakes, until we do something that someone doesn't like or agree with. Then it's ok to burn down their apartment, keep them from getting an education or a job, steal any or all of their items, lie as much as possible about them to everyone for over fifty years, or any otherwise treat them as sub-humans. Because this is the humane thing to do and since we all make mistakes, treating them as sub-humans is acceptable.

So make sure to stay agreeable or you will face the punishment we decide you deserve. Since we know everything, we don't even need to self-check whether this is right or not. If we've done it, it's automatically right all the time.

10. Whatever the issue, the gradient trend over time amounts to the same idea which in many cases is already legal - "We reserve the right to stalk you, destroy you, and wreck your mind."

11. Those who over-value acts of violence and award them with fear, typically fail to recognize that separation is a passive act of violence that over time, does light years greater damage than the overt.

12. We push the envelope while claiming that there isn't one. We claim there are no limits or boundaries as we push everyone in the universe past all of them, then laugh and blame them for any subsequent reaction. Any consequence directly traceable to us is denied almost before it can form. We think we're invisible. We imagine our presumed perfection grants us rights to murder, steal, and destroy. We tow the malevolent line of hate, denying the existence of logic or reason, and slavishly worship, cower from, and without any payments whatsoever, spread the sacred gospel of our all-knowing, immaculate

- Ideological Drug Lords

13. Addicted To Separation

Addicted to separating people
Addicted to tearing apart marriages
Addicted to severing children from their parents
Addicted to lame excuses for screwing children out of their parents
Addicted to molesting children with the absence of their families

Obsessed with separating lovers for no reason
Obsessed with tearing children away from their parents so they may then be used for sick, perverted purposes
Obsessed with emotional damage caused by screwing children out of their parents
Obsessed with separation for any reason imaginable
Obsessed with separation via victim-blaming
Obsessed with going too far to separate people who never gave you permission to separate them
Obsessed with separating the survivors of murderers
Obsessed with causing as much psychological pain and damage as possible in a lifetime
Obsessed with separation based on reasons flooded with nonsense

Addicted to separation under the pretense of furthering scientific knowledge when the truth is that sadism is the only real reason

Addicted to sadistic separations

Addicted to separation and genital mutilation

This is what God wants, oh yes, you must believe this is what God wants

If you don't believe this, we will separate you from your family and steal all of your children

Addicted to tearing families apart because families together are just too boring for us anymore

Addicted to ripping the hearts out of children by taking away their parents for no reason via murder, lies, and psycho-babble

Addicted to separation
Obsessed with separation
Separation is God!
Addicted to separation
Addicted to separation

We're never wrong, so all this has to be right
If you don't believe us, you're crazy
The psychiatrist will see you now.....

The New Leaf

Seckelwary 7th: Unseen snowdrifts spill endlessly through unimaginable tundra blessed by the sissabric mortar ambivalence.

Squoosel Lazenby argem moosra pulgenta ciochrinon darsinghi toofen sloosel sitch. Marchimbry quoozel azen sicher tocky bibbler shocky echol reesen sader. Armos thwoosergury holpen sigler.

Sueshell allery porphindery greyshen squoosel mibry, calerinsurrus, allen forshiry tin treef may zoosush. Gloosarmyn kwalcharsky sipper naggin forley ablominintube. Ackten sorcric yentiliser thor tink cloven syllic.

Clarpy squckel limbin torf, scattle goognyr sek. Splippyn tarker jilly gymbar bloofyn squekyl mibley. Tarbiliquyn subnerfan klasher ellig mabner grandilocyn. Tennebilferyin skribnuk squooche puck snilpy. Amberifen sybillinic jasmer jylpy cligoryn cheq secner jokwee snoodens lacher. Blasser Glassynk starfin choop if rejenel gaber Libly. Silnaefyn stooshy smubblepock glamberferyn. Narcyl nakey bib pot.

Glagner Clucknintzle chortled dekscropingly adelphin storber dastle, kinkeli clarbin jerquoolyn sarferinyl. Kellquillian quiabler dintzel treepin charper poolpryapen.

Sarquellian chaysynax torpyn tagler millcule derjyn naper negrin phorillysytok. Porchinzyll grabex chablin forsoolia tigra morsoferin clabderinys thilen kreebaf tear, smiles into forced domination acceded by the New Leaf.

Chartoolery 21st: The dry sand caked in large clumps to the bottoms of his shoes. A murderer's desire for popularity and subsequent ego engorgement was wryly frustrated by the earth-bound angel. She refused to allow the utterance of his name, which destroyed it. Time, the razor-sharp destroyer of men, knew that its days were also numbered. This is alluded to even within time itself; for anything circular or cyclical, there is no time since each end only starts the beginning over again. Through this contemplation, one can easily gaze into the future and accurately predict thousands of events.

Ego Wars were waged full-scale on the desolate slopes of the Glass Box city. Each person involved in the war was convinced they were responsible for winning it single-handedly while shutting out all controverting evidence. When you can't win the court case, say the evidence isn't. Lacquered dreams drifted rapidly out of memory, robbing the owner of their mind-balancing message. "Hope not for solutions," they cried, "since they bring truths which run counter to your beliefs. Just smile and live in the lies you've spent so many years fabricating." Science will not save you, neither will the fortune teller. It's better to study the illusion of stationary objects. Though they appear to move not, they are moving, and taking you with them. 6:07pm

Jyncyljorx 37th: Once the orange bay showed up, it was a short work of time before what had been seen 1.04 billion seconds earlier came and went with no further trouble, no misunderstanding, no false perception, no broken word. The value of trust and faith in words had been restored. But the sky above the bay was not without cloud. Large squadrons still clasped their false knowledge with steel skulls as a locket bequeathed by an ancient loved one, sealed by a dying curse to possess forever.

Poetic Emetic

1. Repetition Forces Lies Into Reality

Sometimes yes means no
Sometimes no means yes
If you have no clear clue when
It's better not to guess

A silent wish has feeble reach
A word goes twice as far
When you bend others to your will
I'll show you what you are

The words are right, the smile wide
All manners circumspect
By evidence you've long withheld
You kill what you protect

You once had asked for reasons
But what if there are none
Except for those you make up
Then have you really won?

Everyone is doing right
According to themselves
Avoid the mirror, hide yourself
Forever all is well

Sometimes yes means no
Sometimes no means yes
If you have no clear clue when
It's better not to guess

Sometimes no means yes
Sometimes yes means no
If you strain and squint and grunt
It means that you don't know.

Sometimes less is more
Sometimes more is less
You can force the opposite
You'll end with nothing less

You can say I'm wrong
Another liar in your night
I only have two things to say:
"No, really?" & "Yeah, right..."

2. A friend helps you fight your enemies,
will encourage you not to lie,
reveals truth behind lies,
protects you from violence,
prevents you from fear,
holds you away from harm,
keeps you from destroying yourself,
teaches you when and whom to love,
is your mirror when you're blind,
leads you to light and health,
and withholds no good thing from your grasp.

3. With what we have to say or send
With every harm or hope that's strong
Does it really matter when
We aren't here for very long?

One thousand years from now who'll say
"I agree when he got mad?"
Or who'll remember all the things
you bought or never had?

The dreams you gave or traits you shaved
The living hate you bore too long
Will it really matter when
We aren't here for very long?

And even this idea itself
If pondering should prove
A way to change a day of blame
Can it matter with a move?

With all of what we think or feel
A wish of hell - A dream of dawn
Does it really matter when
- We Aren't Here For Very Long

4. The sun is large & fluffy
It tells us what to do
It opens all our presents first
It burns up all our shoes

The sun has failed at driving
It knows not whence it came
Its expertise is cooking eggs
It blinds you with its flames

When the sun comes dancing
Asking for some milk
Hold up your driver's license
And laugh until it wilts

- Play With Fire

5. The Purpose of Cloud

Other moogs and shooper tubes
May well enough display
A cautious indiscretion
At the light of full dismay

But reason hates as reason be
Most solitary lamps
Black sugar crates with sugar fates
Of worldwide whorish tramps

One crippled glaperoptomy
(Who ever really cared?)
While Syllibeth rose-watered breath
Arose with thought and stared

Well far beyond this fragile bond
We made before we died
To see a sow who clapped and frowned
Controlled to live a lie

But other rogues and moper fugues
Who cry to make the hay
Whose parabolic bandy rut
Chance told me where to stay

So if a brick could free your mind
Just think what you could do
When you ignore the sellsword droll
I'll leave that up to you

6. Gingerly, gingerly broach the subjects
What gingerly, gingerly lie
Gingerly, gingerly trove the aspects
So ingenious Ginger won't die
- Antique (14 billion BC) proverb created 18 minutes ago

7. A thought was walking, sadly stalking
Arrested by stern measures
But all, in true, it sought to do
Was chance on gleaming treasure

Not for itself, for time as well
Arrests all subtle meaning
But see the way a minute stays
Expand the soulless ceiling

8. Think your opinion such a fact
You'll kill some for a naught
But you never prove one thing you say
Since that requires thought

9. When the Dead Rule

You reward those who tell you the truth
With death and insults
You asked for the facts - these we gave you
You called us both liars
If baby keeps crying
It wants something else
We fed it some fat lies
All quiet now still
You think you can blame us for lying
But had you not asked....
Lies don't corrupt from telling, only
Upon believing

10. Ought the otter over aught
With other otters over-fraught
Oppose with opprobrious onslaught
For aught it ought not do?

- Otter Oughts

11. A man thought he knew what was wrong
What was true
But he had no concern with his eye off the balance
He did not to others as they did to him
But when he becomes you, you object and pretend

When you
Ride through the canyon that you didn't make
See a time start to flame that you didn't take,
I thought
You knew the reason but found that you didn't
To trust you so long then to see you knew nothing at all
– not at all

A lady was slighted so used all her might to
Record every wrong she thought had been made
But she
Only excused all the ones who abused her
And she never saw what they were which you see as

They build towered cities but can't build a future
That holds anyone who follows the guide of
Concern or compassion are concepts forgotten
We flail in our death throes and kill everyone sent to help
– to help

A mystery eluded, confused, and deluded
The ones looking out who never look in

While the
Judges expand over sea, sky, and land as the
Facts waxing wan yet uncovers their sin that

Of course, several seasons could pass without treason
Extortion or greed, but Oh, God! How they love them!
They've mastered the sky yet still
No one can fly and the
Decades drag past while we
Create a world no one wants
– or cares

- The Towered Cities

12. It doesn't really matter much
If you know the right words anymore
All they'll do is judge you
And throw their second guess on the floor

The rain fell on the moon
And life was there and gone
No one ever trusts you
Unless you take too long

We took you to December
And dropped you in a hole
A brace can wreak and render
The one fooled was the mole

For all of your demanding
You don't give what you get
You hurt yourself to hurt me
And nurse life with regrets

- Hurt Yourself

13. Upon the Point of Death

A Phase shall soon begin to ebb,
Which now appears to rise
To blacken all the golden spheres
Entomb the massive skies

The leaders of this damnéd troupe
Believe that death can sail
But it will crush their feeble whim
Then all their hope shall fail

No need to run headlong into
The thief with arms outstretched
For time will bring it soon to pass
And you (its prey) shall catch

No more the interruptions streaming
Stalwart callow scale
Death shall arrest deceiving mouths
And rend in twain the veil

And silky time - that embalmed shrine -
Was shattered on the floor.
While quarks and neurons razor breath
Lie waiting at the door.

No more the shuttered windows vast -
Like clouds against the sky.
For truth shall shred the scornful past
And lighten every eye.

No more the lies which cloud men's minds
And withhold useful breath.
For all shall fully be revealed
Upon the point of death.

Sources Cited

1. p24, https://www.dictionary.com/browse/collude
2. 1 Cor. 15:56
3. G. Sadler, Half Hour Hegel, Sense Certainty, Paragraph 109-110
4. Proverbs 1:26
5. J.G. Bennett, Creative Thinking, pp6-7
6. Finney's Systematic Theology, Human Government, p365
7. Luke 10:18
8. Romans 12:19
9. Heb 3:19
10. Heb. 4:12
11. James 4:17
12. The Allegory of the Cave, Plato, The Republic, Book VII
13. Jiddu Krishnamurti quote
14. Psa 146:3
15. https://www.cement.org/cement-concrete-applications/how-cement-is-made
16. Romans 1:25
17. https://www.azquotes.com/quotes/topics/action-andreaction.html
18. John 3:19
19. Hegel, Phenomenology of Spirit, ¶54.
20. Anaxagoras
21. I Cor. 15:22
22. Mal. 1:14
23. Job 2:4
24. Prov. 26:12

25. Informal Logic, Douglas N. Walton, p239

26. Rom. 14:12

27. Nicholas Cusanus, Of Learned Ignorance, Book I, p8-9

28. 1 John 4:1

29. ibid

30. Jerem. 17:5

31. I Cor. 14:33

32. ibid

33. The Call of Cthulhu, H.P. Lovecraft, ¶1

34. Eccl. 2:24

35. Prov. 12:15

36. Deut. 30:15

37. Isa 1:18

38. II Pet. 3:10

39. I John 2:15

40. https://www.dictionary.com/browse/word

41. Wikipedia, Galileo Affair

42. Plato, Lysis

43. Jam. 3:16

44. Plato, Euthydemus

45. Heb. 12:1

46. Luke 5:21

47. ibid

48. 2 Cor. 10:4

49. Matt. 9:4

50. Prov. 1:22

51. Job 3:25

52. James 4:2b

53. Erasmus-Luther, Discourse on Free Will, p120

54. Matt. 15:11

55. Plato, Euthydemus

56. Rom. 11:25

57. Wikipedia, Heisenbug

58. Hegel, Philosophy of Right, Abstract Right, ¶90

59. Luke 6:38

Pre-Afterword

After which words should we then rest?
After whose words are we yet blessed?

It could be said that any or all
This book is much aloof,
But that would be redundant
And would still require proof.

Afterword

Many documents were lost in the fire in 1998, including the actual birth certificate proving Thomas' link to his father, among many other things which may have contributed to the solution since the memories hadn't fully returned yet. Only the fake birth certificate remains. More written communication with various people who helped him from one point to the next describing the details of what the criminals did was also destroyed either by the many methods of manipulation available to the criminals or because Thomas was trying to burn the memory of them and everything they did from existence for the sake of sanity. Using hypnosis to get Ralene and himself to say things to get people them agitated enough to either try to kill them or abuse them further to any extent possible was carried out perfectly short of either of them dying, which is only by a miracle.

It is still maintained that there is sufficient evidence in the first book to solve this case for any who are sufficiently skilled. Seeing the case has no apparent end, this book, and a third seem to be a requirement. The third will contain stories with more of the aforementioned illustrations which this book may be lacking. This is assuming the companies of quidnuncs engaged in attempting to kill the author don't actually succeed. The mystery remains, however, how that all those who sporadically remind him of various events as his brain performs its normal job of cutting all the insanity out of the picture don't instead remind themselves of how they can shift events into a positive direction instead of the negative one on which their current focus is cemented.

After this much, only a few relevant questions, in addition to those raised previously, still remain:

1. How is it not clear when someone says repeatedly they're lying that they're lying in that moment when they had spent the last twenty minutes asking the five to ten men surrounding them, all lawyers and legal professionals of some sort, or so they claimed, that what was about to be said was done under threat of future murders?

2. How are we protecting the innocent or what methods are even available in this particular case of being forced to lie under threat of death?

3. Why was this protection not afforded to Thomas?

4. If this isn't the sum of forgotten memories, is it not highly likely that there were an entire other series of rapes and crimes done before this one about which some groups keep asking that Thomas hasn't yet remembered and the other groups keep blaming him for covering up while preaching about how hypnosis can't do any of this?

5. Against the objection: "Many of your statements aren't clear" (which dates all the way back to 1968), it may be asked - Can there be any reason to say or do anything clearly where there yet exists no clear reason for anyone's statements or actions over the last fifty years?

6. If we use these and many other available tools to reveal the invisible aspects of who we are, can we use them to create a more positive atomic record for the future to inherit, or will we still be reading this book after we die?

What the actual transcript of the court records should look like:

"Judge: Since the sentence of the first trial was execution, the defendants will be executed on October 6, 1970 and no later under penalty of incarceration for any party found to be the cause the delay. Justice will not be delayed nor denied."

Since there is a punishment beyond imagining for any who harass a rape victims for over fifty years or who allow any three-year-olds to be raped then award the rapists fifty years of free meals, any attempt at a description would be an utter failure, and so won't be recorded here. But since punishment was asked for repeatedly, it is most definitely on its way.

In order to permanently disable The Blinder, it may be a requirement that we look deeply into The Obfuscatory Oblivion of the Obvious, which may require a good understanding of Proverbs Book XXI and every book which preceded it, and pass beyond The Language Barrier to see the pandemic concept that Our Brains Are Very Tall runs in stark contrast to the many books populating the shelves describing the billions of facets of reality which clearly reveal What You Don't Know. We may need to begin to Prove All Things to ensure that in no place on earth we stand ready to Believe The Lie. This will necessarily produce the road of Frictional Ascension, but will simultaneously arrest, expose, and frustrate the expanding Lethal Subculture, who are grossly Addicted to Separation. It will also begin the era of The New Leaf which could have an indifferent effect on the several volumes of Poetic Emetic, but from which something far better and usable should appear.

J.C.

Printed in the United States
By Bookmasters